A BEGINNER'S GUIDE TO OPERA

JEREMY NICHOLAS

WITH AN INTRODUCTION BY

HARRY ENFIELD

EBURY PRESS

IN ASSOCIATION WITH

CHANNEL FOUR TELEVISION COMPANY LTD

THANKS TO:

JPR, of course, and her small back-up team of one,
who made the writing of this book possible.
Robin Lough, who dreamt up the idea for the television series,
and invited me to help develop it.
Douglas Rae of Ecosse Films who produced the television series. Susanna Yager of
Channel Four Publishing for her confidence in me and finding ...
Rowena Webb of Ebury Press who provided solid support, advice and fun.
Caroline Johnson for her work on the first draft and Sarah Lenton
for her useful comments on the plot outlines.
Martin Lovelock who has designed the whole thing so brilliantly
and Ben Goold for his expert assistance.
My friends Lesley Coleman who did the picture research,
Alison Wylton who compiled the index, and Bryan Crimp whose
pertinent remarks were, as usual, invaluable.

Photographic and illustration credits

Page 4 Mike Prior. Pages 17, 21, 36, 144, 145, Zoë Dominic. 20, 22, 25, 28, 34, 51, 54, 56, 61, 98, 100, 101, 125, 131, 132, 134, 137, 141, 146-147, Mary Evans Picture Library. 24, 34, 37, 45, 72-73, 75, 77, 81, 86, 89, 90, 96, 112, 116-117, 151, 154, Clive Barda/Performing Arts Library. 30, 149, 150, Courtesy Culver Pictures. 33, 47, 114, 121, 122 (David Low), 150, Mander & Mitchenson Theatre Collection. 39, 58-59, 62, 69, 78, 85, 104-105, 106, 108, Opera North, photographs, Hanson. 41 Richard H Smith/Dominic Photography. 48, 83, courtesy the Metropolitan Opera Archive. 52, 57, Catherine Ashmore. 53 Opera News, New York. 64-65 Deutsches Theatermuseum, Munich. 66 Justin Pumfrey. 71 Siegfried Lauterwasser/Bayreuther Festspiele. 79, 80, 103, 128, 138, 147, Houston Rogers/Theatre Museum Collection, courtesy the Board of Trustees of the Victoria & Albert Museum. 82, 147, Kobal Collection. 87 Weidenfeld and Nicolson Archive. 88 courtesy Education Department, Metropolitan Opera Guild/William Harris. 93 Royal Opera House Archives. 120, 126, 130, E.T. Archive. 122 Mansell Collection. 123 SCALA/Museo Teatrale alla Scala, Milan. 145 Hulton-Deutsch.

p17, *Placido Domingo as Calaf and Dame Gwyneth Jones as Turandot
in the Royal Opera House's 1984 production of* Turandot.
p58-59, *Janice Cairns as Madam Butterfly in Opera North's production.*
p64-65, *The National Theatre of Munich's 1818 set design for* The Magic Flute.
p72-73, *Kenneth Woolem as Walther and Janice Cairns as Eva
in English National Opera's production of* Die Meistersinger.
p104, *Bruce Budd in Opera North's production of* Tosca
p116-117, *The Welsh National Opera's 1984 production of* The Merry Widow.
p141, *Leporello and his list in Act 1 of* Don Giovanni.

First published 1993 by Ebury Press
an imprint of the Random House Group
Random House · 20 Vauxhall Bridge Road · London SW1V 2SA

Copyright © 1993 Jeremy Nicholas

The right of Jeremy Nicholas to be identified as the author of this work has been asserted by him
in accordance with the Copyright, Designs and Patents Act 1988.

Catalogue record for this book is available from the British Library.

ISBN 0091775191

Designed by Martin Lovelock

Printed and bound in Italy by New Interlitho S.p.a., Milan

CONTENTS

INTRODUCTION BY HARRY ENFIELD
Page 5

A GUIDE TO THE GUIDE
Page 6

TIME CHART
Page 8

A BRIEF HISTORY OF OPERA – IN FIVE ACTS
Page 10

AN A-Z OF OPERA TERMS
Page 12

BEFORE YOU BEGIN ...
Page 18

THE OPERAS
Page 19

THE COMPOSERS
Page 119

THE ARTISTS
Page 143

INDEX
Page 155

ABOUT THE AUTHOR
Page 160

INTRODUCTION

In 1710 a columnist in *The Spectator* writing about opera said: 'There is no question but our great grandchildren will be very curious to know the reason why their forefathers used to sit together like an audience of foreigners in their own country, and to hear whole plays acted before them in a tongue which they did not understand.' Over two hundred years later some of us are still doing it. Why? What the heck do we think we're up to?

I came to opera pretty recently. It was never part of my childhood. I had a vague impression of fatties ruining quite nice background music by warbling and screeching to their dangerously overworked heart's content. Opera seemed far too complicated. To understand it you had to be an expert. But then I was given a CD of highlights from Verdi's *La Traviata* and after a couple of plays I found I liked some of the tunes – I didn't know what they were singing about, but I didn't know what Bob Dylan meant when he seemed to sing 'Chooder yeaner perner greut, chreamaner raeee!' and that's never bothered me. So then I bought the whole of *La Traviata*, discovered a whole lot more tunes I liked, then bought *Rigoletto* and before I knew it I'd accumulated a whole collection of Verdi operas, a bit of Mozart and a couple of Puccini's. I'd approached opera by the same method as I'd approached pop music as a fat child – I'd liked a single, bought an LP, bought a group's next LP and become a fan. Getting to like opera wasn't nearly as frightening as I'd thought it would be.

This excellent book gives you a step-by-step guide to all the famous operas, tells you what they're about and recommends the recordings worth buying. The stupid thing is that when you say you like opera everyone thinks you're frightfully clever and you'll know all about every opera ever written. Opera lovers are constantly trying to outdo each other by trying to prove that they know the most. I went to a production of *Boris Godunov* recently, and the next day bumped into an elderly opera buff acquaintance. 'I went to *Boris Godunov* last night,' I announced, all pleased with myself. 'Really?' he replied. 'Which version? The original or the re-write?' Imagine my shame and his joy when I confessed that I didn't even know there were two versions. Well now I think it's time for all of us who are quite new to opera and only know a little bit about it to come out into the open and start a 'Proud to be Thick' campaign. Every time someone tries to catch us out by asking a question that they think anyone should know the answer to, and we don't, we should say 'Dunno – I'm thick, I'll look it up in this book.'

Opera shouldn't be the preserve of the intellectual or pseudo intellectual. Everyone likes a good tune with lots of passion in it, so why should that be considered to be highbrow? Why is everyone so serious about opera? My favourite quote about opera comes from Gerard Hoffnung, who loved it, but never took it too seriously: 'Some people say that it's neither proper theatre, nor is it music and that one interferes with the other. And then of course they grumble about the fat heroines. Well I don't agree, I think that good opera is both music and theatre and I think it's absolutely marvellous and I don't mind the fat heroines a bit – I think they're half the fun, and why shouldn't they be fat? I look forward to my Mimi in *La Bohème* lying in bed, a whacking great whale of a woman with another great jelly of a Rodolfo bending over the solitary leg of mutton which is offered to him singing "Your tiny hand is frozen" – I love it.'

HARRY ENFIELD

A GUIDE TO THE GUIDE

This is not a dictionary of opera or a 'complete guide to opera'. It is a guide for those who need a few signposts as they stumble tentatively from the Three Tenors and Pavarotti In The Park to the Piazza at Covent Garden. It does not pretend or attempt to be definitive.

You won't, for instance, find mention of many composers working before Gluck or after Puccini; the omission of Monteverdi, Berlioz and Tippett will perhaps cause some raised eyebrows, but only among those who know a bit about opera already – and this book is not primarily for them. The limits of a slim volume like this have to be drawn somewhere and in this case it's dictated by my own belief that opera began with Mozart and ended with Puccini. (Howls of protest!) Well, there you are – I have compromised by including Gluck, Handel, Britten and a few other interlopers.

If an opera seems to me to be too difficult, inaccessible or boring it hasn't been included and works acclaimed by critics, aficionados and musicologists as masterpieces have not necessarily received an entry – so no *Pelléas et Mélisande*, no *Lulu*, *Les Troyens* or *Parsifal*. *Tristan und Isolde* only just scraped in.

This choice may be subjective but is not meant to be provocative. *The Knot Garden* or *Elektra* would not be among my first choices to introduce someone to opera. The musical language of these works is difficult enough to anyone whose normal theatre-going embraces *Cats*

and *Carmen Jones*, without the strange idea of people singing instead of speaking to each other – and doing it, by and large, in a foreign language.

The vast majority of people (including me) are frequently baffled by some music written even as long as a century ago, let alone the dissonant cacophony of much contemporary classical work. When all *we* hear is drone and din, it's hard to own up to disliking such pieces when our more cultured, educated friends tell us that what we've been listening to is a masterpiece. It leaves us feeling defensive and slightly out of it. And ultimately we don't want to bother. Opera, I think, with all its peculiarities, *is* worth bothering about. It's an entertainment form, like cinema or musicals, that's worth getting to know and making an effort over. After all, on occasions it has been the vehicle for some of man's loftiest thoughts and most inspired creations. So this selection, while not without its challenges to those whose usual listening is primarily to lighter music, is intended to lead gently by the hand.

The average music lover neither knows nor cares that Puccini wrote his operas over a hundred years later than Mozart, and is bewildered by airy references to '*coloratura* arias', 'Wagner's use of *leitmotiv*' and a role 'having a high *tessitura*'. It's no wonder that the world of opera, frequently seen as an élitist pastime for the educated, the wealthy or the musically literate, is a closed book for many people. 'Callas made her debut in Santuzza' – how are we supposed to know that Santuzza is not a town somewhere in Italy, but a role in *Cavalleria Rusticana*?

When the inspirational sound of Domingo or Sutherland excites an interest – who and what to turn to? There are opera guides, handbooks and dictionaries by the dozen, written by the connoisseur for the lover. Coals to Newcastle. This book is for those whose ears have just been jolted into new sensations, perhaps from hearing *'Nessun dorma'* for the first time, and realizing that out there somewhere is a whole different sound world of which they were only vaguely aware before; for those for whom the act of buying a ticket to go to an opera house is, well, worrying; for whom there is no one to go to and say 'I don't want to make a fool of myself by asking all the wrong questions, but I am completely pig-ignorant about opera and all that serious stuff. I really like the little bit I've heard, but I don't know where to start. I haven't got the bread to go experimenting at £25 for a double full-price CD, let alone at £90 a seat, so what should I listen to and what should I avoid?'

Opera is by far the most complex art form in music. In order for it to work it relies on the successful mixture of a number of elements: music, words, lighting, acting, singing, orchestral playing, scenery, story-telling, mood evocation, and the way in which all these are welded together (or not). Above all, it needs an audience on its side, willing it to work. Ultimately, for opera to succeed, it needs *you* there in the theatre; just as Shakespeare hardly ever transfers well to the small screen, or indeed to cinema, opera rarely works on television. You can listen at home to the works on compact disc in perfect sound and comfort. But Mozart and Rossini and Verdi were men of the theatre, working on big canvases, hoping that all the elements had been combined in such a way that their public, sitting together, side by side, would laugh and weep and be exalted *with* them.

Finally, did you know that every opera aria ever composed can be sung to the words 'I come from Leeds'? I do hope you enjoy singing all those listed in the book – and the thousands of others – to this inspiring text. Someone once calculated that since people began writing operas, more than 42,000 arias have been composed. At a conservative estimate of ten arias per opera …

Jeremy Nicholas
Barley Fen
1993

By matching up the composers below with their operas, you can see at a glance who was writing what, when and where.

Timeline (years): 1700 1710 1720 1730 1740 1750 1760 1770 1780 1790 **1800** 1810 1820 1830 1840 1850 1860 1870 1880 1890 **1900** 1910 1920 1930 1940 1950 1960 1970 1980 1990

BRITISH

PURCELL 1659 ~ 1695

HANDEL 1685 ~ 1759 (German born)

BALFE 1808 ~ 1870 (Irish)

(Gilbert and) SULLIVAN 1842 ~ 1900

BRITTEN 1913 ~ 1976

ITALIAN

MONTEVERDI 1567 ~ 1633

ROSSINI 1792 ~ 1868

DONIZETTI 1797 ~ 1848

BELLINI 1801 ~ 1835

VERDI 1813 ~ 1901

PONCHIELLI 1834 ~ 1886

BOITO 1842 ~ 1918

LEONCAVALLO 1857 ~ 1919

PUCCINI 1858 ~ 1924

MASCAGNI 1863 ~ 1945

CILEA 1866 ~ 1950

GERM

GLUCK 1714 ~ 1787

BEETHOVEN 1770 ~ 1827

WEBER 1786 ~ 1826

MEYERBEER 1791 ~ 1864

WAGNER 1813 ~ 1883

R. STRAUSS
1864 ~ 1949

WEILL
1900 ~ 1950

AUBER
1782 ~ 1871

GOUNOD
1818 ~ 1893

OFFENBACH
1819 ~ 1880 (German born)

SAINT-SAËNS
1835 ~ 1921

DELIBES
1836 ~ 1891

BIZET
1838 ~ 1875

MASSENET
1842 ~ 1912

CHARPENTIER
1860 ~ 1956

MOZART
1756 ~ 1791

J. STRAUSS II
1825 ~ 1899

F. LEHÁR
1870 ~ 1948

SMETANA
1824 ~ 1884

JANÁČEK
1854 ~ 1928

BORODIN
1833 ~ 1887

MUSSORGSKY
1839 ~ 1881

TCHAIKOWSKY
1840 ~ 1892

GERSHWIN
1898 ~ 1937

GLASS
1937 ~

FRENCH   AUSTRIAN   CZECH   RUSSIAN   AMERICAN

1700 1710 1720 1730 1740 1750 1760 1770 1780 1790 **1800** 1810 1820 1830 1840 1850 1860 1870 1880 1890 **1900** 1910 1920 1930 1940 1950 1960 1970 1980 1990

A BRIEF HISTORY
OF OPERA ~ IN FIVE ACTS

OVERTURE
ORIGINS

In the late sixteenth century, during the Renaissance ('rebirth') artists, writers and architects became interested in the ancient culture of Greece and Rome. In Florence, a group of aristocrats debated how the ancient Greek dramas were actually performed. They experimented with the plays of Aeschylus and Euripides, declaiming the more poetic passages, and using roughly the same speech rhythms as normal speech but with a few chords of instrumental music accompanying them. Doesn't sound like much, but this was different to any form of musical composition at the time, which was all madrigals and polyphony (i.e. the interweaving of many melodies). Now, people sang solo to tell the story and this rapidly developed into a sort of recitative. Music was made to be as important as the words and actions. This was called *dramma per musica* ('drama by means of music') to emphasize the idea of a play with a musical setting.

ACT ONE

1600 Though *Dafne* (1594 or 1597) by Jacopo Peri (1561–1633) is considered to be the first work written in this way, it's now lost, so for the sake of convenience, the earliest surviving opera is said to be *Euridice* by Jacopo Peri and Giulio Caccini (1546–1618).

1607 *Orfeo* by Claudio Monteverdi (1567–1643). It was pure good luck that a composer of genius should be around at the time to develop these ideas. Characters are given florid songs that halt the action of the play and comment on their feelings, etc.; there are also choruses that are sometimes jolly dances, sometimes tragic laments; and orchestral interludes to accompany stage action and scene changes. With this one work, Monteverdi mapped the future possibilities of opera.

1637 The first theatre built for this new form of entertainment opened in Venice. Previously, only the rich and privileged had been invited to these private amusements; now anyone could go. Soon there were sixteen opera houses in Venice alone, and they were mushrooming elsewhere like movie houses at the beginning of the twentieth century.

1642 *The Coronation of Poppea*, also by Monteverdi. Soon the original idea of recapturing the spirit of Greek tragedy was abandoned. In this, his last opera, Monteverdi drew on Roman history. His followers in Venice (Pier Cavalli and Marc'Antonio Cesti) developed a type of flowing, lyrical song inspired by the flow of spoken Italian – **bel canto**. *Bel canto* **arias** displaced dramatic recitative in popularity.

1650 The term 'opera' (from the Italian meaning 'work') was coined to describe the new music. Already, composers realized the public demand for 'tunes' and showy vocal display. Thus the aria became a convention. So did spectacular scenes on stage. Gods descended from clouds to untangle the plots; battles, shipwrecks and storms were staged. In 1680, one opera featured 100 horsemen in armour, two lions, two elephants, horse-drawn chariots, bears and deers – as well as a few singers!

ACT TWO

1700–1750 In the first half of the eighteenth century, the singer became the dominant feature. Opera descended into being little more than an evening of vocal items strung together with a plot loosely based on legend, mythology or ancient history, more like a vocal recital. Dramatic action was slight. Performers, especially the **castrati** who flourished at this time, were fêted throughout Europe and were highly paid. The chorus was still fairly primitive as far as its dramatic and musical importance was concerned (armies or crowds, mostly) and the orchestra contributed nothing more than a discreet accompaniment for the display of vocal pyrotechnics. To be fair, the gymnastic skill and beauty of tone demonstrated by the singers in those days must have been great indeed, but their virtuosity was not always matched by an equivalent musical sensitivity. Before long changes occurred.

ACT THREE

1762 *Orfeo ed Euridice* by **Gluck**. Using the same subject Monteverdi had used a century and a half earlier, a single composer of genius with a single work once more turned opera on its head and pointed the way forward. Gluck made the action continuous, like a play; the arias were incorporated into the plot, not just stuck in to display the talents of the singer; and musically they had to fit the mood and style of the piece; the overture had to be of the right character to prepare the audience for what followed; the music had to complement and colour both the characters and the story. Here is a first sight of opera as an organic unity, an idea that can be followed through to **Mozart** to **Weber** to Berlioz and ultimately to **Wagner** (the apotheosis of the total expression of music-drama) and **Richard Strauss**.

Something else happened to opera at this point. Italy had invented it and dominated its progress. Gluck was a German. The whole genre, to put it simplistically, was now divided in two: you either wrote in the German way (as above) or continued in the Italian style. The French found a middle way – very successfully – with the likes of **Bizet, Gounod, Offenbach** and **Massenet**, whilst the English school of opera lay virtually moribund from the death of **Purcell** to the flowering of **Benjamin Britten**.

ACT FOUR
NINETEENTH CENTURY

The Italian style placed the singer firmly at the centre of attraction and continued to set thrilling operatic challenges through the works of **Rossini, Bellini** and **Donizetti**. The plot subjects changed, however. No longer based on ancient myths and legends, they often used the romantic tales of such writers as Sir Walter Scott, Byron and Goethe. The music was as dramatic and passionate as the plots were melodramatic. **Verdi**'s long career bestrode the two worlds, the German and Italian, like a colossus, culminating in such works as *Aida*, *Otello* and *Falstaff*, masterpieces that combine the lyricism of the Italians with the dramatic realism of the Germans.

ACT FIVE
TWENTIETH-CENTURY DEVELOPMENTS

The blossoming of opera in the nineteenth century (as can be seen from the chart on pp8–9) occurred in a remarkably short time: Gluck died three months before Rossini was born; by the time Rossini died, Wagner had written most of the *Ring* cycle, Verdi was at the height of his powers and **Puccini** was a lad of ten. *His* career takes us well into the twentieth century. Composers since then may have written in a different musical language to these but the methods, ingredients and actual styles that Berg, Birtwistle, **Britten**, Stravinsky and others have used to write their operas are much the same. In this respect, opera has not made any advance in its development since the end of the nineteenth century.

AN A–Z OF OPERA TERMS

ARIA
Italian: 'air, tune'

A song for a solo voice in an opera. There are any number of elaborate classifications given to the different types of aria, from *aria d'abilità* (an aria requiring special ability, such as those of the Queen of the Night from Mozart's **The Magic Flute**) and *aria cantabile* (expressing sorrow or yearning with a smooth and even melody) to *aria buffa* (a comic aria) and *aria di mezzo carattere* (an aria expressing more restrained emotions and an accompaniment that might become elaborate). Nobody cares much about these niceties now – arias are, quite simply, the famous bits that stick out from the rest: *'Nessun dorma'*, *'Casta diva'*, *'Una voce poco fa'*, etc.

BARITONE
Greek: from bari, *meaning 'deep'*
and tone, *meaning 'sound'*

The middle category of male voice, much darker and with a range roughly four or five notes lower than a tenor's. Rarely the hero, often the villain or second lead to the tenor. Famous ones: **Thomas Allen**, Geraint Evans, Dietrich Fischer-Dieskau, **Tito Gobbi**, **Robert Merrill**.

BASS
Italian: from basso, *meaning 'low'*

The deepest category of male voice with a range from F below middle C to D nearly two octaves below – and beyond (BASSO PROFONDO). Usually devils and villains (Boris, Mephistopheles) or buffoons (Don Basilio in **The Barber**). Famous ones: **Fyodor Chaliapin**, **Boris Christoff**, **Ruggero Raimondi**, **Samuel Ramey**.

BEL CANTO
Italian: 'beautiful singing'

A widely used yet rather imprecise term to describe the traditional Italian style of singing that emphasizes beauty and evenness of tone (sound), fine legato (smooth) phrasing and perfection of technique. This contrasts with the German style of a more dramatic approach with more emotional expression.

If a singer is 'noted for *bel canto* roles' it means he or she is good at **Handel, Bellini, Donizetti, Rossini** and early **Verdi**, for example. If a singer is unmusical but loud, he or she is known in the business as a *can belto*.

CADENZA
Italian: 'cadence'

A cadence is the rounding-off of a musical phrase or close of a piece. 'Cadenza' has come to mean the flashy flourish just before the cadence. It is the opportunity given to the artist in an aria or instrumental piece to show his or her agility in performing trills, runs, arpeggios and other acrobatic feats of the greatest difficulty with the greatest of ease. It generates a *frisson* and elicits (hopefully) a rapturous reception. **Rossini** was among the first to write out his own cadenzas after too many artists took too many improvised liberties with his work. Soon everybody followed suit. An example is the end of *'La donna è mobile'*, which features a brief flourish, or cadenza. In twentieth-century music, cadenzas are thought unnecessary.

CASTRATO
Italian: 'castrated'

Oh yes they did – and they did it until comparatively recently. During the seventeenth and eighteenth centuries, the testicles of young boys would be removed before puberty, thereby preventing the vocal chords from maturing, and thus preserving their high voices: there was great demand for 'angelic' voices in certain roles. The origins of this barbaric practice lay in the Roman Catholic Church's interpretation of St Paul's words (1 Corinthians XIV, 34) to the effect that women should keep silent in church. Since women were not available for the taxing high vocal lines in church music and since boy sopranos had unreliable voices, there was, apparently, only one alternative. The Sistine Chapel choir still had a professional castrato at the turn of this century. Alessandro Moreschi died in 1922 and the dozen or so records he made in 1902 when he was forty (he was the first and last castrato to record, though he never sang in opera) reveal an unearthly, spectral wailing that sends a shiver up the spine (*Moreschi – The Last Castrato*, Pearl Opal CD 9823).

The remains of Moreschi's voice were probably not typical of the castrato sound. The music written for these emasculated men, who were the greatest vocal stars of their day and commanded huge fees, was both brilliant, florid and highly virtuosic; compared to the female voice, it was stronger, more agile and capable of producing lower notes, though with a limited emotional range.

As the demand for dramatic truth increased towards the end of the eighteenth century, castrati were heard less and less, but **Rossini** wrote a part for the castrato Giovanni Velluti (1780–1861) in *Aureliano in Palmira* as late as 1813. **Meyerbeer** was the last significant composer to write for the castrato voice – another role for Velluti in *Il Crociato in Egitto* (1824).

The most famous castrato singer in history was Carlo Farinelli (1705–1782) who spent twenty-five years at the court of Spain. During the last ten years of the life of King Philip V, Farinelli sang the same four songs to him and nothing else every evening.

CLAQUE

French: 'clap'

Still popular in Italy, where opera is more a way of life than elsewhere, but generally out of favour now, is the long-established custom of hiring people to clap. Impresarios and singers, anxious that their endeavours should prosper – or to contradict self-evident failure – have been willing to dispense large sums for the service.

Though paying someone to support (or attack) a performer is as old as deceit itself (Suetonius writes of Nero enjoying the benefits), the systematized use of hired applause in the opera house arrived in France in the early nineteenth century. An agency entitled *L'Assurance des succès dramatiques*, run by a certain Monsieur Sauton, engaged a team of *claqueurs* who received their applause/booing instructions from a *chef de claque*. There were several categories of *claqueurs*:

tapageurs: provided vigorous applause.

connaisseurs: gave exclamations of approval.

pleureuses: had smelling-salts to encourage tears.

bisseurs: clapped for encores.

chatouilleurs: produced witty remarks and offers of sweets.

commissaires: praised production/singer in interval.

chauffeurs: 'warmed up' the audience before and after.

Such a well-spread group could operate their varied roles throughout the house without the audience knowing anything was amiss. Towards the end of the nineteenth century the price for these services were:

Ordinary applause....5 francs

Enthusiastic applause....15 francs

Expressions of horror....5 francs

Groans....12.50 francs

Murmurs of alarm....15 francs

Hissing a rival singer....25 francs

Wild ovations at curtain call....by arrangement

COLORATURA

German: from Koloratur, *meaning 'coloured'*

A term meaning the elaboration of the melody in the form of runs, cadenzas, trills, etc. – a vocal line demanding great agility. Often originally written for specific performers, there are *coloratura* arias for all types of voice, but it's usually associated with a high voice. Thus a *coloratura* soprano (such as **Joan Sutherland**, **June Anderson**, or, from a bygone era, **Amelita Galli-Curci**) specializes in the roles requiring this ability. Listen to the two arias for the Queen of the Night (***The Magic Flute***), the Mad Scene from ***Lucia di Lammermoor*** or the Bell Song (***Lakmé***). Two well-known examples for mezzo-soprano *coloratura* are Rossini's '*Una voce poco fa*' (***The Barber of Seville***) and '*Non più mesta*' (***La Cenerentola***).

CONTRALTO

Italian: against or contrasted with the high voice

The lowest category of female voice, with a range of roughly F below middle C to two Fs above it. Famous contraltos: Marion Anderson, **Kathleen Ferrier**, Grace Bumbry, Dame Clara Butt.

COUNTER-TENOR

The highest naturally produced male voice which covers the soprano and contralto range without the need for drastic surgery. Popular from medieval times to the days of Purcell and Handel, recently there has been a slight revival of interest in writing for this voice. Not to be confused with falsetto. Famous counter-tenors: Alfred Deller, James Bowman.

CURTAIN CALLS

The bows at the end of a scene or act. Unlike the performance of a play in a theatre where, almost universally, the only bows are those taken at the end of the evening by the players, opera has different customs, which vary from country to country. In England, the main applause is given at the end of the performance (though individual arias can receive applause in the course of the evening) and on special occasions includes a seemingly unending procession of people besides the artists: conductor, producer, designer, chorus-master, *et al.* In Italy, all the calls (including solo calls) are made during the performance so that the audience gets up and leaves as soon as the final curtain falls. German houses tend not to like solo calls and elsewhere some have banned them. When he ran the Met in New York, Rudolf Bing forbade them.

DIVA

Italian: 'divine woman'

Used of a great female singer when even *prima donna assoluta* seems inadequate. The term has imperious overtones of a bygone era.

ENCORE!!

The one meaning this French word doesn't have in France is the one for which English speakers use it: 'Please play it again' or 'More, please'. The French cry *'Bis!'* or *'Répétez!'* if they want extra helpings. *'Encore'* to them simply means 'yet', 'still' or 'longer'. An English tenor was engaged for a *lieder* recital in the Austrian capital, to be sung in German. He was honoured but at the same time apprehensive, for he knew that the Viennese are among the most knowledgeable and demanding of critics. He began nervously but well, feeling in fine voice. After the fourth item there was a surprising and gratifying chorus demanding he sing the song again. He obliged and repeated the selection. Again, its finish was greeted with loud roars . Again he sang the same song. 'Once more', they shouted as soon as he ended. Smilingly, he signalled for silence and said how kind, but could he proceed now with the rest of his programme? 'No,' came the reply, 'not until you've sung the last one properly.'

INTERMEZZO

Italian: 'interlude'

In its original sense, the intermezzo was a short musical entertainment performed during the course of a more serious one. It developed into a genre of its own in the eighteenth century, providing the beginning of *opera buffa*. Nowadays it is associated exclusively with an orchestral interlude typically played between two scenes or acts to denote the passage of time or a change of scene. The Intermezzo from Mascagni's **Cavalleria Rusticana** is the most famous example.

LEITMOTIV

German: 'leading motif'

A term first coined in 1871 in a discussion of the works of **Weber** who made much use of the device in *Der Freischutz* and *Euryanthe*. All it is is a short musical phrase identified with a particular person, emotion, event or idea. It's a term very much associated with **Wagner** because he, more than anybody, consciously developed the *leitmotiv* as an integral part of an operatic score. Not only did he use these little figures (which he preferred to call 'remembrance motifs', 'idea motifs' etc.) to create subtle evocations of moods, events and characters, but he did so in musically ingenious ways, so that, in his words, 'they are contrasted with one another, supplement each other, assume new shapes'. Music was thus lent a kind of unity unlike anything previously heard in opera.

The influence of Wagner's use of 'leading motifs' was enormous; there is hardly an opera written since that does not have them. **Richard Strauss, Humperdinck, Janáček**, Berg, Schoenberg – all of their music is indebted to Wagner's practice.

Wagnerites are obsessed with *leitmotiv* and, like train-spotters, compile catalogues, cross-referencing them and pointing out the similarities of, say, the leading motif of the *Liebestod* from **Tristan und Isolde** with that of the Holy Grail in *Parsifal*.

LIBRETTO

Italian: 'little book'

The text of an opera, the story, the book of words that are sung and spoken, requiring from the audience 'the willing suspension of disbelief'. We don't know very much about opera librettists. Their names are, with the exception of Gilbert (of **Gilbert and Sullivan**), scarcely known to any but opera fanatics. There must be (and is) a very good reason for this. A libretto which is as rewarding, as convincing and as timeless as the music to which it is set is a rare commodity. Don't let's fool ourselves: most opera libretti are, at the worst, tosh, or, at the best, not Shakespeare. A great composer can make a weak libretto into a masterpiece (e.g. *Il Trovatore*) or at least passable entertainment (e.g. *The Pearl Fishers*). A weak composer has never had a triumph with an opera boasting a brilliant libretto. Many good libretti, too, have had to undergo the debilitating effect of mediocre translations which doesn't help the cause.

Gilbert and Sullivan is the best-known example of a successful librettist and composer team, but others have been Calzabigi and **Gluck**, Da Ponte and **Mozart**, Hofmannstahl and **Richard Strauss**. **Wagner** and a few others wrote their own. **Boito** wrote his own and other people's (Verdi's *Otello* and *Falstaff*) besides composing.

The majority of libretti will not be clearly heard or understood by the audience. Most are highly implausible, too. An opera-goer, in the words of Nicolas Slonimsky, must leave his scepticism with his hat in the cloakroom.

MEZZO-SOPRANO

Italian: 'half-soprano'

The middle category of the female voice, a few notes lower than a soprano at both ends of the scale. Famous ones: **Janet Baker**, **Teresa Berganza**, **Marilyn Horne**, **Christa Ludwig**, **Conchita Supervia**.

OPERA

Italian: 'work'

A drama (frequently, but not always, a tragedy) in which all or most of the characters sing and in which music constitutes the dominant and unifying part. OPERETTA (Italian: little opera) is a more light-hearted opera, almost exclusively a mid-nineteenth- to early twentieth-century European phenomenon, and is virtually the same as LIGHT OPERA. The MUSICAL or MUSICAL COMEDY is an American or English light operetta of the nineteenth and twentieth centuries, usually less unified musically and often requiring the principals to sing and dance *simultaneously*. This is why **Pavarotti** sticks to opera.

There are other subdivisions:

OPÉRA BOUFFE (pronounced: *Boof*) (French: comic opera) A term taken from the Italian (see below), although historically not quite the same. A type of satirical, light opera, especially by **Offenbach** and his ilk.

OPERA BUFFA (pronounced: *Boof'-a*) (Italian: comic opera) Often with stock comic characters and plots involving disguises, mistaken identities, intrigues and unlikely endings. Especially associated with eighteenth-century works.

OPÉRA COMIQUE A French term that, confusingly, does *not* mean a 'comic opera'. The form began in the eighteenth century when the word *comique* was attached to entertainments that were intended to send up Grand Opera and – the important thing – had *spoken dialogue*. The Paris Opéra banned spoken dialogue; its rival, the Opéra-Comique, made a feature of it. The description 'comique' embraced the tragedies of *Faust* and *Carmen* because, in their original versions, both had spoken, rather than sung recitatives.

GRAND OPERA One of those bandied-about phrases that has a somewhat vague meaning. Operas which involve grand emotions, grand spectacle and grand themes all fall into this category, which, frankly, can embrace anything from **Handel** to **Meyerbeer** to **Verdi**. Grand Opera tends to have no spoken dialogue, frequently includes ballet and other interludes – and never has any jokes.

OPERA SERIA (Italian: serious opera) The opposite of *opera buffa* and the same sort of thing that is meant by Grand Opera, but specifically of the seventeenth and eighteenth centuries. It should contain at least three acts (and as many as five) and deal with emotional, tragic, disastrous entanglements involving murder, death and suicide. In fact, plenty to sing about.

PRIMA DONNA

Italian: 'first lady'

Before about 1700 this was the title given to the leading artists of the day, since vocal writing required ever-increasing skill from the singers. Later, the term came to mean a highly paid, celebrated soprano. Later still (today) it came to mean an overpaid, temperamental artist. As in 'He/she's a bit of a prima donna', i.e. spoilt, selfish and apt to behave in public the way overpaid, temperamental but musically gifted artists are expected to behave. (See also **Diva**.)

PRIMA DONNA ASSOLUTA

Italian: 'absolute first lady'

Just to rub the point in. Because she could sing '*Vissi d'arte*' from Puccini's *Tosca* lying face down on the floor, Maria Jeritza (1887–1982) was known as *la prima donna prostrata*. It's not known whether or not it was she who complained to Sir Thomas Beecham of having to perform the aria while lying flat on her face, but Beecham replied, '*Madam, I have given some of my best performances in that posture.*'

RECITATIVE

The bits in between the arias where there are no tunes and everyone is half singing, half talking. In fact the plot and the action happen almost exclusively in recitative. As the nineteenth century progressed, the gap between the end of the story-telling recitative and the beginning of the reflective aria became less and less obvious. With Wagner, recitative and aria became one, i.e. 'through-composed', an endless melody. (Hence the difficulty of playing chunks of Wagner.)

SINGSPIEL

German: 'song-play'

A German opera written with spoken dialogue separating the musical numbers (pantomime style), as opposed to a work with continuous musical accompaniment, recitative, etc. First applied in the eighteenth century to plays using the occasional bit of music, it developed into a distinct (and highly popular) form in its own right, culminating in *The Magic Flute*, *Fidelio* and *Der Freischütz*.

SOPRANO

Italian: from sopra, *meaning 'above'*

The highest female voice. The normal range is two octaves, from middle C upwards, but some roles require even higher and lower notes. Usually the heroine. Opera houses (but never composers in their scores) classify the different soprano voices according to the character of the roles. For example:

DRAMATIC SOPRANO For roles needing a powerful voice and the ability to declaim. Brünnhilde (*The Ring*), Tosca.

LYRIC SOPRANO or SOPRANO LEGGIERO Needed for roles which are lighter, less histrionic. Arabella, Countess (*Figaro*), Mimi (*La Bohème*), Lakmé.

COLORATURA SOPRANO For the parts which demand neat, acrobatic agility and a wide range. Queen of the Night (*Magic Flute*).

LIRICO SPINTO (literally 'lyrically pushed') Desdemona (*Otello*) and **Madam Butterfly**.

Famous sopranos: **Montserrat Caballé, Maria Callas, Kiri Te Kanawa, Jessye Norman, Joan Sutherland.**

SURTITLE

The equivalent of subtitles in the cinema, a device that offers a visual translation of the foreign language being sung on stage. On the one hand it tells you what they're singing about; on the other you may find it disconcerting when the audience reacts well after the character has spoken the line. Or, even worse, before.

TENOR

Italian: from tenore, *meaning 'holding';*
originally the voice that 'held' the plainsong

The high male voice, with a range of two octaves, from C below middle C to the C above it. One mark of a great tenor voice is the quality and duration of the top C (thus Pavarotti's nickname, 'King of the high Cs'). Usually the hero. Like sopranos, opera houses have useful categories for ease of casting each part. For example:

HELDENTENOR (German: heroic tenor) A voice made for the dramatic demands of the heavy roles, particularly associated with **Wagner**. **Lauritz Melchior** was the archetypal example.

LYRIC TENOR Corresponding to the Lyric Soprano. Max (*Der Freischütz*).

LIRICO SPINTO ('pushed', i.e. requiring vigour and attack) Rodolfo (*La Bohème*).

TENORE DI FORZA For roles where a robust voice, full of vigour, is necessary to convey strong passions – Otello, for example.

Famous tenors: **Jussi Björling, José Carreras, Enrico Caruso, Placido Domingo, Luciano Pavarotti.**

TESSITURA

Italian: 'texture'

You'll hear opera buffs referring to such-and-such a role as having 'a high tessitura'. This doesn't mean that the role has particularly high notes, but that most of the role is written using the upper range of the voice (for example many *coloratura* parts). Equally, if there are frequent low notes, the part is said to have a low tessitura.

TRAVESTI

French: from travestir, *meaning 'to disguise'*

In English we call it a 'trouser role' or 'breeches part', for example Cherubino (*The Marriage of Figaro*), Orlovsky (*Die Fledermaus*) or Octavian (*Der Rosenkavalier*), in other words male characters sung by women. The cross-dressing tradition flourishes in pantomime (Dandini, Prince Charming, etc.).

VERISMO

Italian: 'realism'

The naturalistic school of opera represented by the works of **Mascagni, Puccini**, Giordano and **Leoncavallo**. *Pagliacci* is often cited as the first of its kind, but *Carmen* has a stronger claim. The subjects of *verismo* operas were not drawn from legend or morality tales but from real life – and more often than not low life (*La Bohème, Louise* and *Cavalleria Rusticana*). *Verismo* works typically present heightened violence and emotions in everyday life.

VIBRATO

Italian: 'vibrated'

The slight fluctuation in the note being sung which keeps the note 'alive'. Violinists use the same technique when they press down the strings to produce a note. When done well, it is admirable; when exaggerated, done badly (or more likely when the voice is past it) and the fluctuation is wide and pronounced, vibrato becomes wobble.

BEFORE YOU BEGIN ...

Before you start skimming through the book, here are a few points:

❖ Generally, the more space devoted to an opera, the more suitable it is for a first visit to the opera; conversely, the less space, the more you should wait for a while or bone up beforehand. The exception to this is the amount of space devoted to Wagner's operas; they simply take up a lot of room to outline.

❖ The opera titles used are those by which the operas are generally known to British audiences. Thus **Madam Butterfly** rather than *Madama Butterfly*, **The Tales of Hoffmann**, rather than *Les Contes d'Hoffmann*, **Die Fledermaus** rather than *The Bat*.

❖ The translations of aria titles are not alway literal; many convey the sense of what is being sung.

❖ Spellings of opera titles, names of characters, performers etc. are as given in Kobbé (10th edition, 1987) and/or Baker's (7th edition, 1984).

❖ All dates given for operas are those of the first performance and not the date of composition, unless otherwise stated.

❖ Lengths of performances of the major operas are approximate and do not include intervals.

❖ In the abbreviations used after the name of the main characters, s = soprano; ms = mezzo-soprano; c = contralto; ct = counter-tenor; t = tenor; bar = baritone; b = bass.

❖ All the plots/stories of the opera have been greatly condensed and are only given in outline. Some, like **The Ring** and **Don Giovanni**, have a far greater depth and significance than can be dealt with here. Just remember that following *any* synopsis of an opera plot will reveal the fact that the action takes at least five times as long to unravel as an ordinary play.

❖ Highlights from each opera are listed only if they are generally well-known. They are cross-referenced in the index. If no highlights are indicated then there are no real 'hits' from the work.

❖ The recommended recordings for each opera are the best, in my opinion, currently available. I have generally opted for quality of performance rather than quality of sound, so that some oldish recordings (perhaps in mono) may be my first choice. I would rather listen to the hiss and crackle of a uniquely magical piece of singing than put up with superb reproduction and a lifeless, lacklustre performance. The added bonus here is that if an older recording is first choice it is often reasonably priced, so you won't have to risk a fortune on something you might then discover you don't like. Recordings listed are complete, but highlights are also recommended for the major operas. Artists are listed first, followed by chorus, orchestra and conductor.

❖ All records are stereo and the numbers are for compact discs unless otherwise indicated.

ABBREVIATIONS

BPO	Berlin Philharmonic Orchestra
Ch	Choir
LPO	London Philharmonic Orchestra
LSO	London Symphony Orchestra
NPO	New Philharmonia Orchestra
NSO	New Symphony Orchestra
O	Orchestra
PO	Philharmonia Orchestra
Phil.	Philharmonic
Philh.	Philharmonia
ROHCG	Royal Opera House, Covent Garden
RPO	Royal Philharmonic Orchestra
RSO	Radio Symphony Orchestra
SO	Symphony Orchestra
VPO	Vienna Philharmonic Orchestra
VSO	Vienna Symphony Orchestra

❖ The composers section is an alphabetical guide to the most celebrated *opera* composers. You won't find any mention of Bach, Brahms or Chopin, for instance, since they didn't write any operas; you won't read much about Beethoven either (he only wrote one) and nothing at all about Debussy (*Pelléas et Mélisande*, his only opera, is not for the uninitiated).

❖ The performers section lists some of the most famous and important opera singers, past and present. You can pick up a fair amount of opera by listening to selected recordings of various artists. It's quite fascinating to compare the way in which two great tenors, say, will interpret a well-known aria in two totally different but equally convincing ways.

For reasons of space, this section includes, with few exceptions, only singers who have had long established international careers. This has, alas, forced the omission of many world-class artists such as Cheryl Studer, Cecilia Bartoli, Anne Sofie van Otter, Sumi Jo, José van Dam, Renato Bruson, Kathleen Battle, Bryn Terfel and many others.

❖ The index allows you to look up the title of an aria (or the name by which it's generally known) and see immediately which opera it comes from. You can also do the same for the principal characters in the major operas. Any word in **bold type** means that it's cross-referenced in its own entry.

THE OPERAS

'Opera is when a guy gets stabbed in the back and instead of bleeding, he sings'

ED GARDNER, 1905 ~ 1963

ADRIANA LECOUVREUR
FRANCESCO CILEA
1902

PRONOUNCED: AD-REE-AR¹-NER
LE-COO¹-VRUH

LIBRETTO: ARTURO COLAUTTI
BASED ON THE 1849 PLAY OF THE
SAME NAME BY ERNEST LEGOUVÉ
AND EUGÈNE SCRIBE

4 ACTS SET IN PARIS IN 1730

The tragedy of a lovers' quartet, based on a true story. Two women are in love with the same man, Maurizio, Count of Saxony (*t*); one of them is loved by a another man, Michonnet (*bar*), the stage-manager of the Comédie Française. The women in question are the famous French actress Adrienne (Adriana) Lecouvreur (*s*) (1692–1730) and her rival, Princess de Bouillon (*ms*). Adriana has one of opera's more unusual demises – she inhales the scent of a bunch of poisoned violets.

RECOMMENDED RECORDING
Scotto/Domingo/
Obratsova/Milnes
Philh. O, Levine
SONY CD 79310

L' AFRICAINE
MEYERBEER
1865

PRONOUNCED: LAF-REE-KEN
LITERALLY 'THE AFRICAN MAID'
LIBRETTO: EUGÈNE SCRIBE

5 ACTS SET IN LISBON, AT SEA AND IN INDIA, EARLY IN THE 16TH CENTURY

This was one of the most popular operas of the nineteenth century but it is rarely seen nowadays. **Meyerbeer** and Scribe worked on the piece for over twenty years (the composer actually died before the first production). The Portuguese explorer Vasco da Gama is shipwrecked off the African coast, having returned to Portugal with two captives – Nelusko (*bar*) and Selika (*s*), the African queen of the title. Feckless

Two scenes from Act 4 of
L'Africaine

Vasco falls in love with her but finally returns to his old love Inez (*s*), leaving Selika to die another unusual death (see *Adriana Lecouvreur* above) – she kills herself by breathing the poisonous scent of the manchineel tree.

HIGHLIGHT

ACT 4 '*O paradiso!*' ('Oh Paradise') Sung by Vasco da Gama as he surveys the wonderful tropical scene before him. Still a favourite with **tenors**.

RECOMMENDED RECORDING
Maggio Musicale Fiorentino
Muti
MEMO HR42 13/5

AIDA

VERDI

1871

PRONOUNCED: EYE-EE'-DAH
LIBRETTO: ANTONIO GHISLANZONI
BASED ON THE ORIGINAL BY CAMILLE DU LOCLE
LENGTH: 2' 30"

This is what **grand opera** is all about. *Aida* has spectacle, intimacy, a strong story, triumphant chorus numbers and memorable arias. In the ABC of operatic popularity, *Aida* comes first, then *La Bohème*, then *Carmen*. It has held its place in the repertoire for over a century and you can see why. With or without the elephants, it provides a thrilling and moving experience.

BACKGROUND

Ismail Pasha, the Khedive (Viceroy) of Egypt, commissioned Verdi to write a piece for the new Opera House in Cairo. (It was not produced for its opening, nor written to celebrate the 1869 opening of the Suez Canal as legend has it.) Verdi requested a fee of $20,000 for the job (a huge sum then) and got it without a murmur. Camille du Locle, a French admirer of Verdi and a former director of the Opéra-Comique in Paris, wrote the libretto in French prose, which was then translated into Italian verse by Ghislanzoni; but it was a famous French Egyptologist, François-Auguste Mariette (also, confusingly, known as Mariette Bey) who in fact came up with the idea for the opera (and also

Ethiopian prisoners huddle before the Pharaoh in the finale of Act 2, Aida

directed the first production). The score was completed by 1870 but by then the Franco-Prussian War had erupted. Paris, from where all the costumes and scenery came, was besieged by the Prussian Army and *Aida* had to wait a year for its premiere.

FIRST PERFORMANCE

Cairo Opera House
24 December 1871

A glittering polyglot audience could follow the story with librettos printed in Italian, Arabic, French and Turkish (the initial print order of 1,000 had to be doubled). The Khedive arrived with his entire harem, which occupied three boxes. So enthusiastic was the reception of some numbers that the conductor, Bottesini, had to turn to the audience and shout angrily, 'That isn't done!' According to the Khedive's assistant, the reaction was one of 'total fanaticism' and he wired the composer: 'We have had a success beyond belief.' Verdi hated such glitzy occasions; he also loathed travelling by sea and so missed the premiere. He did, however, conduct the first performance in Italy at La Scala, Milan on 8 February 1872, when

Enrico Caruso as Radames in 1908

he was presented with an ivory baton and a diamond- and ruby-studded star.

STORY

4 acts set in Memphis and Thebes during the time of the Pharaohs (c. 2000 BC)

PRINCIPAL CHARACTERS
AIDA, an Ethiopian slave (s)
RADAMES, Captain of the Egyptian Guard (t)
AMNERIS, an Egyptian princess (ms)
KING OF EGYPT, father of Amneris (b)
AMONASRO, King of Ethiopia and father of Aida (bar)
RAMPHIS, High Priest of Egypt (b)

Radames hopes he will be given command of the Egyptian Army in order to win the heart of Aida, the Ethiopian slave with whom he has fallen in love. He does not know that she is really the daughter of the Ethiopian king, nor that he himself

is loved by Amneris, daughter of the Egyptian king. Radames' wish is granted and he goes to the temple to invoke the blessing of the gods on his endeavours. Suspecting that Aida loves Radames, Amneris tricks her into admitting this and threatens to have her killed.

Radames returns victorious. Among his prisoners is the Ethiopian King Amonasro, disguised as a simple soldier. Aida recognizes her father but is begged not to reveal his identity as he implores clemency. The Pharaoh rewards, as he thinks, Radames with his daughter's hand, while Radames requests the freedom of his prisoners. This is granted except for Aida and her still unidentified father who are kept as hostages.

Amneris prepares for her marriage on the banks of the sacred

Nile while Radames and Aida secretly meet to say adieu. Amonasro attempts to persuade his daughter to extract from Radames the Egyptian Army's plans. Instead, she and Radames plan their escape together and he, unwittingly, betrays his country by telling her which pass is unguarded at present. Amonasro appears and reveals his true identity. Amneris and Ramphis have overheard the scene and, as Aida and her father flee, Radames surrenders to them.

Amneris confronts Radames as he is taken to prison and promises to save him from being buried alive if he will renounce Aida. Radames refuses. Amneris regrets her jealousy but can do nothing now to save her love from the sentence pronounced by the priests. In his living tomb, Radames hears a sound and discovers Aida beside him. She has returned to share his terrible death. Amneris prays for Radames' peace and happiness while the two lovers glory in their love and sing farewell to life on earth.

HIGHLIGHTS

ACT 1 *'Celeste Aida'* ('Heavenly Aida') Radames sings the praises of his 'divine' Aida. Usually spoilt by the arrival of latecomers as it comes so near the beginning of the opera. A great tenor recital favourite.
'Ritorna vincitor' ('Return victorious') Aida is torn between her feelings for her lover and her father.
ACT 2 *Grand March*. The triumphal victory thanksgiving.
ACT 3 *'O patria mia'* ('O my native land') Aida recalls happier days in Ethiopia.
ACT 4 *'O terra, addio'* ('O Earth, farewell') The final duet between Aida and Radames.

AKHNATEN
PHILIP GLASS
1984
PRONOUNCED: ARK-NAR'-TUN
LIBRETTO: GLASS IN ASSOCIATION
WITH SHALOM GOLDMAN

3 ACTS AND AN EPILOGUE SET IN
EGYPT IN 1370 BC AND
THE PRESENT DAY

As with the stage works of Birtwistle, Maxwell Davies and other contemporaries, Glass's *Akhnaten* falls outside the accepted definition of opera. With no narrative, it's more a succession of episodes, some symbolic, some factual, that together add up to a theatrical experience with minimalist music. There's not much singing, but there is chanting, dancing, mime and speaking – all elements of traditional opera, though not the main one which has tended to emphasize the voice-beautiful singing. There's no doubt that it provides a memorable evening – for a variety of reasons. Its early productions captivated the more adventurous culture-vultures. However, if your preference for an evening out is *The Sound of Music* with *La Bohème* as a bit of high art, better leave this one for a bit.

There is no story as such, but an imaginative evocation of life in the time of Akhnaten (*ct*) King of Egypt and his wife Queen Nefertiti (*alto*). Ancient texts sung in the

original language are used to build a portrait of Ancient Egypt, from its rituals and dances to the historical events which led to the eventual overthrow of Akhnaten. Finally, tourists are guided around the ruins of his city (Akhetaten), the spirit of the Pharaoh still hovering around them.

RECOMMENDED RECORDING
Stuttgart State Op.Ch. & O,
D. R. Davies
CBS CD42457

UN BALLO IN MASCHERA
VERDI
1859
PRONOUNCED:
UN BAL'-O IN MASK'-UR-OH
'A MASKED BALL'
LIBRETTO: ANTONIO SOMMA
BASED ON ONE BY
EUGÈNE SCRIBE

3 ACTS SET IN
18TH CENTURY SWEDEN

The story is based on fact (King Gustave III was assassinated at a masked ball in Stockholm in March 1792). *Gustavus III*, as **Verdi** originally called his work, was to have been staged in 1858, shortly after the attempted murder of Napoleon III. The authorities banned any work dealing with the murder of a monarch and Verdi eventually agreed to change the location (bizarrely) to Boston, Massachusetts. For King Gustavus III read Riccardo, Count of Warwick and Governor of Boston; for Anckarstroem read Renato and for Mlle Arvidson read Ulrica, a Negro sorceress. Nowadays, the Stockholm version is preferred.

❖

K ing Gustavus III of Sweden (*t*)

loves Amelia (*s*), the wife of his friend and secretary, Captain Anckarstroem (*bar*). Mlle Arvidson (*c*), a fortune-teller, predicts the death of Gustavus at the hands of a friend. The Captain, having learned that there is a plot afoot to kill his master, hurries to warn the King of the danger but encounters him with a veiled lady – his wife, Amelia. Believing she has been unfaithful, Anckarstroem joins in the plot to murder the King at a masked ball.

HIGHLIGHT

ACT 3 *'Eri tu che macchiavi quell'anima'* ('Would you have sullied a soul so pure?') sung by Anckarstroem.

RECOMMENDED RECORDING

L. Price/Bergonzi/Merrill
RCA Italian Op. Ch. & O,
Leinsdorf
BMG/RCA GD 86645

THE BARBER OF SEVILLE

ROSSINI

1816

ORIGINAL ITALIAN TITLE: 'IL BARBIERE DI SIVIGLIA'
PRONOUNCED: EEL BAHR-BE-AY'REH DEE SEE-VEEL'YAH
LIBRETTO: CESARE STERBINI AFTER THE COMEDY BY BEAUMARCHAIS
LENGTH: 2' 30"

For many people Rossini's *The Barber*, as everyone calls it, is the perfect comic opera and provides all the principal singers with splendid opportunities, especially the soprano or mezzo appearing as Rosina. The score bubbles with wit, charm and all the elements of **opera buffa** – some spirited classical **recitative**, wonderful tunes, a tightly-knit plot, splendid stage effects and genuine comic invention. It is so full of

Dr Bartolo discovers he's been tricked, in Welsh National Opera's 1987 production of The Barber of Seville

joyous good humour and high spirits that many of its melodies (to say nothing of the overture) are known and loved even by those who have never heard a complete opera. *The Barber* has never been out of the repertoire and remains among the most popular operas ever written. Deservedly so.

BACKGROUND

The Barber is based on the first of three plays concerning the lovable rogue, Figaro (the barber of the title), by the French dramatist Pierre Augustin Caron de Beaumarchais. His *Le Barbier de Séville* (1775) was followed in 1784 by *Le Mariage de Figaro* – the one on which **Mozart** based his opera – and in 1792 by *La Mère Coupable*.

There were at least four other musical versions of Beaumarchais's play doing the rounds when Rossini decided to write his. The most popular was by Giovanni Paisiello, written in 1783. Under contract to provide the Teatro di Torre Argentina in Rome with an opera, the busy twenty-four-year-old Rossini left the work until the last minute and, desperate for a story, obtained 'permission' from Paisiello to use the Beaumarchais play. The 600 pages of *The Barber* were

written in thirteen days, according to Rossini (nineteen according to his biographer), an incredible feat, although he did borrow suitable bits of music from some of his earlier operas to help him. The famous overture, for example, is a reworking of material from his earlier failures *Aureliano in Palmira* and *Elisabetta, Regina d'Inghilterra*, and the first-night audience didn't take too kindly to it when they recognised it as such!

FIRST PERFORMANCE

Teatro Argentina, Rome
20 February 1816

The premiere was a fiasco. Entitled *Almaviva ossia l'inutile precauzione* ('Almaviva or The Futile Precaution') to distinguish it from Paisiello's version, there were various technical hitches on stage – one of the singers tripped and had to sing with a bloody nose; a cat wandered on stage and distracted everyone's attention. But it was the off-stage antics of the followers of Paisiello which created the impression of a first-night failure. Furious at Rossini's impudence in re-using material already successfully set by their hero, they booed, whistled and catcalled throughout the performance. Legend has it that the singers, anxious to console Rossini,

Cover for the vocal score of The Barber of Seville

hurried round to his house afterwards. They found him totally unconcerned – he was already in bed, sleeping peacefully. After some quick rewrites the following day, Rossini watched the second performance – a triumph. Soon afterwards, he also changed the title. Paisiello's version was already consigned to oblivion.

STORY

2 acts set in Seville in the 17th century

PRINCIPAL CHARACTERS
COUNT ALMAVIVA (t)
FIGARO, the barber of Seville (bar)
DOCTOR BARTOLO (bar)
DON BASILIO, a music-teacher (b)
ROSINA, ward of Bartolo (s, ms or c)

Count Almaviva is in love with Rosina, the rich ward of Dr Bartolo who keeps her under lock and key. The ingenious Figaro, the city's popular barber and Mister Fixit, is the perfect person to help the Count, and after Rosina has

In Act 2, Rosina is given 'a music lesson' by the Count. The original Rossini manuscript was long said to be lost. This gave Rosina the chance to interpolate any favourite song of her choosing, often nothing to do with Rossini and frequently written years after the opera. **Adelina Patti** *liked to sing 'Home Sweet Home', while Marcella Sembrich (1858–1935) would sit down at the piano* and sing, to her own accompaniment, Chopin's 'Maiden's Wish' in Polish. **Nellie Melba (1861–1931)** *preferred to accompany herself in Tosti's 'Mattinata' while* **Amelita Galli-Curci (1882–1963)** *went for 'The Last Rose of Summer'. Nowadays, Rosina sings what Rossini wrote – 'Contro un cor che accende amore' ('Against a heart inflamed by love').*

managed to pass a letter to the Count under her guardian's nose asking him to reveal his name, Figaro manages the affair. Bartolo, anxious to marry his ward himself and get his hands on her dowry, has heard of the Count and with his old friend Don Basilio they plot to spread rumours that will force him to leave Seville. Figaro suggests the Count should dress up first as a drunken soldier pretending he has been billeted on Dr Bartolo (this nearly gets him arrested by the police) and then as a music teacher sent in to replace Rosina's usual teacher, who is, apparently, ill. This ruse is successful and the two lovers are plotting their elopement when the real music master appears. A bag of gold persuades him that he really *is* ill and he departs. Bartolo, meanwhile, has obtained a letter the Count has written to Rosina and, when they are alone, he persuades his ward that Almaviva has written it to another woman. Rosina believes him and, in a jealous fury, decides to marry her guardian. Figaro once more saves the situation in the nick of time, and the notary who was to have married the doctor and his ward performs the ceremony for the Count and Rosina. For once in an opera everybody ends up happy – even the doctor. He is given Rosina's dowry as recompense.

HIGHLIGHTS

Overture

ACT 1 *'Ecco ridente in cielo'* ('See, smiling in the sky') Almaviva serenades his love in the grey light of dawn.

'Largo al factotum' ('Make way for the factotum') Figaro's introduction of himself and perhaps the best known of all operatic tongue-twisters ('Figaro, Figaro, Figaro!').

'Una voce poco fa' (variously translated as 'A little voice I heard just now', 'A voice in the distance' and 'A little voice within my heart' – known irreverently to pros as 'Do not poke it up too far') Among the greatest of all operatic *coloratura* arias, sung by Rosina after hearing the Count's serenade from her balcony.

'La calunnia e un venticello' ('Slander is like a breath of wind') Dr Bartolo, with the help of Don Basilio, agrees to hatch a plot to slander the Count.

Sextet: *'Fredda ed immobile'* ('Frozen and motionless') Confusion and bewilderment all round at the end of Act 1.

ACT 2 *'Buona sera, mio signore'* ('Fare you well, good sir') The quintet in which Basilio is hustled away.

RECOMMENDED RECORDINGS

complete:
De los Angeles/ Alva/Cava
Glyndebourne Festival Ch., RPO, Gui
EMI CMS7 64162 2
(also at bargain price on cassette
CFP TC-CFPD 4704)
highlights: Callas/Alva/Gobbi
Philh. Ch. & O, Galliera
EMI CDM7 63076 2
video: La Scala, Abbado
DG 072 404-3GH

THE BARTERED BRIDE
BEDŘICH SMETANA
1866
ORIGINAL CZECH TITLE: 'PRODANÁ NEVĚSTA'
LIBRETTO: KAREL SABINA

3 ACTS SET IN A VILLAGE IN 19TH-CENTURY BOHEMIA

*T*he Battered Bride (as it's known in the trade) is the only one of Smetana's operas still performed regularly. He made five versions of this comic masterpiece which beautifully conjures up Czech rural life. The delightful score is filled with dance rhythms and folk-songs.

❖

It tells the story of two lovers, Mařenka (*s*) and Jenik (*t*). Mařenka's parents have decided that she shall marry the son (whom she has never seen) of the wealthy Tobias Micha, as arranged by Kečal (*b*) the village marriage broker. The son turns out to be a simpleton, Vašek (*t*), and Mařenka successfully persuades him to have nothing to do with her; meanwhile Kečal gives Jenik 300 crowns if he will finish with Mařenka so that she can marry Vašek. Vašek himself falls in love with Esmerelda (*s*), a circus dancer. The bitter Mařenka decides that after all she *will* marry Vašek – who then turns out to be Jenik's half-brother. Jenik has outwitted the marriage broker – he can keep the money and marry his love.

HIGHLIGHTS

Overture
ACT 1 *Polka*
ACT 2 *Furiant*
Dance of the Comedians
ACT 3 *'Our dream of love'*

RECOMMENDED RECORDING
Benackova/Vesela/ Mrazova
Czech Phil. Ch. & O, Kosler
SUPRAPHON 35112

LA BOHEME

PUCCINI

1896

USUALLY TRANSLATED AS 'THE BOHEMIANS', OR 'BOHEMIAN LIFE'
LIBRETTO: GIUSEPPE GIACOSA AND LUIGI ILLICA
AFTER THE NOVEL BY HENRI MURGER 'SCÈNES DE LA VIE DE BOHÈME'
LENGTH: 1' 30"

How many people have become hooked on the whole experience of opera from hearing this most romantic of pieces for the first time? You couldn't make a better choice than *La Bohème* for your introduction to the genre. Here you have a touching tale of love, laughter and tears, with some of the best-known **arias** ever written. The bustling brilliance of the score, which contrasts moments of high passion and drama with heart-rending lyricism, will have you reaching for the tissues. For many people, this is the quintessence of what they understand by Italian opera.

BACKGROUND

La Bohème was Puccini's fourth opera (after *Le Villi*, *Edgar* and *Manon Lescaut*) and the one that finally established him as a major operatic composer. He came to write it through his friendship with fellow composer Ruggiero Leoncavallo, one of several collaborators on the *Manon Lescaut* libretto. The two met in the streets of Milan in March 1893 and, so it goes, Leoncavallo told Puccini that he had commenced work on an opera based on the dramatization of Henri Murger's novel *Scènes de la vie de Bohème*, a subject he had previously suggested to Puccini but which Puccini had rejected. On being told this news, however, Puccini insisted that he had already started on his own version of the story. The next day Leoncavallo wrote an angry letter to the papers, staking his claim; Puccini replied indolently, 'Let him compose his opera, and I will compose mine. The public will judge.' And judge it did. Although Leoncavallo's version, first performed in May 1897, sticks to the original more faithfully, it never equalled the success of Puccini's, so rapidly did this achieve its wide popularity.

FIRST PERFORMANCE

Teatro Regio, Turin, Italy
1 February 1896
The conductor on this occasion was the young Arturo Toscanini, just beginning to make a name for himself (he recorded the opera many years later). Though the audience took to it immediately, its reception was far less enthusiastic than it had been for *Manon Lescaut* and the critics' reactions were, at first, decidedly cool. 'Unsuccessful,' they said. 'Deplorable decline.' '*La Bohème*', wrote the respected critic of one Turin paper, 'will not leave much of a mark in the history of Italian opera.' *La Bohème* has been regularly performed the world over ever since, perhaps the best loved of all operas, and one of the most strikingly original.

STORY

4 acts set in the Latin Quarter of Paris, *c.* 1830

PRINCIPAL CHARACTERS
THE BOHEMIANS:
RODOLFO, a poet (t)
MARCELLO, a painter (bar)
SCHAUNARD, a musician (bar)
COLLINE, a philosopher (b)

BENOIT, a landlord (b)
MIMI, a dressmaker (s)
MUSETTA, a grisette* (s)
**(a young working-class French girl, usually poorly paid but who always likes a good time.)*

It is Christmas Eve and the four inseparable Bohemians – poet, painter, musician and philosopher – lead a precarious life of feast or famine. In Rodolfo's and Marcello's garret they meet, work, raise each others' spirits, struggle to keep warm and wonder how to pay the rent. Into Rodolfo's life comes the beautiful little consumptive seamstress Mimi, who knocks at the door asking for a match. It's love at first sight. Suddenly life seems very beautiful to them and, having agreed never to part, they declare what the future holds for them – love alone.

Full of Christmas spirit, they join their friends who are at a nearby café in the Latin Quarter, when Musetta, an old flame of Marcello's, comes to a neighbouring table with an ageing (and wealthy) admirer. No one has thought how to pay the bill, so as a regiment of guards passes by, they leave the café – and the bill – in the hands of Musetta's

Opposite: Cover for the vocal score of La Bohème

elderly dupe. Come February and both sets of lovers (Marcello and Musetta are back together) have had bruising quarrels. Rodolfo and Mimi have decided to part, Musetta and her flirting are having their effect on Marcello and *everyone* is cold. Back to the Bohemian life as before. In the attic, Schaunard and Colline arrive to share a scanty meal, which is joyfully magnified into a sumptuous banquet by their vivid imaginations. Suddenly, Musetta bursts in with the news that Mimi is dying. They bring her weak body, racked with coughing, into the room and lay her on Rodolfo's couch. The lovers are reconciled, but all attempts to save her are too late. Mimi fades away even as the friends reassure Rodolfo that all is well.

HIGHLIGHTS

ACT 1 *'Che gelida manina'* ('Your tiny hand is frozen') Rodolfo takes

Nellie Melba was the first singer to appear as Mimi at the Met, but although she was largely responsible for the opera's first successes at Covent Garden and in New York (both managements were initially reluctant to take it), she could not resist the temptation of giving the audience a bonus after she had expired, and came before the curtain to offer the Mad Scene from Donizetti's Lucia di Lammermoor.

Another famous Mimi, Frances Alda, authenticated the story that during one performance in Philadelphia, Andres de Segurola, the bass playing Colline, was taken ill while on stage in the final act. Caruso (her Rodolfo), with his back to the audience, sang the whole of Colline's aria, 'Vecchia zimarra'. No one except the conductor and those on stage knew the difference.

Mimi's hand as she enters. It's as cold as ice. He promises to warm it, tells her his name and that he is a poet who writes verses to beautiful eyes like hers.

The music matches the emotion as Rodolfo falls head over heels in love. One of the most popular of all **tenor** arias, known in the trade as 'you're tiny – and it's frozen'. *'Si, mi chiamano Mimi'* ('Yes, they call me Mimi') Mimi tells Rodolfo that she is a seamstress who makes artificial flowers for a living. Lonely and longing for the sunshine, she yearns for the real flowers of the countryside. *'O, soave fanciulla'* ('O lovely girl') The love duet between Rodolfo and Mimi before they leave for the café at the end of the act.

ACT 2 *'Quando me 'n vo'* ('When I am out walking', Musetta's Waltz Song) The enchanting Musetta, trying to attract Marcello's attention, sings of how much she enjoys being desired.

ACT 3 *'Addio, dolce svegliare'* ('Farewell, sweet awakenings') The unorthodox but beautiful quartet, sung by Rodolfo and Mimi who are parting with regret, Musetta and Marcello who are quarrelling as ever.

ACT 4 *'Ah Mimi, tu più non torni'* ('Ah Mimi, you will never come back') Rodolfo and Marcello sing

THE BOHEMIAN GIRL
MICHAEL WILLIAM BALFE
1843
LIBRETTO: ALFRED BUNN

3 ACTS SET IN PRESBURG, HUNGARY IN THE EARLY 19TH CENTURY

Together with *Maritana* (by Wallace) and *The Lily of Killarney* (by Benedict) the three were known for years as The English Ring. One of opera's more improbable stories didn't prevent this from remaining immensely popular up until the 1930s.

❖

Little Arline (s), the daughter of Count Arnheim (bar), is stolen by Devil's Hoof (b), a gypsy chieftain, and grows up among the gypsies. The Gypsy Queen (c) is in love with Thaddeus (t), a Polish exile who lives with the gypsies; he is in love with Arline. The Queen unjustly accuses the girl of stealing and she is brought before Count Arnheim to be tried. He recognizes his long-lost daughter, she reclaims her inheritance and the Gypsy Queen gets her come-uppance after the bullet she fires at Arline misses, ricochets and kills her.

HIGHLIGHTS

ACT 2 *'I dreamt I dwelt in marble halls'*, sung by Arline to Thaddeus, recalling her childhood. A greatly popular ballad in its day.

RECOMMENDED RECORDING
Thomas/Power
RTE Phil. Ch
National SO Ireland, Bonynge
ARGO 433 324-2ZH2

BORIS GODUNOV
MUSSORGSKY
1874
LIBRETTO: MUSSORGSKY
BASED ON THE PLAY BY
ALEXANDER PUSHKIN AND
NICOLAI KARAMZIN'S 'HISTORY
OF THE RUSSIAN STATE'

---

4 ACTS WITH A PROLOGUE
SET IN RUSSIA AND POLAND
BETWEEN 1598 AND 1605

The plot of this long, brooding work is complex enough, but the story of its evolution is almost as intricate. Books have been written on the subject. It was first produced in 1874, but only after two revisions of the original version, completed in 1868, had been rejected. Nowadays it is mostly seen in Rimsky-Korsakov's reorchestrated version. In essence, the story, which is based on real events, concerns the remorse of Tsar Boris (*b*) after he has killed Dmitry, the rightful heir to the throne of Russia. After his rise to

*Chaliapin as Boris Godunov
in 1921*

supreme power he himself comes to dread a second usurper, Grigory (*t*), a novice monk who poses as the young tsarevitch. The Pretender Dmitry raises a popular revolt in Poland and is acclaimed as the rightful Tsar. Boris, racked with guilt, loses his mind and, in a famous scene, dies after advising his son Fyodor how to rule.

The point of this complex (it is essential to follow it with an English translation) and lengthy work (over three hours) is not so much its succession of grand historical scenes as its examination of the personality of Boris, his personal tragedy in parallel with the tragedy of his nation. **Mussorgsky's** raw and innovative music (many feel that Rimsky's 'smoothed-out' version emasculates the original) and the lack of set-piece **arias** (the story is told largely with expressive and fast-moving recitative) make this a very different experience to the Italian operas being written at the same time. Difficult at first hearing, but ultimately rewarding and regarded as one of the greatest epic operas.

HIGHLIGHTS

PROLOGUE *Coronation Scene*
ACT 2 In the town of Kasan, Varlaam (*b*), a vagabond monk with whom Grigory has escaped to an inn on the Lithuanian border, sings a rollicking drinking-song recalling the deeds of Tsar Ivan the Terrible.
ACT 4 *The Death of Boris*. The tolling of the bells and the people praying for their dying sovereign form the background for Boris' terror. A famous show-piece for the title role. The Bulgarian bass-baritone **Boris Christoff** and before him the great Russian bass **Feodor Chaliapin**, are the two singers of different generations who made the role their own.

RECOMMENDED RECORDINGS
complete:
Arkhipova/Piavko/Vedernikov,
USSR TV Large Radio Ch & O,
Fedoseyev
PHILIPS 412 281
video: Bolshoi, Morozova
CAST CV12041

CARMEN

BIZET

1875

LIBRETTO: HENRI MEILHAC AND LUDOVIC HALÉVY
AFTER THE NOVELLA BY PROSPER MÉRIMÉE
LENGTH: 3 HOURS

With its succession of classical 'pops', compelling story and exotic settings, it's no wonder that *Carmen* is the most frequently performed of all operas and among the best-loved works in the repertoire. It's that rare thing, a truly great work that is universally popular. Everyone can find something in it: there are four or five tunes you can sing in the bath; there is the fast-moving and dramatic story with a charismatic heroine and a score that matches it moment for moment.

BACKGROUND

Bizet's opera career had been less than successful (the librettos he'd been landed with nowhere matched his talents as a composer) so using Mérimée's story for his next venture was, to say the least, brave. A risqué, low-life tale of passion and murder was not exactly the sort of stuff that the puritanical middle-class audiences of Paris's Opéra-Comique were used to. 'Mérimée's *Carmen*? Isn't she killed by her lover?' demurred the head of the Opéra-Comique when apprised of Bizet's intentions. 'And that background of thieves, gypsies and cigarette-makers! Death on the stage of the Opéra-Comique! Such a thing has never been seen!' Nevertheless, two of Paris's leading librettists, Meilhac and Halévy (a cousin of Bizet's wife), were persuaded by Bizet to adapt the book. (Mérimée had been inspired to write this after a visit to Spain in 1830. He had come across a 'swarthy waitress' whom his guide feared was a witch; her name was Carmencita.) During the lengthy rehearsals, Bizet fought hard against a reluctant management to retain the earthy realism of the story, revising many parts so as to tighten the action and heighten the dramatic tension, and cutting and rewriting sections (the first Carmen, Célestine Galli-Marié, instructed Bizet to rewrite the famous 'Habanera' no less than fourteen times in order to accommodate her voice). The composer had also to persuade the chorus – used to posing in tableaux – to act as individual characters. This was tantamount to revolution.

FIRST PERFORMANCE

Opéra-Comique, Paris
3 March 1875

After the struggle to mount the opera, the public reception of the work must have struck Bizet a terrible blow. Halévy wrote in his diary: 'Act 1 well received ... second act less fortunate ... Great effect from the Toreador's entry, followed by coldness. The coldness more marked in the third act ... The fourth act was glacial from first to last ... *Carmen* failed.'

The fact is the audience had come unprepared for this sort of subject-matter. The sight of girls smoking on stage, for instance, was quite a shock, and the depraved (to their minds) character of Carmen herself was not at all the sort of thing they were used to. The critics were keen to compare the score unfavourably with the work of **Wagner**. 'A definite and hopeless flop,' Bizet pronounced after enduring the unenthusiastic response.

Not entirely accurate, but Bizet was a bit like that. For a start, it was included in the next season of the Opéra-Comique, which would certainly not have happened had

---

SOME FIRST REACTIONS TO CARMEN

'*Carmen must stand on its own merits – and those are very slender. It is little more than a collocation of couplets and chansons ... and musically, is really not much above the works of Offenbach. As a work of art it is naught*'
New York Times, *24 October 1878*

'*The composer of* Carmen *is nowhere deep; his passionateness is all on the surface, and the general effect of the work is artificial and insincere. Of melody, as the term is generally understood, there is but little. The air of the Toreador is the only bit of "tune" in the opera, and this scarcely rises above the vulgarity of Offenbach ... Bizet aimed at originality, and he undoubtedly obtained it, but obtained monotony at the same time*'
Boston Gazette, *5 January 1879*

Carmen been an out-and-out disaster. It had a respectable run of thirty-seven performances. Added to this, Bizet had been paid 25,000 francs for the score by his publisher and made a Chevalier of the Légion d'honneur on the eve of the premiere – hardly the trappings of failure.

It's often said that the disappointing reception of the first performance of *Carmen* was partly responsible for the death of Bizet, three months later, from a broken heart. Not so, though it is a cruel irony that had he lived just three months more, he would have seen his work acclaimed as a triumphant success, something for which he had hoped all his life. However, it was not to be, and on the evening of the 31st performance of *Carmen* Bizet died of a heart attack, brought on by the throat affliction (probably cancer) from which he had suffered for years. Within three years his opera had been produced in almost all the major opera houses of Europe.

ANOTHER 'FIRST' PERFORMANCE

The second production was in Vienna – Bizet signed the contract for this the day before he died – but the Austrians saw a different *Carmen* to the Parisian one. Instead of spoken dialogue – an integral form of the **opéra-comique** for which Bizet had been commissioned – Bizet's pupil and colleague Ernest Guiraud replaced most of the spoken dialogue with **recitative**. The Viennese, it was thought, would prefer it sung. This version was the one that secured the initial success of the opera, and it was the one invariably seen in all non-French opera houses for well over three-quarters of a century: it had the effect of toning down and making more palatable some elements of the story.

Carmen was first recorded complete (on thirty-six sides!) as early as 1908.

The first film of the original Mérimée story was made the year after in France with Victoria Lepanto. Since then no less than thirteen other versions have been made (Theda Bara, Pola Negri and Rita Hayworth among the Carmens) not including the 1954 film of Oscar Hammerstein II's stage adaptation Carmen Jones (1945). In this all-black version (given a superb revival in London in 1991) Carmen works in a parachute factory, Escamillo becomes Husky Miller, a boxer and Micaela is renamed (of all things) Cindy-Lou.

Many composers have written instrumental variations and fantasies on the best-known melodies from Carmen, including Sarasate and Waxman (for violin) and Busoni and Horowitz (for piano). These can be enjoyed independently of the opera, as can the two Carmen Suites – orchestral arrangements of the opera's main vocal themes.

Strange that such a popular work should achieve its popularity in a form that the composer would probably never have sanctioned. Only comparatively recently has the original come to be preferred and the strengths of Bizet's intentions seen for what they are.

STORY
4 acts set in Seville
about 1820

PRINCIPAL CHARACTERS
DON JOSE, a corporal (t)
ZUNIGA, a captain (b)
MORALES, a corporal (bar)
MICAELA, a peasant girl (s)
ESCAMILLO, a matador (bar)
CARMEN, a gypsy (s) or (ms)
FRASQUITA, a gypsy (s)
MERCEDES, a gypsy (s)

Carmen, the daring, dark-eyed gypsy girl who has left her people and come to Seville to work in a cigarette factory, emerges for a break in the town square with her work mates. Soldiers from the barracks opposite have come off guard and she flirts with one of them, Don José. After she has returned to the factory, Micaela, Don José's sweetheart, arrives with a message from his mother.

Suddenly there is a fight in the factory. Carmen has stabbed one of the girls and Zuniga sends José to arrest her. Carmen works her charms on the soldier and persuades him to free her. Don José is imprisoned and demoted for his trouble. A few days later, at Lillas Pastia's tavern, a haunt of gypsies and smugglers, Zuniga and other soldiers watch as Carmen and her friends dance. Escamillo, the popular bull fighter, pays a visit to the tavern and sets eyes on Carmen. Once he has gone, Don José arrives, now released, and declares his passionate love for Carmen, a love that leads him to quit the troops and join the smugglers and gypsies.

In the rocky mountain pass where the smugglers have their camp, Carmen reads her fortune in the cards and foresees death. She is already tiring of Don José who, while disenchanted with the new life, is totally under Carmen's spell and consumed with jealousy

*Galli-Marié as the first
Carmen in 1875*

towards Escamillo. Micaela comes to the camp to tell José that his mother is dying. She is followed by the bullfighter, who is looking for the bewitching Carmen. The two men fight and José, torn between duty and passion, leaves with Micaela to the sound of Carmen's taunts. For the final act, Seville is *en fête* outside the bullring where Escamillo is appearing. The haggard José, driven close to insanity, approaches Carmen and begs her to return to him. She now loves Escamillo and pushes him away. José stabs her. Escamillo emerges triumphant from the arena to find her dead with Don José nearby, sobbing his confession.

HIGHLIGHTS

ACT 1 *'L'amour est un oiseau rebelle'* ('Love is a bird that's hard to tame') This is the famous *Habanera* (so-called because it is written in the rhythm of the Cuban dance, the Habanera). In fact, the tune, one of the most famous from *Carmen*, is not by Bizet. Mistaking

it for a folk-song, Bizet inserted it in the opera (with slight alterations), not knowing that it was a song called *'El Arreglito'* by the Spanish composer Sebastián de Yradier (1809–1865).

'Près des remparts de Séville' ('Near the ramparts of Seville'). Known as the *Seguidilla* (a popular Spanish dance), this aria has Carmen seductively inviting Don José to dance with her once she is free. It works.

ACT 2 *'Les tringles des sistres tintaient'* ('To the sound of tambourines'). Better known as the *Chanson Bohème*, this is Carmen's wild gypsy dance at the inn of Lillas Pastia.

'Votre toast je peux vous le rendre' ('To your toast I drink with pleasure) This is the popular Toreador's Song. Escamillo describes his triumphs in the bullring. Carmen is fascinated by him. Perhaps the best-known **baritone** aria in all opera.

'La fleur que tu m'avais jetée' ('The flower that you threw me') Known as the Flower Song, this is the beautiful aria in which Don José declares his love for Carmen.

CAVALLERIA RUSTICANA

MASCAGNI

1890

PRONOUNCED: KAH-VAHL-LEH-REE'-AH ROOS-TIH-KAH'-NAH
'RUSTIC CHIVALRY'
LIBRETTO: GIOVANNI TARGIONI-TOZZETTI AND GUIDO MENASCI
ADAPTED FROM THE STORY BY GIOVANNI VERGA.
LENGTH: 1' 10"

This popular work is affectionately known as *'Cav'* (as in *'Cav* and *Pag'* – *Pagliacci*, another one-act opera with which it is customarily programmed). Together they are certainly the most frequently performed one-acters (*Pag* actually has two acts, but they are generally played as one). *Cav* has one of the strongest of all libretti and the score is one of total inspiration from beginning to end, not to mention its middle, the famous **Intermezzo**. Mascagni spent the rest of his life vainly trying to equal it (he wrote a further sixteen operas, usually trying to avoid the style that had made him famous).

BACKGROUND

Mascagni was twenty-six years old when he wrote *Cavalleria Rusticana*. Until then, his life as a

Cavalleria Rusticana at The Royal Opera House, 1982

musician had been a struggle; with this one work he found wealth and fame. In 1889, the music publisher Sonzogno offered a prize for the best one-act opera to be submitted to him. Mascagni took Verga's story (which the author had also turned into a play, providing a vehicle for the great actress Eleonora Duse) and, having set it to music in an incredibly short time, entered the competition and won first prize.

FIRST PERFORMANCE
Teatro Costanzi, Rome
17 May 1890
Before the performance was half over, the somewhat small audience was wild with enthusiasm. It received no less than sixty curtain calls and in ten months had taken its place in the European repertoire. So great was the opera's success, that medals were struck in Mascagni's honour, his native city of Leghorn welcomed him home as a hero with a torchlight procession, and the King of Italy bestowed on him the Order of the Crown of Italy, something that even **Verdi** was not given until middle age.

RECOMMENDED RECORDINGS

complete:
Milanov/
Björling/
Merrill
Robert Shaw Chorale
RCA O, Cellini
BMG/RCA GD86510 (mono)
highlights:
Cossotto/Bergonzi/Guelfi
La Scala Ch & O, Karajan
DG 427 717 (cassette)
video: La Scala, Pretre
PHIL 070 103-3PH

The Intermezzo is one of those imperishable melodies that, although hackneyed, always manages to sound fresh and to stir emotions (especially when heard in context). When a satirical version of Cavalleria was produced in Vienna, the Austrian burghers loved the first half and were doubled up in their seats with laughter. Then came the Intermezzo. The writers had racked their brains for a comic idea and thought that an oily old Italian with a monkey and a barrel organ grinding out the tune would be just the thing. The house listened in dead silence, then burst into loud applause. Even this crude treatment could not undermine the nobility of this marvellous tune.

STORY
1 act (2 scenes) set in
a Sicilian village on Easter Day
in the late 19th century

PRINCIPAL CHARACTERS
SANTUZZA, a village girl (s)
LOLA, wife of Alfio (ms)
TURIDDU , a young soldier (t)
ALFIO, a teamster (bar)
MAMMA LUCIA, mother of
Turiddu (c)

This passionate Sicilian love tragedy begins with Turiddu serenading his old love, Lola. After returning from military service, he finds he's still in love with her and she with him, although she has meanwhile married Alfio and Turiddu has taken up with Santuzza, making her pregnant. On Easter morning, as the villagers make their way to the service, Santuzza has proof of Turiddu's preference for Lola. Santuzza begs Turiddu to stay with her, but Turiddu, seeing Lola on her way to church, leaves Santuzza to follow Lola. Santuzza denounces Lola and Turiddu to Alfio, who vows revenge. Traditional rustic chivalry means he must challenge Turiddu, who knows he cannot but accept. This done, Turiddu bids farewell to his mother and, in case anything should happen, asks her to look after Santuzza. He goes to meet Alfio. Seconds later, we hear that Turiddu has been killed.

HIGHLIGHTS
'*O Lola*' The opening aria, known as the *Siciliano*, resembles a typical Sicilian love song, in which Turiddu serenades Lola. Unusually, it's sung off-stage.
'*Inneggiamo, il Signor non è morto*' ('Let us sing of the Lord now victorious') Known as the Easter Hymn, this magnificent Resurrection chorus is sung by the villagers kneeling in the square, led by Santuzza.
'*Voi lo sapete*' ('Now you shall know') Santuzza tells Mamma Lucia of her love and her disgrace.
Intermezzo Among the most celebrated of opera 'hits', this is played between the two scenes, while the stage is empty, to denote the passage of time before Turiddu offers wine to the people coming out of church.
'*Viva, il vino spumeggiante*' ('Here's to the flowing wine'). The *Brindisi* (toast or drinking-song), with the devil-may-care Turiddu singing of the pleasures of wine, outside the tavern, shortly before the final tragic events.

LA CENERENTOLA
ROSSINI
1817

PRONOUNCED: LA CHAY-NAY-
REN'TOW-LAH
'CINDERELLA'
LIBRETTO: JACOPO FERRETTI
AFTER ÉTIENNE'S TEXT FOR
SOUARD'S OPERA

2 ACTS SET IN DON MAGNIFICO'S
HOUSE AND THE PRINCE'S PALACE

There are the ugly sisters Clorinda (*ms*) and Tisbe (*s*) and their father Don Magnifico, Baron of Mountflagon (*b*), mistreating their stepsister Angelina (*ms*), known as Cinderella. With slight variations on the familiar story – the fairy godmother, for instance, is Alidoro (*b*), the tutor of Prince Ramiro (*t*), and the glass slipper becomes a silver bracelet – everybody lives happily ever after.

If you like *The Barber of Seville*, this is a good one to follow it with. The action is quick-fire, Rossini's invention is astonishing and the succession of brilliant ensembles, *coloratura* writing and deft patter songs can't help but leave you in a warm, happy glow.

HIGHLIGHTS
Overture
ACT 1 *'Signor, una parola'* ('Sir, one word!') the quintet between Cinderella, Prince Ramiro (disguised as his valet Dandini), Dandini (disguised as Ramiro), Magnifico and Alidoro.
ACT 2 *'Nacqui all'affanno ... Non più mesta'* ('I was born to sorrow ... No longer sad beside the fire') Known as the Rondo Aria. Cinderella forgives her stepsisters and her stepfather and concludes the opera with a sparkling vocal display.

RECOMMENDED RECORDING
complete:
Terrani/Ravaglia/
Schmiege/Dara,
Capella Coloniensis
Ferro
SONY CD 46433

COSÌ FAN TUTTE
MOZART
1790

PRONOUNCED: COZ-EE'
FAN TOO' TAY
LITERALLY: 'THUS DO ALL
[WOMEN]', IT IS USUALLY GIVEN
AS 'THAT'S WHAT ALL WOMEN
DO' OR 'WOMEN ARE LIKE THAT'
LIBRETTO: LORENZO DA PONTE

2 ACTS SET IN NAPLES
IN THE 18TH CENTURY

The opera's subtitle tells you its subject: *'La Scuola degli Amanti'*, or 'The School for Lovers'. The story is supposed to have been based on something that happened in Trieste at about this time and was the subject of much gossip in Vienna. The suggestion that it be used as an opera came, it is said, from Emperor Joseph II himself, who commissioned the work. Throughout the nineteenth century the supposed immorality of the plot led it to be tampered with, ignored or frowned on and it's only in this century that it's been hailed as a masterpiece and performed all over the world.

On one level, *Così* (which is what it's called by all the buffs) is a small-scale comedy; on another, it's a cynical, clinical look at love and relationships. Mozart himself could identify only too well with the

*Kiri Te Kanawa
as Fiordiligi in Act 1
of* Così Fan Tutte

simple plot: he had fallen in love with the singer Aloysia Weber, been rejected and married her sister Constanze.

❖

Ferrando (*t*) and Guglielmo (*b*) are two officers in love with two sisters, respectively Dorabella (*s*) and Fiordiligi (*s*). An old philosopher and cynic, Don Alfonso (*bar*) bets them that their women will not be faithful when they're away. To try his theory, he tells the ladies that their lovers are departing, called away on active service. Tearful farewells are made and the men leave. Despina (*s*), the ladies' maid, is taken into the plot Alfonso has devised, though without being told the identities of the two 'foreigners' who turn up to make love to her mistresses. The two disguised officers are unsuccessful, pretend to take poison and are magically resuscitated by Despina, disguised as a doctor. The men try once more. This time, progress is made, but it's Guglielmo who makes progress with Dorabella and Ferrando with Fiordiligi, so much so that Despina (now a 'lawyer') draws up marriage contracts. When Don Alfonso informs them that the two officers

are returning, the 'foreigners' flee to return moments later in their true guises and be handed the marriage contracts by Don Alfonso. They refuse to listen to their betrotheds' excuses but finally Don Alfonso reveals all and the couples are reunited. But which ones?

HIGHLIGHTS

ACT 1 *'Soave sia il vento'* ('May the breeze be gentle') Don Alfonso joins Fiordiligi and Dorabella as they bid farewell to their lovers. This trio is one of the most sublime creations in all music.

'Come scoglio' ('Like a rock') Fiordiligi's aria in which she maintains her faithfulness to Guglielmo. It's a prodigiously difficult test-piece (some would say a parody) of the **soprano's** agility with tremendous vocal leaps. It is said to have been written both as a showy vehicle for the original singer and to poke fun at her: she was Da Ponte's mistress and not in Mozart's best books.

'Un' aura amorosa' ('Her eyes so alluring') Ferrando's beautiful aria in which he sings of his love.

ACT 2 *'Per pietà, ben mio, perdona'* ('Ah, my love, forgive my madness') Another show-piece (a rondo) for Fiordiligi of taxing but thrilling **coloratura**.

RECOMMENDED RECORDINGS
complete:
Schwarzkopf/Ludwig/Kraus
Philh. Ch & O
Boehm
EMI CMS7 69330 2
highlights:
Te Kanawa/ Murray/McLaughlin
VPO, Levine
DG Dig 431 290

Act 3 of English National Opera's 1988 production of The Cunning Little Vixen

THE CUNNING LITTLE VIXEN
LEOŠ JANÁČEK
1924
LIBRETTO: JANÁČEK

3 ACTS SET IN AND AROUND
A FOREST IN MORAVIA

Probably the best of Janáček's nine operas to try first, though it's by no means an instantly accessible work. A bilingual libretto would be essential even for Czech listeners as Janáček wrote it in the Brno dialect, the equivalent to an English audience of being sung to in Geordie. He based the libretto on a story by journalist Rudolf Tešnohlídek, published in instalments in a Brno newspaper, which was in turn inspired by a series of drawings by Stanislav Lolek.

The story (a parable) is of great interest and originality, although switching as it does between humans and animals, means that stagings of the opera are more than usually complex and not always successful affairs. Sharpears (*s*), the vixen, is captured by the Forester (*bar*) and kept as a pet. She escapes, takes over the lair of a Badger (*b*), eventually mating with Goldenmane (*s* or *t*) before being shot by Harašta (*b*), the poacher.

The Forester misses his vixen but, waking after a doze in the forest, he sees the vixen's daughter, exactly like her mother, and comforts himself in the knowledge that the forest eternally renews itself.

RECOMMENDED RECORDING
complete:
Popp/Randova/Jedlinka,
Vienna State Opera Ch,
VPO,
Mackerras
DECCA 417 129

DIDO AND AENEAS
HENRY PURCELL
1689
PRONOUNCED: DYE'-DOH
AND AN-EE-US
LIBRETTO: NAHUM TATE
BASED ON THE FOURTH BOOK OF
THE AENEID BY VIRGIL

3 ACTS SET IN CARTHAGE IN
CLASSICAL TIMES

The first performance was given in Josias Priest's Boarding School for Girls and the parts were taken by the pupils. After this, with the exception of two productions in 1700 and 1704, it was not given in its authentic form again until 1895. It is Purcell's only full-scale opera, though he wrote some forty other stage works. Many, like *The Fairy Queen* and *The Indian Queen*, could almost be called 'operas with spoken dialogue'.

❖

Dido, Queen of Carthage is unhappy because she's fallen in love with Aeneas (*t*), a Trojan prince. Belinda (*s*), Dido's lady-in-waiting, and the entire court encourage her to marry the prince and unite the two thrones. Finally, Dido accepts him as her husband-to-be. In the cave of the witches, the Sorceress (*ms*) invokes her cronies to plot the downfall of

Dido, sending one of their number, an elf (*s* or *t*) disguised as Mercury, to Aeneas with a false charge from Jove that he must set sail that very night, despite the storm that has arisen. It will destroy the Trojan fleet. The witches' 'plot is took', for Aeneas admits he must do the god's bidding, though it pains him. The heart-broken Dido cannot live without him and dies.

HIGHLIGHT
ACT 3 *'When I am laid in earth'*. Known as Dido's Lament, the Queen's final aria is among the most moving passages of music ever composed.

RECOMMENDED RECORDING
Flagstad/Schwarzkopf,
Mermaid Singers and O.
Jones
EMI References CDH 7 61006 2

DON CARLOS
VERDI
1867
LIBRETTO: FRANÇOIS-JOSEPH
MÉRY AND CAMILLE DU LOCLE
BASED ON THE TRAGEDY BY
FRIEDRICH SCHILLER

5 ACTS SET IN 16TH CENTURY SPAIN

More than one opera fanatic will tell you that here is the zenith of **grand opera** and Verdi. Others, while acknowledging its many powerful scenes and thrilling, richly wrought score, its deft characterizations and taut, realistic drama, admit that its complexity, length and sprawling structure put it beyond popular acclaim.

The original version, written in French, has five acts; it's now usually given in Italian in one of two revised versions, one with four acts, the other five. And if you think that's complicated, wait till you see the opera! It has one of the most convoluted of all story-lines. A summary can't begin to indicate all the sub-plots or the many political, moral and personal themes it explores, but at its heart lies the conflict between Church and State.

❖

The action is set in France and Spain during the middle of the sixteenth century. Don Carlos (*t*), son of Philip II of Spain (*b*), is in love with Elisabeth de Valois (*s*), daughter of Henry II of France. For reasons of state, the French King gives his daughter to Philip. Rodrigo, Marquis de Posa (*bar*) sees trouble coming and tries to persuade Don Carlos to leave court and join the Spanish Army in Flanders. Carlos and his new stepmother are violently in love and Princess Eboli (*ms*), former mistress of King Philip and also fruitlessly in love with Carlos, tells the King of his young Queen's affair with his son. Philip orders his son's arrest and throws him into prison, where he is visited by de Posa. An assassin shoots him, Carlos is released and meets Elisabeth secretly to say farewell before going to Flanders, but they are discovered. The King hands his son to the Inquisition, accused of plotting against Church and State.

RECOMMENDED RECORDINGS
complete:
Carreras/Freni/
Ghiaurov/Baltsa/ Raimondi,
BPO, Karajan
EMI CMS7 69304 2
highlights:
Domingo/Caballé/ Verrett/Milnes
ROHCG, Giulini
EMI CDM7 63089 2

DON GIOVANNI

MOZART

1787

PRONOUNCED: DON JOH-VAHN¹-NEE
LIBRETTO: LORENZO DA PONTE, BASED ON THE DON JUAN LEGEND
LENGTH 2' 45"

At least thirty other operas besides Mozart's have been written around the legend of Don Juan/Giovanni, the seducer and blasphemer who mocks the conventions of man and God. Men, it seems, are fascinated by his courage, women by his reputation. But it's the mixture of the comic and serious, the pace at which events move and, above all, Mozart's music that make this the only operatic version of any consequence.

BACKGROUND

The Marriage of Figaro had been a great success in Prague, and, as the second most important city in the Austro-Hungarian Empire, it was quite natural that Mozart should be invited to write a follow-up. What the burghers of Prague got for their money was not the light-hearted ebullience of *Figaro* but a mixture of dramatic power and subtle characterization with elements of tragedy relieved almost incidentally by comedy. Neither *opera buffa* nor *opera seria* but a *dramma giocoso* – 'joyful drama' – was how Mozart and **Da Ponte** described it.

John Connell as the
Commendatore in Don Giovanni
(Opera North, 1992)

FIRST PERFORMANCE

National Theatre, Prague
19 October 1787

The overture, so legend has it, was not written by the eve of the première. Mozart was passing the evening with some friends, who reminded him of this fact. He left them and began composing around midnight, his wife by his side telling him stories to keep him awake. In three hours he had written the overture, a work that comments on the opera itself.

A contemporary journal reporting on the first performance said: 'Connoisseurs and artists say that nothing like this has been given in Prague. Mozart himself conducted, and when he appeared in the orchestra, he was hailed by a triple acclamation.' *Don Giovanni* was a triumph on its first hearing and has been hailed as one of opera's masterpieces ever since.

STORY

2 acts which take place in and around 17th-century Seville

PRINCIPAL CHARACTERS
THE COMMENDATORE, DON PEDRO, Commandant of the Knights of Malta (b)
DONNA ANNA, his daughter (s)
DON OTTAVIO, engaged to Donna Anna (t)
DON GIOVANNI, a young nobleman (bar)
LEPORELLO, his servant (b)
DONNA ELVIRA, a lady of Burgos (s)
ZERLINA, a country girl (s)
MASETTO, a peasant engaged to Zerlina (b)

The story is based around the various seductions attempted by Don Giovanni. His first is of Donna Anna in the Commendatore's palace. She resists and cries for help. Her father rushes in, sword drawn, and is killed by Giovanni who then escapes. While Donna Anna and Ottavio vow revenge and swear their love for each other, Giovanni continues his amatory 'adventures' until he is unmasked and denounced. Reading on the statue raised to the Commendatore the words, 'Here I await Heaven's vengeance on him who slew me', Giovanni mockingly invites the statue to dine with him. The statue speaks its acceptance. One of the Don's conquests, Elvira, who still dotes on him, begs him to mend his ways. He refuses. Surrounded by his friends in the banqueting hall, Giovanni hears a knock and the statue of the Commendatore appears. The guests flee, Giovanni laughs his defiance and is dragged down to hell by the apparition, still unrepentant.

HIGHLIGHTS

Overture
ACT 1 *'Madamina'* ('Madam') Known as the Catalogue Aria: Leporello lists his master's many conquests to Donna Elvira (a total of 2,065 from all over Europe, of all sorts and conditions). Hardly tactful – she has been one of them.
'Là ci darem la mano' ('Give me your hand') Giovanni's beautiful overture of love to the peasant girl Zerlina, who is about to be married to Masetto. One of opera's gems.
'Dalla sua pace' ('Mine be her burden') Ottavio sings of his love for Donna Anna.
'Fin ch' han dal vino' ('Wine, flow like a fountain') Known as the Champagne Aria. Don Giovanni breathlessly anticipates the drunken revels he has instigated.
'Batti, batti, o bel Masetto' ('Scold me, scold me, dear Masetto') Zerlina begs Masetto's forgiveness for flirting with Giovanni.
ACT 2 *'Il mio tesoro'* ('My treasure') Don Ottavio vows to defend and comfort his beloved Anna. Regarded as the touchstone of classic **arias** for tenors.
'Non mi dir' ('Say no more') Donna Anna sings this meltingly lovely reassurance of her feelings for Ottavio.

DON PASQUALE
DONIZETTI
1843
PRONOUNCED: DON PAHSS-QUAH'-LEH
LIBRETTO: DONIZETTI AND GIOVANNI RUFFINI

3 ACTS SET IN ROME IN THE EARLY 19TH CENTURY

One of Donizetti's most delicious comic creations, *Don Pasquale* is fun, sparkling with good humour and full of tunes. The title role is a rich, crusty old bachelor Don Pasquale (b), who, though he has never seen her, won't allow his nephew Ernesto (t) to marry the pretty and witty young widow Norina (s). Doctor Malatesta (bar) is an old friend of Pasquale – and also of the young couple. Sympathetic to them, he devises a plan in which he tells Pasquale he should get married to his sister 'Sofronia', fresh from a convent. 'Sofronia' (Norina in disguise) marries the old bachelor in a mock ceremony and proceeds to make his life hell, spending all his money and showing she has a vile temper. Malatesta suggests that the marriage should be annulled, Pasquale agrees and Ernesto gallantly offers to marry 'Sofronia' himself. Pasquale, admitting he's been fooled, gives his blessing to Ernesto and Norina.

HIGHLIGHTS

ACT 1 *'Quel guardo il cavaliere'* ('Glances so soft and bright').
ACT 3 *'Com' è gentil'* ('How lovely it is') (*Serenata*) Ernesto pretends to lure Sofronia away from her husband.

RECOMMENDED RECORDING
complete: Freni/Bruscantini
Philh. O, Muti
EMI CDS7 47068 2

RECOMMENDED RECORDINGS

complete: Sutherland/ Schwarzkopf/ Sciutti/Alva/ Frick
Philh. Ch & O, Giulini
EMI CDS7 47260 8
highlights: Baltsa/Battle/Ramey
BPO, Karajan
DG dig.431 289
video: La Scala/Muti
CAST CV12061

L'ELISIR D'AMORE
DONIZETTI
1832

PRONOUNCED: LAY-LEE-SEER'
DAH-MOH'REH
'THE ELIXIR OF LOVE' OR
'THE LOVE POTION'
LIBRETTO: FELICE ROMANI
BASED ON 'LE PHILTRE', A
COMEDY BY SCRIBE, ITSELF
BASED ON 'IL FILTRO' BY SILVIO
MALAPERTA

2 ACTS SET IN AN ITALIAN VILLAGE
IN THE 19TH CENTURY

Luciano Pavarotti as Nemorino in the Royal Opera House's 1991 production of L'Elisir d'Amore

A mong Donizetti's best (and most famous) comic creations and containing some of his most memorable melodies – including one of opera's all-time favourite **arias**, *'Una furtiva lagrima'*. It is said that the libretto was written in eight days and the music in fourteen. Good going even for Donizetti. 'You know what my motto is?' he asked. '"Quickly!" It may be reprehensible but the good things I've written were always written quickly; and often the accusation of carelessness is made against the music that cost me most time.' It was certainly written in a hurry – in order to fill a gap in the theatre's schedule. His forty-first opera, it was instantly successful – and has been ever since. The effervescent *Elisir* together with his **Don Pasquale**, are among the best of all Italian comic operas of the nineteenth century.

❖

Adina (*s*) is a wealthy and independent young lady who is loved by the peasant Nemorino (literally 'little nobody') (*t*) and the sergeant Belcore (*bar*). She herself fancies Nemorino but he is too shy to make any approach. To the village comes the quack doctor Dulcamara (*b*) who has a love potion to sell. 'Works wonders, never fails, only twenty scudi!' Nemorino uses his last coin to buy some. It's only wine in the bottle, and when Nemorino becomes drunk and makes a fool of himself, Adina is furious at his behaviour. Belcore sees his chance, proposes and is accepted.

Nemorino goes back to Dulcamara who recommends another bottle. To get enough money to buy it, Nemorino has to join the army, signing on under the auspices of his rival, the recruiting sergeant Belcore. News arrives of the death of Nemorino's rich uncle. Suddenly, all the village girls find him attractive. Adina regrets her hasty decision but is consoled by Nemorino. All ends happily with Adina buying back the soldier's contract, the gallant Belcore declaring that there are plenty of other women in the world and Dulcamara triumphantly proclaiming the benefits of his elixir. As the curtain falls, the village peasants crowd round to buy his worthless potion.

HIGHLIGHTS
ACT 2 *'Una furtiva lagrima'* ('A furtive tear') One of the most popular of all tenor arias, this beautiful melody is sung by Nemorino as he sees Adina's tears of regret. A good example of **bel canto** singing. All the great lyric tenors have loved playing Nemorino, from **Caruso** and **Gigli** to Di Stefano and **Pavarotti**.

RECOMMENDED RECORDING
complete:
Ricciarelli/Carreras/Trimarchi
Turin Radio Symph. Ch & O,
Scimone
PHILIPS 412 714

EUGENE ONEGIN
TCHAIKOVSKY
1879
PRONOUNCED:
YOO'-JEEN ON-YAY'-GIN
ORIGINAL RUSSIAN TITLE:
'YEVGENY ONYEGIN'
LIBRETTO: TCHAIKOVSKY AND
CONSTANTINE SHILOVSKY
BASED ON THE POEM OF THE
SAME NAME BY PUSHKIN

3 ACTS SET IN THE LATE
18TH CENTURY IN AND AROUND
ST PETERSBURG

The most popular of Tchaikovsky's ten operas, 'Eugene One Gin' as it's irreverently nicknamed, is also his most successful. When the big tunes come, they *really* come.

❖

Tatyana (*s*) and Olga (*c*) are the daughters of the widowed Madame Larina (*ms*) who has an estate outside St Petersburg. Olga is engaged to Lensky (*t*) who comes to visit his fiancée with his elegant friend Eugene Onegin (*bar*). The gauche Tatyana falls head over heels in love and writes him a letter. Onegin, telling her to control her emotions better, advises her to forget him. At a ball given for Tatyana's birthday, Onegin flirts with Olga and Lensky challenges his friend to a duel that results in Lensky's death. Six years pass and Onegin,

having left Russia in a state of remorse, returns to St Petersburg and, at a ball in the Imperial Palace, meets a middle-aged cousin of his, Prince Gremin (*b*), a retired general. Gremin introduces Onegin to his wife – the now radiant and sophisticated Tatyana. It's Onegin's turn to fall head over heels in love. She has not forgotten her first love and struggles against her emotions. Duty conquers and she sends Onegin away irrevocably.

HIGHLIGHTS
ACT 1 *The Letter Scene* Tatyana releases her pent-up feelings of love and writes her letter to Onegin. The first part of the opera Tchaikovsky composed.
ACT 2 *The Waltz* The guests are dancing at the party given in Tatyana's honour.
Lensky's Aria A moving, lyrical outpouring of farewell before the fateful duel.
ACT 3 *The Polonaise* Played at the ball in St Petersburg when Onegin reappears.

RECOMMENDED RECORDINGS
complete: Kubiak/Burrows
ROHCG, Solti
DECCA SET 596-8
highlights:
Freni/Allen/Schicoff/Von Otter
Staatskapelle Dresden, Levine
DG 431 611

The completion of Eugene Onegin *was among the first fruits of the emotional and financial security Tchaikovsky had found in his platonic relationship with Nadezhda von Meck, a wealthy widow and passionate music lover. This followed his disastrous marriage in 1877 to Antonina Miyukova, a pretty but neurotic 28-year-old music student who was also a nympho-maniac. Distraught, the homosexual Tchaikovsky had fled to his sister's estate and, some weeks later, attempted to drown himself.*

FAUST
CHARLES GOUNOD
1859
LIBRETTO: JULES BARBIER AND
MICHEL CARRE
AFTER GOETHE'S POEM

5 ACTS, SET IN 16TH CENTURY
GERMANY

Tastes in opera change. For the first two decades of this century, *Faust* was by far the most popular and most frequently performed opera in the world. Now, after a long period of neglect, it is coming back into favour. Like many other very successful operas, its initial reception was indifferent. It was criticized for the librettists' melodramatic treatment of Goethe's poem, and for its sentimental music. In Germany they normally produce it as *Margarete* or *Gretchen* to dissociate it from their great poet. Gounod revised the score, introducing a ballet between Acts 4 and 5, and, following its second première in 1869, Paris's Grand Opéra alone gave more than 1,000 performances of *Faust* during the following eight years.

It's true there aren't any laughs, but Gounod knew as well as Verdi how to write for the voice and orchestrate a tuneful and dramatic score. The work contains any number of memorable moments, and there are three tremendous lead roles that singers have always been grateful to seize.

❖

The ageing philosopher Faust (*t*) makes a pact with Mephistopheles (*b*): his soul in exchange for eternal youth and the lovely Marguerite (*s*). At an Easter fair, Valentine (*bar*), Marguerite's brother, entrusts his sister to the care of his young friend Siebel (*ms* or *s*, i.e. a *travesti* role) as he is about to go off to the wars. The rejuvenated Faust meets Marguerite for the first time but she turns him down. The Devil presents Faust with a casket of jewels to tempt Marguerite and, while he diverts her companion Martha (c), Faust woos and wins Marguerite.

By Act 4, Faust has deserted Marguerite, who prays in church for forgiveness, tortured by the voice of the unseen Mephistopheles. The soldiers return home from the war, watched by Faust and Mephistopheles. Valentine is among them and, hearing the Devil insult his sister's name, he challenges Faust to a duel. He is killed, cursing his sister as he dies. Finally, Faust repents. But Marguerite has been imprisoned for killing her child and, her mind wandering, she refuses Faust's help to escape. Her prayers are answered and she is taken up into Heaven; the despairing Faust is dragged down to Hell by Mephistopheles.

HIGHLIGHTS

ACT 2 *'Avant de quitter ces lieux'* ('Before I leave this place') Valentine's serene prayer for Marguerite's protection.

Finale The townspeople, soldiers and students dance a waltz during which Faust introduces himself to Marguerite.

ACT 3 *'Salut! demeure chaste et pure'* ('Hail, saintly dwelling!') A familiar **tenor** aria. Faust, deeply in love with Marguerite, salutes her simple home.

'Il était un roi de Thule' ('Once there was a king in Thule') Marguerite's thoughts drift to the handsome stranger.

'Ah! je ris de me voir' ('I am laughing with joy') Known as the Jewel Song, a favourite recital piece for **sopranos**. Sung by Marguerite as she examines the jewels Faust

An 1882 Punch *cartoon of Gounod*

has given her.

ACT 4 *'Gloire immortelle'* ('Immortal glory') The celebrated Soldiers' Chorus. The soldiers return triumphantly from their exploits. Welsh male voice choirs love this one. Gounod originally wrote it for his unfinished opera, *Ivan the Terrible.*

Ballet Music Played before the final act when Mephistopheles shows Faust a tempting vision of seduction.

ACT 5 *'Anges purs!'* ('Holy Angels!') A powerful trio. The distracted Marguerite prays to

Heaven for forgiveness while Faust and Mephistopheles entreat her to hurry away with them.

RECOMMENDED RECORDINGS
complete: Studer/Leech/van Dam, Toulouse Capitole Ch & O Plasson
EMI CDC7 54358
highlights: Sutherland/Corelli/ Ghiaurov, LSO, Bonynge
DECCA CD421 861

LA FAVORITA
DONIZETTI
1840
PRONOUNCED:
LAH FAH-VOOR-EET'-A
LITERALLY: 'THE FAVOURITE'
LIBRETTO: ALPHONSE ROYER,
GUSTAVE VAËZ AND EUGÈNE
SCRIBE
AFTER BACULARD D'ARNAUD'S
PLAY 'LE COMTE DE
COMMINGUES'

4 ACTS SET IN SPAIN IN 1340

Not so well known as *Lucia di Lammermoor*, *La Favorita* is a tragedy well worth investigating and has some of Donizetti's most inspired writing, even if the libretto is second-rate.

Donizetti's Leonora is 'La Favorita' of the title. She is loved by Fernando (*t*), a novice in a monastery who has seen her come to pray there. Little does he suspect that she is Leonora de Gusman (*ms*), the mistress of Alfonso (*bar*), King of Castile. Baldassare (*b*), the prior, advises Fernando to go back into the world – he's not suitable for the order – and the would-be monk eventually marries Leonora. On finding out about her past he is appalled and returns to the monastery to take his vows. Leonora is there disguised as a novice, dying of grief and remorse. She begs his forgiveness, he relents but it is too late and she dies in his arms.

HIGHLIGHTS
ACT 1 *'Una vergine, un angiol di Dio'* ('A virgin, an angel of God') *Romanza*. Fernando confesses his love for the unknown woman.
ACT 4 *'Spirto gentil'* ('Spirit so fair') Donizetti at his simplest and most sublime. A **tenor** aria, when Fernando says goodbye to the

outside world and welcomes the gentle spirit of divine love.
RECOMMENDED RECORDING
complete:
Pavarotti/Ghiaurov/Cotrubas,
Teatro Comunale Ch & O
Bonynge
DECCA 430 038

FIDELIO,
ODER DIE EHELICHE LIEBE
BEETHOVEN
1805
PRONOUNCED: FEE-DAY'-LI-OH
LITERALLY: 'FIDELIO, OR
CONJUGAL LOVE'
LIBRETTO: JOSEPH
SONNLEITHNER
BASED ON A GERMAN VERSION OF
BOUILLY'S 'LÉONORE, OU
L'AMOUR CONJUGAL'

2 ACTS SET IN 18TH-CENTURY SPAIN
AT A FORTRESS NEAR SEVILLE

Beethoven, that giant among composers, wrote only one opera; indeed he was generally happier writing for instruments than for the voice. Yet here, as in the Choral Symphony, he takes the listener beyond the expectations of the medium into another realm. *Fidelio* is not just the story of a faithful wife rescuing her husband but about the redemptive power of love and revolutionary idealism.

Don Pizarro (*bar*), the governor of the state prison, has unjustly thrown the nobleman Florestan (*t*) into jail. Disguising herself as a lad named Fidelio, Florestan's wife Leonore (*s*) gets a job under Rocco (*b*), the chief jailer. Marzelline (*s*), Rocco's daughter, falls in love with Fidelio, much to the annoyance of her lover, the turnkey Jacquino (*t*). When Don Fernando (*bar*), the Minister of State, sets out to investigate rumours of false imprisonment, Pizarro decides to do away with Florestan before he arrives. He is about to kill him in his dungeon when Leonore/Fidelio threatens him with a pistol, just as the Minister arrives. Florestan and Leonore are united, many prisoners released and Pizarro disgraced.

HIGHLIGHTS
Overture But which? Leonore No. 3 is a masterpiece – a résumé of the whole opera. (But see below.)
ACT 1 *'Mir ist so wunderbar'* ('I see such wonder') The quartet in which

---

FOUR FIDELIO OVERTURES

There are no less than four overtures to choose from and two of them – often heard separately in the concert hall – serve as an excellent way of getting to know the opera. Three of them are called Leonore, *the name by which the opera was first known. It's a bit confusing. The first to be written was* Leonore No. 2, *played at the first performance but not used today.* Leonore No. 3, *the greatest of the four, was the next to be composed, and nowadays is usually played between the final scenes as*

an interlude, although it doesn't really fit. Leonora No. 1 *was written for a performance in Prague that never took place. The* Fidelio *Overture that begins the opera today was written for the first performance of the revised version Beethoven made in 1814, when the original three acts were reduced to two. (In a further twist, this new overture wasn't played on that occasion; Beethoven hadn't finished it and his overture* The Ruins of Athens *was substituted!)*

Fidelio, Rocco, Marzelline and Jacquino hope for joy to come – for different reasons.

'*O welche Lust*' ('What happiness') Known as the Prisoners' Chorus. Leonore persuades Rocco to let the prisoners have a few moments in the sunlight.

ACT 2 '*O namenlose Freude!*' ('O indescribable joy!') Leonore and Florestan are reunited.

RECOMMENDED RECORDINGS
complete:
Ludwig/Vickers/Frick/Berry
Philh. Ch & O, Klemperer
EMI CMS7 69324 2
highlights:
Rysanek/Haefliger/
Fischer-Dieskau/Frick
Bavarian State Opera Ch & O
Fricsay
PICKWICK IMPX9021

DIE FLEDERMAUS

JOHANN STRAUSS II

1874

PRONOUNCED: DEE FLAY'DER-MOUSE
LITERALLY: 'THE BAT'
LIBRETTO: CARL HAFFNER AND RICHARD GENÉE
LENGTH: 2' 30"

This was Strauss's third opera and the only one by the waltz king of Vienna actually set in that city. Still the most famous operetta ever written, *Die Fledermaus*, with its elegant sets and gowns, the infectious gaiety of its music and the lively, mocking spirit of its story is, above all, *fun*.

Lesley Garrett as Adele sings her audition song in Die Fledermaus

A disastrous feature film called Oh Rosalinda! *(1955) attempted to modernize* Die Fledermaus. *It starred Michael Redgrave as Eisenstein and Ludmilla Tcherina as Adele, with Anthony Quayle, Mel Ferrer and Dennis Price amongst others. 'Lumbering attempt ...' says* Halliwell's Film Guide, *'... totally lacking the desired ... touch and a sad stranding of a brilliant cast.'*

A good choice for a first visit to the opera – even an average production can hardly fail to whisk you off into the enchanting world of delicious waltz tunes, mistaken identities, comic intrigue and romance.

BACKGROUND

Johann Strauss I and Joseph Lanner between them had popularized the waltz throughout Europe. Johann Strauss II followed in his father's footsteps and by the 1860s was known universally as 'The Waltz King' (his *Blue Danube* waltz appeared in 1867). The 'King of Parisian Operetta' was the French composer **Jacques Offenbach** and he it was who encouraged Strauss to try his hand at something for the stage. *Die Fledermaus* was Strauss's third such work. A Viennese impresario passed on to Strauss a disappointing drama called *Le Réveillon* written by Meilhac and Halévy, the librettists of *Carmen* (it's possible that Offenbach had already turned it down). Genée and Haffner adapted it to Viennese tastes, after which Strauss was so inspired by the project that he completed the entire score in forty-three days.

FIRST PERFORMANCE

Theater an der Wien
Vienna, 5 April 1874

The work had a brilliantly successful premiere in Vienna on Easter Sunday 1874, but was taken off after only sixteen performances owing to a series of disasters on the Stock Exchange. It quickly made a triumphant progress through Europe (Berlin, Hamburg, Paris and London) and New York, becoming the epitome of Viennese operetta.

STORY

3 acts set in Vienna in the
late 19th century

PRINCIPAL CHARACTERS
GABRIEL VON EISENSTEIN, a young
man about town (t)
ROSALINDE, his wife (s)
ALFRED, her lover, an Italian
singer (t)
FRANK, governor of the prison (bar)
PRINCE ORLOFSKY, a wealthy
Russian (ms or t)
DR FALKE, a friend of Eisenstein
(bar)
DR BLIND, Eisenstein's attorney (t)
ADELE, the Eisensteins' maid (s)
IDA, Adele's sister, an actress (s)
FROSCH, the gaoler (actor)

Baron Eisenstein has been sentenced to a week's imprisonment for contempt of court. Before he goes to jail, he's persuaded by his friend Falke to go in disguise to a ball being given by Prince Orlofsky. Three years earlier, Falke, disguised as a bat for a fancy-dress ball, has been made to walk home in broad daylight as a joke by Eisenstein and, ever since, he has been plotting his revenge. Rosalinde, Baroness Eisenstein sees her husband depart, as she thinks, for prison, and admits her lover, Alfred. The prison governor arrives to collect Eisenstein

and believes Alfred to be him. To protect the lady's reputation, Alfred reluctantly volunteers to go to prison as her husband.

At Prince Orlofsky's ball, Adele has gained admission by dressing up in one of her mistress's gowns. The Baron flirts outrageously with her watched by his wife whom Falke has disguised as a Hungarian Countess. The fickle Baron then transfers his attention to the mysterious Countess, who manages to get hold of his watch during their tête-à-tête. Eisenstein arrives at the prison to give himself up. He's amazed to find himself being impersonated by Alfred and furious when he discovers his wife has a lover. Rosalinde counters her husband with the watch the 'Countess' obtained at the ball and the evidence of her own eyes – the Baron's flirtation with her own maid. It's a case of tit for tat, and Falke arrives to explain that the whole thing was a joke to get revenge. Mutual reconciliations and champagne all round.

RECOMMENDED RECORDINGS

complete:
Popp/Rebroff/
Kollo
Bavarian State
Opera Ch &
O, C. Kleiber
DG 415 646
highlights:
Popp/Baltsa/Domingo/Rydl
Munchner
Rundfunkorchester
Domingo
EMI CDC7 49866 2
video: Bavarian State Opera
C. Kleiber
DG 072 400-3GH

HIGHLIGHTS

Overture A masterpiece in its own right – and often heard independently of the operetta – mixing several of the work's best known melodies into a mouth-watering curtain-raiser.

ACT 2 *'Mein Herr Marquis'* ('My dear Marquis') Known as the Laughing Song, Adele's famous aria in which she pretends to object to being taken for a lady's maid. Still a firm recital favourite with **sopranos**.

'Klänge der Heimat' ('Strains of my homeland') (*Czardas*) The fake Hungarian Countess (Rosalinde) sings of her native land. Could any genuine Hungarian have done it so movingly and convincingly? A thrilling display piece of enormous difficulty.

Waltz First heard in the Overture and now danced at Prince Orlofsky's ball.

THE FLYING DUTCHMAN
WAGNER
1843

ORIGINAL GERMAN TITLE:
DER FLIEGENDE HOLLÄNDER

PRONOUNCED: DAIR FLEE'-GEN-
DEH HOL-LAYN'-DER

LIBRETTO: WAGNER
BASED ON AN ARTICLE BY
HEINRICH HEINE

3 ACTS SET IN A NORWEGIAN FISHING
VILLAGE IN THE 18TH CENTURY

The best way to get into the daunting world of Wagner is to listen to extracts from some of the operas (the overture to *Tannhäuser*, for example, Siegfried's 'Journey to the Rhine' from *Götterdämmerung*, the Liebestod from *Tristan und Isolde* or the Prelude to Act 3 of *Lohengrin*). But the best complete opera to listen to first is this one. Musically and dramatically it is a bridge between his earlier works (influenced by **Meyerbeer**) and the later epics (*The Ring, Tristan, Die Meistersinger et al.*).

Wagner wrote *The Flying Dutchman* after a particularly rough crossing in the North Sea in 1839. The ship was nearly wrecked three times and was once forced into the safety of a Norwegian harbour. During the voyage, Wagner heard the legend of the Wandering Jew of the ocean condemned to sail the seas for eternity after boasting he could round the Cape of Good Hope in any conditions. Allowed to put into port once every seven years, the curse would only be lifted if he found a woman who would be faithful to him to death.

❖

A seven-year period has ended and the ghostly Flying Dutchman (*bar*) puts into port beside the Norwegian Captain Daland (*b*) who takes the stranger to his home. Here he meets Daland's romantically inclined daughter, Senta (*s*). She knows the story of the Flying Dutchman (she even has his picture on the wall) and when she sees him, she knows that it is her destiny to save the man from his eternal perdition.

They fall in love and the wedding is announced when Erik (*t*), a huntsman and Senta's former love, returns and unsuccessfully begs to be reunited. The Dutchman overhears the scene and, misunderstanding what has passed, is possessed with the thought that if Senta has been unfaithful to Erik, then Senta could also be unfaithful to him. His dream of fidelity is shattered and he immediately weighs anchor, heading out into a terrible storm. Standing on the cliffs, Senta sees her Flying Dutchman sailing away from her and in despair throws herself into the sea. The wind carries her cry of 'I will be faithful unto death' to the storm-tossed vessel, which sinks in the full force of the gale. The sea calms and two figures rise from the waters – the Dutchman and his Senta whose faith has redeemed him.

HIGHLIGHTS

Overture Almost a précis of the opera, it includes one of the mightiest of orchestral storms.

Senta (right) leaps from the rock to save the Dutchman's soul in the original 1843 production of The Flying Dutchman

Rosa Ponselle as Leonora in La Forza del Destino in 1918

ACT 2 *Spinning Chorus.* In Senta's home, a crowd of girls are busy spinning. Senta does not join them but sits looking at the portrait of the 'Flying Dutchman' that hangs on the wall.

'Traft ihr das Schiff' Known as Senta's Ballad. The heroine tells the spinning maidens the legend of the sailor and his phantom ship.

RECOMMENDED RECORDINGS
complete:
Silja/Adam/Talvela
BBC Ch & Philh. O
Klemperer
EMI CMS7 63344
highlights:
Vejzovic/van Dam/Moll
BPO, Karajan
EMI CDM7 63449

LA FORZA DEL DESTINO
VERDI
1862

PRONOUNCED: LAH FORT'-ZAH
DEL DES-TEE'-NOH
LITERALLY: 'THE FORCE OF
DESTINY'
LIBRETTO: FRANCESCO PIAVE
BASED ON A PLAY CALLED 'DON
ALVARO, O LA FUERZA DEL SINO'
BY ANGEL DE SAAVEDRA, DUKE
OF RIVAS

4 ACTS SET IN SPAIN AND ITALY IN
THE MID-18TH CENTURY

Written after the successes of *La Traviata* and *Trovatore*, *The Force of Destiny* is musically more advanced than either of its predecessors. Verdi is limbering up for the later perfection of *Aida* and the orchestral writing here is more colourful, varied and vivid. There is a greater seriousness of purpose and more emphasis on dramatic atmosphere without (this being Verdi) any loss of melody.

Verdi's Leonora is the daughter of the Marquis of Calatrava (*b*), who is accidentally killed by her lover, Don Alvaro (*t*). (Another of opera's unlikely demises: Alvaro's pistol is thrown to the floor where it explodes and mortally wounds the Marquis.) Alvaro disappears and Leonora, disguised as a man (again! see **Fidelio**), flees from Seville and takes refuge in a monastery. Her brother, Don Carlo (*bar*), seeks Alvaro to take vengeance. Five years later, the tragedy ends with the two men meeting at last in Leonora's presence at 'a wild spot near [the monastery of Hornacuelos'. They duel and Carlo is fatally wounded. Alvaro and Leonora, each thinking the other long dead, rush into each other's arms but the unforgiving Carlo stabs his sister who dies in her lover's embrace.

HIGHLIGHTS

Overture
ACT 2 '*La vergine degli angeli*' ('May angels guard thee') The monks at the monastery pray for the protection of Leonora.
ACT 3 '*Solenne in quest'ora*' ('In this solemn hour') The poignant duet between Carlo and Alvaro, who have become friends, neither knowing the other's identity.

RECOMMENDED RECORDINGS
complete:
L. Price/Tucker/ Merrill
RCA Italiana Opera
Ch & O, Schippers
BMG/RCA GD 87971
highlights:
Freni/Domingo/Surian
La Scala Ch & O, Muti
EMI CDC7 54326

DER FREISCHÜTZ
CARL MARIA VON WEBER
1821

PRONOUNCED: DAIR FRY'-SHOOTS
LITERALLY: 'THE FREE-SHOOTER'
LIBRETTO: FRIEDRICH KIND
BASED ON APEL AND LAUN'S 'GESPENSTERBUCH'

3 ACTS SET IN 18TH-CENTURY BOHEMIA

The opera's title is usually translated as *The Free-shooter*, a marksman who uses magic bullets.

You can appreciate this magnificent work on two levels: as a piece of music drama and as one of the most important operas ever written. With this one work, Weber established German (as distinct from Italian) opera. Discarding the plots of mistaken identity and intrigue, he based his work on the legends of his own country, involving magic, the supernatural and religious themes. It's easy to see how this led to **Wagner** and the German school of Romanticism and nationalism, for the monumental ***Ring*** cycle is based entirely on the same ideas. When he was nine years old, Wagner saw Weber himself conduct *Der Freischütz* in Dresden. He admired the work immensely, as did Berlioz.

As for Weber, despite the immense popularity of his opera – its melodies were whistled everywhere in Germany, and in

London two theatres produced it simultaneously – he made no great fortune from it. Understandably, it annoyed him to see others doing so, and consequently all mention of *Der Freischütz* was banned in his company.

❖

Echoes of the **Faust** legend here: in exchange for a man's soul, the evil spirit of the forest can provide magic bullets able to hit any target.

The Bohemian Prince Ottokar (*bar*) has a head ranger, Cuno (*b*), who in turn has two assistants, Max (*t*) and Kaspar (*b*), both excellent marksmen. Max is in love with Cuno's daughter Agathe (*s*), who has promised to be his bride if he can prove himself to be the best shot in the Prince's shooting contest. In a preliminary trial, Kilian (*t*), a rich peasant, beats Max, who, despondent at his defeat, allows Kaspar to lead him to the Wolf's Glen, much to Agathe's disquiet. Kaspar is in the power of the evil wild huntsman Samiel (*speaking part*). In the depths of the Glen, amid a scene of supernatural horror, Samiel casts seven mystical bullets. The first six will hit any target Max desires; the seventh will be directed by Samiel.

During the contest, Max impresses the Prince with his uncanny marksmanship but with his final shot he is asked to shoot a white dove on the wing. This seventh shot not only kills Kaspar, who has been watching events in a tree, but also Agathe. Max admits his pact with Samiel and is banished by the Prince, but a mysterious hermit (*b*) appears, revives Agathe and successfully pleads for Max to be forgiven.

HIGHLIGHTS
Overture A brilliant concert favourite and the first of its kind to

include not only thematic material from the opera but to quote complete melodies.

ACT 2 'Leise leise, fromme Weise' ('Gently, gently, lift my song') The beautiful aria known as Agathe's Prayer, in which Agathe looks out of her window in the moonlight and sings of her love for Max.

RECOMMENDED RECORDING
complete: Grummer/Otto/Schock/
Kohn, BPO, Keilberth
EMI CMS7 69342 2

GIANNI SCHICCHI
PUCCINI
1918
PRONOUNCED: Jᴵ-ANNᴵ-Y SKEEᴵ KY
LIBRETTO: GIOVACCHINO
FORZANO
BASED ON AN EPISODE IN
DANTE'S 'INFERNO'

ONE ACT SET IN FLORENCE IN 1299

This, Puccini's only light opera, is the comic third part of his *Trittico* (Triptych), the other two being *Il Tabarro* ('The Cloak') and *Suor Angelica* ('Sister Angelica').

❖

Gianni Schicchi (*bar*) is a wily Tuscan peasant whose daughter Lauretta (*s*) is going to be married to Rinuccio (*t*), a relative of a wealthy man who has just died, leaving all his money to the Church. At Rinuccio's suggestion, Schicchi devises a plan to change the will so that his grasping relatives will inherit the money instead. Not only does he revise the

will, but, except for a few hand-outs, keeps all the money himself.

HIGHLIGHT
'O mio babbino caro' ('Oh my beloved father') A justly famous **aria** (used with great effect in the Merchant–Ivory film of *A Room With a View*) sung by Lauretta to her father when asking him to help the disinherited relatives, her lover among them.

RECOMMENDED RECORDING
complete:
Cotrubas/Domingo/Gobbi,
LSO, Maazel
CBS/SONY CD79312

LA GIOCONDA
PONCHIELLI
1876
PRONOUNCED: LA JOH-KONᴵ-DAH
LITERALLY: 'THE JOYFUL GIRL'
LIBRETTO: ARRIGO BOITO
BASED ON VICTOR HUGO'S
'ANGELO, TYRAN DE PADOUE'

4 ACTS SET IN 17TH CENTURY
VENICE

Although this is Ponchielli's only lasting success, *La Gioconda* is an important Italian opera. Inspired by the example of **Wagner**, he set out to make the music more continuous, more closely suited to the action, with a richer sound and more symphonic texture than had previously been heard in Italian Opera. Yet he still retained the Italian tradition of beautiful melodies and ***bel canto*** singing. Ponchielli was also important as the teacher of **Puccini** and **Mascagni**.

❖

La Gioconda (*s*) is a street singer who loves the sailor Enzo Grimaldo (*t*), an exiled noble-man. He,

however, does not return her love, preferring Laura (*ms*), the wife of Alvise (*b*), brutal lord of the Inquisition. Gioconda refuses the attentions of the Inquisition's spy, Barnaba (*bar*). In revenge, he arrests Gioconda's blind mother, La Cieca (*c*), accusing her of witchcraft. Laura pleads with her husband to save the old woman's life and, in return, La Gioconda, though she is heart-broken at her unrequited love, helps Enzo and Laura escape the vengeance of Alvise. La Gioconda buys the freedom of the man she loves by offering herself to the hated Barnaba. As he arrives to claim her, she kills herself.

HIGHLIGHTS
ACT 2 'Cielo e mar!' ('Heaven and ocean!') In this celebrated aria, beloved of tenors, Enzo is on board his ship waiting for Laura, and gives expression to his joy.

ACT 3 *Dance of the Hours* In the great hall of the Palace, Alvise has put on a ballet for his guests that represents the hours and the symbolic struggle between darkness and light. The music is a classical pop (it's one of the numbers from Walt Disney's *Fantasia*) but is known equally well as sung by Alan Sherman with the words 'Hello muddah, hello faddah, here I am at Camp Granada!'

ACT 4 'Suicidio!' ('Yes, suicide!') La Gioconda threatens to kill her rival, the sleeping Laura, and then kill herself. She can't bring herself to do either and drops weeping to the ground.

RECOMMENDED RECORDING
complete:
Callas/Cossotto/
Ferraro/Cappuccilli
Ch & O La Scala, Votto
EMI CDS7 49518 2

THE GONDOLIERS
GILBERT AND SULLIVAN
COMPOSER:
SIR ARTHUR SULLIVAN
LIBRETTO: SIR W. S. GILBERT
1889

2 ACTS SET IN THE PIAZETTA, VENICE, AND THE PALACE OF BARATARIA IN 1750

This, the twelfth Gilbert and Sullivan collaboration, has the longest vocal score of any of the Savoy Operas and, arguably, the wittiest libretto. Its sunny Venetian setting, the inspired lunacy of the plot and characters, the memorable melodies following one after the other in quick succession, all make *The Gondoliers*, in many ways, the supreme achievement of the partnership. It was also their last great success and a minor miracle that it came to be written at all.

After *The Mikado* and *The Yeomen of the Guard* the two men had quarrelled frequently. Sullivan wanted to concentrate on more serious work and told Gilbert so. The next work had to be one 'where the music is to be the first consideration – where words are to suggest music, not govern it'. The sensitive Gilbert was stung into waspish response: 'If you are really under the astounding impression that you have been effacing yourself for the last twelve years ... there is certainly no *modus vivendi* to be found that shall be satisfactory to both of us. You are an adept in your profession, and I am an adept in mine. If we meet, it must be as master and master – not as master and servant.'

As usual, the impresario D'Oyly Carte got them to bury the hatchet. Gilbert's Venetian plot appealed to Sullivan and, whilst it took them far longer than usual (five months), the

Sketches from The Gondoliers *at the Savoy Theatre in 1889*

result was an immediate success (although not in America, where it failed at the box-office and was known as 'The Gone Dollars').

The morning after the first night Gilbert wrote to Sullivan: 'I must thank you for the magnificent work you have put into the piece. It gives one the chance of shining right through the twentieth century with a reflected light.' 'Don't talk of reflected light,' replied Sullivan. 'In such a perfect book as *The Gondoliers* you shone with an individual brilliance which no other writer can hope to attain.'

Shortly afterwards Gilbert went off on a cruise to India with his wife. He returned home to find that £500 of the partners' money had been spent on new carpets for the Savoy Theatre. A furious row ensued and it was to be three years before another G & S work appeared.

❖

Giuseppe (*t*) and Marco (*bar*) are the two gondoliers in question. They have chosen (blindfolded) their brides from a number of girls, Tessa (*c*) being caught by Giuseppe, Gianetta (*s*) by Marco. The impoverished Duke of Plaza-Toro

(*bar*), his wife the Duchess (*c*), their daughter Casilda (*s*) and attendant Luiz (*t*) appear. Twenty years ago, baby Casilda was married by proxy to the baby son of the King of Barataria. The baby heir was stolen by Don Alhambra del Bolero, the Grand Inquisitor (*b*), who arrives to tell them that the boy was raised by an old gondolier. This gondolier had a son of his own and the two boys got mixed up, the result being that no one knows which of them is the rightful king. Giuseppe and Marco discover they are the supposed 'brothers'. After a brief joint reign, the two gondoliers (republicans at heart) return with their wives to the simple life, the young King's foster-mother, Inez (*c*), having turned up and revealed that the royal babe was not stolen. She had substituted her own son and kept the prince herself – and his name is Luiz. Thus the Duke's attendant, who in any case is in love with the Duke's daughter, ascends the throne and marries Casilda.

HIGHLIGHTS

Overture
ACT 1 'The merriest fellows are we'.
'Buon' giorno, signorine!'
'In enterprise of martial kind'.
'I stole the Prince (No possible doubt whatever)'.
'When a merry maiden marries'.
'A regular royal Queen'.
ACT 2 'Rising early in the morning'.
'Take a pair of sparkling eyes'.
'Dance a cachucha'.
'A Duke or a Duchess'.
'I am a courtier grave and serious'.

RECOMMENDED RECORDING
complete:
Sansom/Toye/Round/Styler/Reed
D'Oyly Carte
NSO, Godfrey
DECCA 425 177

HANSEL AND GRETEL
ENGELBERT HUMPERDINCK
1893

ORIGINAL GERMAN TITLE:
'HÄNSEL UND GRETEL'
LIBRETTO: ADELHEID WETTE
(THE COMPOSER'S SISTER)
BASED ON GRIMM'S FAIRY TALE

3 ACTS SET IN THE FOREST

'If you go down to the woods today ...' Dark forests have a fascination for Germans: *Der Freischütz, Siegfried* and other operas all make significant use of them, but none to such magical effect as this perennial favourite. And how rare to find an opera that children *and* adults can enjoy equally. Based on the Brothers Grimm fairy tale, the work began life in the form of some verses that Humperdinck's sister wrote for her children and which she sent to her brother to set to music. The first performance was given as a Christmas entertainment in a private

Hansel and Gretel nibble at the Witch's house in English National Opera's 1987 production

theatre in Frankfurt and subsequently elaborated into a full-length opera.

You wouldn't know it, but Humperdinck, who was close to Wagner and worked with him, adopted the latter's then fashionable **leitmotiv** technique and other orchestral devices in the score. But it's all handled so lightly and melodically that, well, who cares? *Hansel and Gretel* is an original and personal work. Humperdinck based much of the material on popular songs and folk-tunes so that it could be accessible to ordinary people. Would that more opera composers shared his sentiments.

❖

Once upon a time there lived a poor broom-maker, Peter (*bar*), and his wife Gertrude (*ms*). They had two children – Hänsel (*ms*), a little boy, and Gretel (*s*), a little girl. One day their mother sent them off into the woods to gather some strawberries. Tired out, she fell asleep. Father returned late and both parents grew worried that the children, who had not come back yet, might have been captured by a wicked witch who lived in the wood and made children into gingerbread. They set out to look for them.

Meanwhile, the children had eaten all the strawberries they'd picked. Before they knew it, it was dark and they couldn't find their way back. They were frightened but the Sandman (*s*) came along to lull them to sleep.

Next morning they were awoken by the Dew Fairy (*s*) to find themselves by a gingerbread house that, because they were so hungry, they began to eat. From inside, a voice asked them who was eating her house. The Witch (*ms*) came out and bewitched the children with her magic wand, locking Hänsel in a cage to fatten him up for eating later before dancing about on her broomstick. But Gretel managed to get hold of the magic wand, speak the magic words and break the spell, releasing Hänsel. The Witch ordered Gretel to look in the oven to see if the gingerbread was cooked, but Gretel pretended to be stupid and asked to be shown how. When the witch looked inside, Hänsel and Gretel pushed her into the oven and slammed the door shut. The oven exploded and all the other little gingerbread boys and girls whom the Witch had enchanted were restored to life. Mother and Father at last found their children. The Witch turned into a giant gingerbread cake, there was enough treasure in her house to keep them happy for life and they all sang and danced for joy – and, of course, lived happily ever after.

HIGHLIGHTS
Prelude
ACT 1 *'Brüderchen komm tanz' mit mir'* ('Brother come and dance with me') *Dance duet.* The children dance to help them forget how hungry they are.
ACT 2 *'Der kleine Sandman bin ich'* ('I am the fairy Sandman') *The*

Sandman's Song. The Sandman sprinkles sand in the children's eyes to send them to sleep.

'*Abends, will ich schlafen gehn*' ('When I lay me down to sleep') *Evening Prayer.* The children kneel to say their prayers, invoking fourteen angels.

Dream Pantomime. The angels appear to protect the sleeping children.

RECOMMENDED RECORDING
complete:
Schwartzkopf/Grummer/Schurhoff,
Philh. O, Karajan
EMI CMS7 69293 2

LAKME
LEO DELIBES
1883
PRONOUNCED: lak'-MAY
LIBRETTO: EDMOND GONDINET
AND PHILIPPE GILLE
AFTER PIERRE LOTI'S
'LE MARIAGE DE LOTI'

3 ACTS SET IN 19TH CENTURY INDIA

Delibes was already famous for his two ballet scores *Coppélia* and *Sylvia* by the time he wrote *Lakmé*, the only one of his twenty-eight other stage-works (including operettas, incidental music for plays and grand operas) heard today.

❖

Nilakantha (*b*) is a fanatical Brahmin priest who guards the sacred temple and awaits the day that the British invaders will be driven from his land. Curiosity leads a young English officer, Gérald (*t*), and his friends to break into the mysterious grounds of the temple and when Nilakantha's daughter, Lakmé (*s*),

*Lily Pons as Lakmé
in a 1932 production*

sees him, it's love at first sight for both of them. But Gérald has trespassed and Nilakantha swears death for the intruder.

To find the foreigner, he orders his daughter, disguised as a street singer, to sing in the market place in the hope that her voice will attract him. The ruse works. Nilakantha sees Gérald and stabs him. Lakmé and her slave Mallika (*ms*) carry the wounded officer to a hut in the forest. There, Frédéric (*bar*), a fellow officer, comes to persuade Gérald to return to his regiment. Martial music is heard in the distance and Gérald realizes that he must go. Lakmé understands that she has lost her lover. Like many other disconsolate operatic maidens, she poisons herself – by biting a leaf of the deadly datura tree – and dies happy in his arms.

HIGHLIGHTS

ACT 1 *'Dôme épais, le jasmin'* ('O thick canopy of jasmine') A languorous and sensual barcarolle sung by Lakmé and Mallika as they prepare to bathe in the temple gardens. Known as the Flower Duet (see also **Madam Butterfly**), it is now practically impossible to hear without thoughts of the world's favourite airline.

ACT 2 *'Où va la jeune Hindoue?'* ('Where is the young Hindu maiden?') This is the Bell Song, among the most testing of *coloratura* arias, in which Delibes's bell-like effects for the singer mingle with a seductive oriental melody. Hugely popular in recitals.

RECOMMENDED RECORDING
complete:
Sutherland/Berbire/Vanzo,
Monte Carlo Ch & O, Bonynge
DECCA 425 485 2

LOHENGRIN
WAGNER
1850
LIBRETTO: WAGNER
BASED ON SEVERAL POEMS AND LEGENDS

3 ACTS SET IN ANTWERP IN THE FIRST HALF OF THE 10TH CENTURY

This is the earliest of Wagner's operas the connoisseurs consider to be a masterpiece. For beginners, it provides an effective initiation into Wagner's world, especially if you're intrigued by his later *Ring* cycle and want to investigate that.

After *Rienzi* (a success) and *The Flying Dutchman* (a relative failure) had come *Tannhäuser* (not an immediate success). In each work, Wagner had developed his style. With *Lohengrin* he went further, replacing the conventional overture with a Prelude concentrating on the story's inner significance. His ability as a dramatist has improved, and he makes significant use of **leitmotivs** associating different musical themes with certain characters. There is also an obvious effort to break away from the set-piece **aria** by using instead seamless **recitative**, a device which, he felt, better expressed the emotional truth and character of what he was writing about.

Picture from Le Petit Journal *of the riot that followed* Lohengrin's *first night*

Wagner finished the score of *Lohengrin* in March 1848, at a point in his career when he had to come up with a hit. In 1849 a wave of social unrest swept Germany and, believing that a more democratic form of government might improve things, Wagner joined the popular uprising. When the May Revolution was crushed by the military, Wagner fled the country, forced to make his escape in disguise. In exile in Switzerland, he wrote to Franz Liszt, begging him to produce *Lohengrin*. At that time, Liszt was the greatest pianist in the world, among the most respected of living composers, courted by kings and universally acclaimed. When he conducted the first performance in Weimar in 1850, he showed a deal of courage and generosity in championing this work by a relatively unknown composer whose revolutionary tendencies had made him an exile sought by the German authorities. Wagner himself did not hear the work until eleven years later in a production in Vienna, after he had been allowed to return from exile.

❖

Elsa of Brabant (*s*) has been accused of murdering her brother by Frederick of Telramund (*bar*) and has a mystic dream of a knight who will defend her from the charge. Her knight (*t*) in shining armour arrives in a boat drawn by a swan. The stranger announces that his aim is to help all those unjustly accused or oppressed; he tells her he can only stay as long as she never asks his name or whence he came. She agrees and her knight defeats Telramund in combat, sparing his life. Elsa and her knight marry but Ortrud (*ms*), Telramund's wife, taunts the bride that she does not know who her husband is. At

length, when Elsa can bear it no more and cries out, 'Who are you?', Telramund and four soldiers rush in with drawn swords. The knight kills Telramund. Then, sadly, he answers Elsa's question: he is Lohengrin, the son of Parsifal, the guardian of the Holy Grail. The swan appears with Lohengrin's boat, when Ortrud emerges to reveal that the swan is none other than Gottfried, Elsa's brother, whom Ortrud had transformed by magic. The swan sinks and, restored to human shape by a timely prayer from Lohengrin, in its place stands Gottfried. Lohengrin steps into the boat, drawn now by a white dove, as Elsa sinks lifeless into her brother's arms.

HIGHLIGHTS

Prelude The music suggests a vision of the Holy Grail, the cup, according to medieval legend, which Christ used at the Last Supper. It descends from Heaven, 'shedding', in Wagner's words, 'glorious light on the beholder like a benediction' before ascending again to the 'ethereal height of tender joy'.
ACT 1 *'Einsam in trüben Tagen'* Elsa's Dream in which she sings of her vision of a guardian knight coming to defend her.
ACT 2 *Wedding Procession.*
ACT 3 *Prelude* A brilliant impression of the wedding festivities – the wedding of Elsa and Lohengrin having closed Act 2 – played before the curtain rises to the strains of the …
Bridal Chorus How many brides have walked down the aisle to this? 'Here comes the bride …
ACT 3 *'In fernem Land'* ('In a far-off land'). Lohengrin's Narrative, in which he tells Elsa (and the

assembled citizens of Brabant) that he comes from a distant land.

LOUISE
GUSTAVE CHARPENTIER
1900
LIBRETTO: CHARPENTIER

4 ACTS SET IN PARIS IN THE 1890S

The fact that *Louise* is not among the best-known operas shouldn't dissuade you from investigating it. It's a one-off work of great appeal, dramatically and musically, and has many original features. Like Wagner, Charpentier provided his own libretto and adopted his use of **leitmotiv** to underline the mood of different characters. Paris, where the opera is set, emerges as a central figure in the work and the composer introduces Parisian street cries and sounds into the score. But there is something of an Italian melodist and romantic in him as well, besides the unusually truthful treatment of the emotions and tensions which the story produces.

Charpentier (not to be confused with his seventeenth-century namesake, Marc-Antoine) was actively concerned in the social problems of the working classes and formed a society for their welfare. More personally, his mistress at the time he was writing the opera was called Louise. She, too, was a dressmaker. Although he

Act 4 of the original Paris production in 1900 of Louise

lived to the ripe old age of ninety-five, he never produced anything else to equal this.

❖

Louise (*s*) is in love with a young poet, Julien (*t*), but her parents are violently opposed to the relationship. Nevertheless, she eventually leaves home to live with her lover in Montmartre. They are blissfully happy when Louise's mother (*c*) arrives to plead with her to return to her father (*b*), who is dying of grief from the loss of his daughter. With Julien's consent, she goes home. Her parents plead with her not to return to Julien, but Louise has tasted the free life of the city with her man and that is all she wants. Her father orders her from the house in a rage. The curtain falls as the old man shakes his fist at the city into which she has disappeared, crying '*O Paris!*'

HIGHLIGHTS

ACT 3 '*Depuis le jour où je me suis donnée*' ('Since the day I gave myself to you') As twilight falls over the city, Louise tells Julien

how happy she is. A rapturously lyrical **aria** which is just as effective out of context.

RECOMMENDED RECORDING
complete:
Cotrubas/Berbie/Domingo
NPO,Pretre
SONY S3K 46429

THE LOVE FOR THREE ORANGES
PROKOFIEV
1921
LIBRETTO: PROKOFIEV
AFTER CARLO GOZZI'S
'FIABA DELL' AMORE DELLE TRE MELARANCIE'

4 ACTS SET IN THE KING'S PALACE, THE WITCH'S DOMAIN AND THE DESERT

Prokofiev's most popular works are *Peter and the Wolf*, the ballet of *Romeo and Juliet* and the orchestral suite *Lieutenant Kije*. All three contain elements of the musical style you can expect in his most popular opera: lyricism – although admittedly there aren't many tunes to hum – spiky, angular rhythms and harmonies, and a fantastic imagination.

❖

The three oranges are three princesses imprisoned in the oranges by the wicked sorceress Fata Morgana (*s*). The King of Clubs (*b*), who rules over a kingdom where the people are dressed as playing cards, has a melancholy hypochondriac son, the Prince (*t*). He is advised that the only cure for the boy is to make him laugh, but as his son has no sense of humour this seems like an impossible task. After various entertainments are put on in an attempt to raise a smile, the wicked

Fata accidentally trips and does a somersault – this does the trick. The Prince falls about laughing and in return the witch condemns him to fall in love with three oranges. After many adventures, the Prince tracks down the monster fruits. Out of the first orange steps a princess who immediately dies. The second and the third do likewise, but the last is revived by the jesters with a bucket of water. The witch is beaten and, of course, they all live happily ever after.

HIGHLIGHT

ACT 2 *March* Its grotesquely pompous tune (the opera's catchiest) is often heard independently, either as an orchestral suite from the opera or in the composer's well-known piano transcription.

RECOMMENDED RECORDING
complete:
Soloists/Lyon Opera Ch & O,
Nagano
VIRG VCD7 91084

LUCIA DI LAMMERMOOR
DONIZETTI
1835
PRONOUNCED: LOO-CHEE'-AH DI LAMMERMOOR
LIBRETTO: SALVATORE CAMMARANO
AFTER SIR WALTER SCOTT'S NOVEL 'THE BRIDE OF LAMMERMOOR', ITSELF BASED ON A TRUE STORY

3 ACTS SET IN SCOTLAND AT THE END OF THE 17TH CENTURY

This is Donizetti's masterpiece and a wonderful vehicle for a great *coloratura* soprano, one of the reasons it has never been out of the international repertoire. (That's not to say the lead tenor doesn't get a look in – he certainly does.) From **Patti** to **Melba** and **Galli-Curci** to **Sutherland**, every major **prima donna** has delighted in the challenges of the title role. Of all the mad scenes in opera, the one in *Lucia* (as it is always called) is the most renowned, requiring enormous technical virtuosity to negotiate the tricky vocal writing. The ensemble numbers, which include the famous sextet, are among the best in Italian opera. Donizetti wrote the score in thirty-six days, though there are some passages not written by him. The chorus in the last act is said to be copied from a Mass by one Simone Meyr!

Katia Ricciarelli as Lucia di Lammermoor in the Royal Opera House's 1980 production

Ravenswood Castle and estate have been usurped by the Ashtons, and Enrico (*bar*) – Lord Henry Ashton of Lammermoor – has not only gone through his family fortune but has weakened his position with politicial activities. Needing both allies and money, he plans to wed his sister Lucia (*s*) to the wealthy Arturo (*t*), laird of Bucklaw. Lucia, however, is secretly in love with Edgardo (*t*), the dispossessed heir to Ravenswood, and he with her. Edgardo is sent to France on duty but his love letters to Lucia are intercepted by Enrico, who forges a letter showing that Edgardo has not been faithful to Lucia. On seeing this, she reluctantly agrees to marry Arturo. The ceremony is taking place when Edgardo bursts in, sees Lucia's signature on the contract and curses her and the house of Lammermoor. In the bridal chamber, Lucia loses her mind, killing the bridegroom and then herself. Edgardo forces a duel with Enrico and waits for him in the burial ground of the Ravenswood family. Here he learns of Lucia's fate and takes his own life by falling on his sword.

HIGHLIGHTS

ACT 1 *'Regnava nel silenzio'* ('In silence reigned the night') Known as Lucia's Cavatina, our heroine sings of her sorrows mingled with ecstasy, as she waits for her secret meeting with Edgardo.

'Verranno a te sull' aure' ('My love will reach you') Edgardo and Lucia's love duet.

'Se tradirmi tu potrai' ('If you betray me') In a duet of thrilling power, Enrico puts pressure on her to marry Arturo.

ACT 2 *'Chi mi frena'* ('What can restrain me?') The finest sextet in opera. Lucia, who has just signed the marriage contract in the Great Hall of the Castle, bemoans her fate, Edgardo bursts in, Enrico begins to show remorse and the other guests express their compassion.

ACT 3 *'Ardon gl'incensi'* ('The incense rises') The Mad Scene. A lexicon of trills, runs, cantabile, duets with flute – a *coloratura tour de force* which must not be sung as a mere show-piece but convey Lucia's sadness and confusion.

RECOMMENDED RECORDINGS
complete:
Callas/Di Stefano/ Gobbi
Maggio Musicale Fiorentino
Ch & O, Serafin
EMI CMS7 69980 2 (mono)
highlights:
Callas/Tagliavini/Cappuccilli
Philh. Ch & O, Serafin
EMI CDM7 63934 2

MADAM BUTTERFLY

PUCCINI

1904

ORIGINAL ITALIAN TITLE: 'MADAMA BUTTERFLY'
LIBRETTO: GIUSEPPE GIACOSA AND LUIGI ILLICA
AFTER DAVID BELASCO AND JOHN LUTHER LONG
LENGTH: 2' 10"

Up near the top in the popularity stakes, *Butterfly* also gets a ten out of ten tissue rating. Even if the story is too sentimental for you – for many people it is all too real – it takes a hard heart not to respond to Puccini's luscious music. Although the score is 'through-composed' (i.e. it doesn't have the old-fashioned stop-start, **recitative-aria** format), it contains some of the most sumptuous and memorable of melodies you'll hear in a single opera. You don't have to be a musicologist to appreciate the subtle ways in which Puccini includes Japanese themes and oriental orchestral effects without losing his essential Italian character.

BACKGROUND

The story of *Madam Butterfly* is said to be based on fact. In any case, the American writer John Luther Long wrote a short story that attracted the attention of the legendary Broadway producer David Belasco. Needing a new play to save a disastrous season, he made one himself out of Long's tragic tale of a Japanese girl abandoned by an American sailor. It was so successful that in 1900 a production was put on in London, and it was this that Puccini came to see. Although he didn't understand a word of it, apparently, he was so deeply moved by what he saw that, according to the colourful Belasco's unreliable memoirs, he embraced the writer-producer with tears in his eyes and begged him for the rights. Impressed by this display of emotion, Belasco agreed at once and Puccini began writing *Madam Butterfly* in the autumn of 1901. A car accident interrupted the work for several months, but he finally completed the orchestration in December 1903.

FIRST PERFORMANCE

La Scala, Milan
17 February 1904
Butterfly is another of those masterpieces which had a disastrous first outing. Whether it was organized or not, the première at **La Scala** aroused hissing during Butterfly's first number (it sounded like Mimi's in *La Bohème* and Puccini subsequently rewrote it) as well as laughter at some of the action. It was a fiasco: the Cio-Cio-San had backstage hysterics that could be heard all over the theatre

and, as a result of all this, it was withdrawn after one performance. Two months later, Puccini had revised the score and in a second production in Brescia, *Butterfly* was given a rapturous reception.

Puccini himself felt that the work was 'the most felt and most expressive opera that I have conceived', and it was his personal favourite of all he wrote. Many would go along with that.

STORY

3 acts set in the early years of the century in Nagasaki, Japan

PRINCIPAL CHARACTERS
MADAM BUTTERFLY (Cio-Cio-San), a 15-year-old geisha (s)
SUZUKI, Cio-Cio-San's servant (ms)
B. F. PINKERTON, a lieutenant in the US Navy (t)
KATE PINKERTON, his American wife (ms)
SHARPLESS, US Consul at Nagasaki (bar)
GORO, a marriage broker (t)
THE BONZE, Cio-Cio-San's uncle (b)
PRINCE YAMADORI, a suitor for Cio-Cio-San (t)

While stationed with the US Navy in Nagasaki, Lieutenant Pinkerton falls for a young geisha and decides to marry the girl. His friend Sharpless tries to dissuade him from the marriage which the Lieutenant sees as a temporary arrangement, although Cio-Cio-San not only considers the ceremony to be binding but has even renounced her religion for it.

Butterfly (Cio-Cio-San's nickname) enters with her relatives. Sharpless learns that she is the impoverished daughter of a nobleman who died by his own

Opposite: *Cover of the score for Madam Butterfly*

hand. She is indeed deeply in love with Pinkerton. The marriage is celebrated, but not without the angry opposition of Cio-Cio-San's uncle, the Bonze, who curses her for forsaking her faith. After the ceremony, the house is cleared and Butterfly and Pinkerton sing of their love.

Three years pass. The Lieutenant, recalled to America, has not returned as promised and the money he left has nearly run out. Butterfly is convinced he will come back (he has never seen his little boy 'Trouble'). Sharpless tries to tell her that Pinkerton has married an American girl and will shortly be visiting Nagasaki, but the trusting Cio-Cio-San doesn't take it in. Goro, a marriage-broker, presents Prince Yamadori as a wealthy suitor, but the girl insists she is married to Pinkerton and refuses him. Sharpless attempts to make her understand what has happened; but she remains sure her husband will return into her life when he knows about the boy.

A cannon shot booms over the harbour announcing the arrival of the *Abraham Lincoln* – Pinkerton's ship. Butterfly decorates the house and with joyful expectancy waits for

him. She waits all night. Pinkerton, his American wife and Sharpless appear. On seeing the situation, Pinkerton cannot bear to stay. When Butterfly is told that he wants to adopt the child, she tells her visitors, without any emotion, that in half an hour they may take the child away. Left alone, she embraces 'Trouble', gently bandages his eyes and gives him an American flag to wave, before killing herself with her father's sword. She dies as Pinkerton and Sharpless rush in. Sharpless takes the child as the American sailor sobs with grief and shame.

Janice Cairns as Butterfly and David Maxwell Anderson as Pinkerton in Opera North's production

HIGHLIGHTS

ACT 1 *'Ancora un passo'* ('There is one more step to climb') Butterfly's entrance. She is heard off-stage encouraging her various relatives on the climb up the hill to the honeymoon cottage.

'Dolce notte' ('Sweet night') The exquisite love duet sung by Pinkerton and his pretty little

Butterfly as they hold each other close under the stars.

ACT 2 *'Un bel dì vedremo'* ('Some day he'll come') 'One Fine Day', as it's now known, is among the most popular **soprano arias** in opera. It's become a little hackneyed from over use – not Puccini's fault! – but it's a clever bit of writing. Butterfly's optimism is real enough but you can hear in the music that her situation is hopeless.

'Tutti i fior' ('Every flower') The lovely Flower Duet in which Butterfly and her maid decorate the house with cherry blossoms to welcome home Pinkerton.

Intermezzo Suggests the passage of time between the end of Act 2 and the beginning of Act 3. This is the Humming Chorus, when the oriental night is delicately evoked.

THE MAGIC FLUTE

MOZART

1791

ORIGINAL GERMAN TITLE: 'DIE ZAUBERFLÖTE'
PRONOUNCED: DEE TSOU-BER-FLUH'-TEH
LIBRETTO: EMANUEL SCHIKANEDER
BASED ON THE STORY 'LULU, ODER DIE ZAUBERFLÖTE'
BY AUGUST JACOB LIEBESKIND,
PUBLISHED IN A COLLECTION OF ORIENTAL FAIRY TALES
LENGTH: 2' 30"

'The opera ... is the only one in existence that might conceivably have been composed by God,' wrote the critic Neville Cardus; **Beethoven** considered it to be Mozart's greatest work. Whether you see this, almost his last completed work, as a fairy tale, an allegorical pantomime or an evening glorifying the brotherhood of Freemasonry (the opera works on many levels), *The Magic Flute* is a work of universal genius. This is artistic endeavour, inspiration – call it what you will – at the highest level, despite its implausible story. What's more, children and adults can enjoy this side by side, for it has slapstick comedy, magic and special effects, goodies and baddies, a human journey of enlightenment mixed with fantastical, mystical, sacred elements and much more – not to mention the incomparably beautiful music.

BACKGROUND

Mozart was hard up and in declining health when his friend Schikaneder asked him for a *singspiel* for his small theatre in Vienna. Schikaneder was an appealing character – baritone, playwright, impresario, considered to be one of the finest Shakespearean actors of his day and, like Mozart, a Freemason. Mozart's successful collaboration with Da Ponte having ended with the latter's dismissal from the Court theatre, Schikaneder supplied the text with its fashionable fairy-tale elements, and hoped that the finished work would save him from financial troubles. Mozart's contribution lifted it out of the realms of straight-forward pantomime into a work of parables, inner meanings and symbols, that managed to combine the three main elements of operatic composition: German richness of harmony and counterpoint, French grace and wit and Italian beauty of melody.

FIRST PERFORMANCE

Theater an der Wien, Vienna
30 September 1791
Josefa Hofer (Constanze Mozart's sister) was Queen of the Night, Schikaneder played Papageno, and Mozart conducted from the fortepiano. The performance began at seven o'clock, as we know from surviving handbills, and was greeted with immediate acclaim. There is the touching story (apocryphal, alas) of the young composer Johann Schenk securing a seat in the orchestra pit at the last minute; after the dead silence that followed the Overture, he crawled up to the rostrum and kissed Mozart's hand. The opera's popularity spread quickly (in the first year alone it was given more than 100 times), Mozart's greatest operatic success. Not that Mozart knew, for little more than two months after the opening night, he was dead.

STORY

2 acts set in Egypt
in legendary times

PRINCIPAL CHARACTERS
SARASTRO, High Priest of Isis (b)
TAMINO, an Egyptian prince (t)
PAPAGENO, the Queen's bird catcher
(bar)
THE QUEEN OF THE NIGHT (s)
PAMINA, her daughter (s)
MONOSTATOS, Sarastro's Moorish
servant (t)
PAPAGENA, Papageno's lover (s)

Tamino is rescued from a dreadful serpent by the three Attendants of the Queen of the Night. Having fainted, he comes round in the belief that Papageno has saved him and Papageno says nothing to disabuse him of this. The attendants produce a picture of Pamina, with which Tamino immediately falls in love. He is told, however, that she is in the clutches of Sarastro and, in order to help rescue her, he is given a

magic flute and Papageno some magic bells. After frightening, then being captured by, and finally escaping from the evil Monostatos, the slave of the sacred temple, they find Pamina. She duly falls in love with Tamino, only to discover that Sarastro is not the baddie at all: it's her mother, the Queen of the Night.

Sarastro sees how the two lovers feel for one another and promises that if they prove themselves in a series of trials, he will grant them a future of happiness. One of the ordeals is a vow of silence for both Tamino and Papageno (who has been told that he too is due eternal happiness with his new love, Papagena). Neither is allowed to speak to any woman – disconcerting for both the ladies concerned. Worse is to come. The Queen of the Night discovers that Tamino has joined the initiates of Sarastro's sacred temple and, in a fury, bids Pamina

kill the High Priest. Poor Pamina is further told that Tamino is to leave her. She decides to take her life, as does Papageno, who has lost *his* love. Both are given hope by the three Genii. Tamino and Pamina have to pass through fire and water (with the help of the magic flute, of course) and are finally welcomed into the fellowship of the temple. Papageno and Papagena are also joyfully reunited. The Queen of the Night, Monostatos and their allies attempt to destroy the temple, but are vanquished for ever by the power of Sarastro.

HIGHLIGHTS

Overture After the initial heavy introductory chords (said to represent knocking on the door of the masonic lodge), this brilliant introduction to the work heads off into a fugue which might have been written to dispel any thoughts that this form has to be dry and academic.

ACT 1 *'Der Vogelfänger bin ich ja'* ('I am the jolly birdcatcher') Papageno introduces himself.

'Dies Bildnis ist bezaubernd schön' ('O loveliness beyond compare') Tamino's beautiful aria (one of Mozart's finest for the **tenor** voice) on seeing Pamina's portrait.

'O zittre nicht' ('O tremble not') This is the first of the two arias for the Queen of the Night that stretch the range and agility of the singer to the limits, the highest note being a top F – an octave above the top note any of us would sing in, say, a hymn. Mozart wrote it for his sister-in-law to strut her stuff, but it's also a good piece of characterization.

'Bei Männern' ('The manly heart') Another exquisite air, a duet between Pamina and Papageno, she reassuring him that love will be his one day.

Alan Opie as Papageno in English National Opera's production

'O Isis und Osiris' ('O Isis and Osiris') This prayer to the gods of Egypt, sung by Sarastro, is as deep as the Queen of the Night's aria is high.

ACT 2 *'Der Hölle Rache kocht in meinem herzen'* ('The pangs of hell are raging') Off she goes again, threatening to disown her daughter in a celebrated *coloratura* show-piece of brilliant vocal arabesques, including *four* top Fs! This is the one usually referred to as 'the Queen of the Night's Aria'.

'Ein Mädchen oder Weibchen' ('A maiden or a little wife') Papageno wistfully yearns for love, accompanying himself with his magic bells.

'Pa-pa-pa' The jolly duet between Papageno and Papagena, finally reunited.

THE TWO MANONS

First came the novel by Abbé Prévost, L'Histoire du Chevalier des Grieux et de Manon Lescaut in 1731; then there was a ballet (Manon Lescaut) by Halévy in 1830, followed by Auber's opera of the same name in 1856, another opera (Manon) by Massenet in 1884 and a third one (Manon Lescaut) by Puccini in 1893.

Only the last two survive in performance today. Both tell the same tragic story of a beautiful but misguided girl who gives in to her weakness for the good things of life at the expense of her true feelings of love. Inevitably, the Frenchman and the Italian go about it in different ways: Puccini follows the novel more closely in four relatively disjointed scenes; Massenet departs from the original more, but achieves greater dramatic unity. The latter wrote much of his version in The Hague, in the very room in which Abbé Prévost had lived.

Puccini was quite daring to take on the same subject – it had been a success only nine years earlier and, moreover, a success for a well-established composer. It was a risk worth taking, however, for Manon Lescaut was Puccini's first resounding triumph and made him an overnight success. It gave him financial independence and, together with La Bohème just three years later, established him as an internationally important composer.

MANON
JULES MASSENET
1884
PRONOUNCED: MAHN-ON
LIBRETTO: HENRI MEILHAC AND
PHILIPPE GILLE
AFTER 'MANON LESCAUT' BY
ABBÉ PRÉVOST

5 ACTS SET IN AND AROUND
PARIS IN 1721

Manon (*s*) is the sort of girl who inspires passion in men without being aware of her powers. In the company of her cousin Lescaut (*bar*), she is en route to a convent to finish her education when she stops at an inn. There and then she meets, falls in love and elopes to Paris with the young, impecunious Chevalier des Grieux (*t*). In Paris, Lescaut's friend, the wealthy nobleman de Brétigny (*bar*), persuades Manon to leave and live with him. Heartbroken, des Grieux enters the priesthood. Manon, meanwhile, is kept in luxury, admired and content, until one day she learns of the fate of her old love. It's *her* turn to be heartbroken now – at her behaviour – and, forsaking de Brétigny, she hurries to St Sulpice to entice des Grieux back into the world before he can take his vows. After a brief struggle with himself he leaves with her. In order to keep her in the style to which she is now accustomed he takes to gambling. He is falsely accused of cheating and Manon is arrested as a prostitute. Due to the influence of his father, the Count des Grieux (*b*), the Chevalier is protected, but Manon is faced with deportation. Des Grieux bribes the guard to let him in to see the imprisoned Manon and tries to persuade her to escape, but she is too weak and dies in his arms.

HIGHLIGHTS
ACT 2 *'Adieu, notre petite table'* ('Farewell, our little table') Manon, tempted into Brétigny's world of luxury, looks sadly at the table at which des Grieux and she had sat.
'En fermant les yeux' ('When closing one's eyes') Known as the Dream Aria. Des Grieux relates a dream he has had – a paradise of Manon's cottage in a beautiful wood. The dream changes and Manon has gone.
ACT 3 *'Obéissons, quand leur voix appelle'* ('Listen to the voice of youth') Manon, now living in the lap of luxury, sings this brilliant Gavotte about her new way of life. *'Ah fuyez, douce image!'* ('Depart, fair vision!') Des Grieux renounces the sweet visions of the past and seeks peace of mind in prayer.

RECOMMENDED RECORDING
complete:
Cotrubas/Krauss
Ch & O of Capitole Toulouse
Plasson
EMI CMS7 49610 2

MANON LESCAUT
PUCCINI
1893
PRONOUNCED: MAHN-ON LES-KOH
LIBRETTO: ILLICA, PRAGA, OLIVA
AFTER 'MANON LESCAUT' BY
ABBÉ PRÉVOST

4 ACTS SET IN THE 18TH CENTURY
IN AMIENS, PARIS,
LE HAVRE AND LOUISIANA

Here, as in Massenet's *Manon*, des Grieux (*t*) and Manon (*s*) fall in love and elope, but Puccini's wealthy nobleman who wants

Manon for himself is Géronte de Ravoir (*b*), the Treasurer-General and an elderly roué. Manon deserts des Grieux for a life of luxury, but when he reappears one day, her feelings are rekindled. Géronte has her arrested as a prostitute, to be transported to the French province of Louisiana. Des Grieux pleads with the captain of the ship to consent to smuggle him on board and the final act takes place in the desert near New Orleans. Manon is in rags and can hardly walk. Des Grieux searches for food and shelter. He returns as Manon dies in his arms, telling him how much she has always loved him.

HIGHLIGHTS

ACT 1 '*Donna non vidi mai*' ('Maiden so fair') Des Grieux has just met Manon and sings that he has never before seen such beauty.

ACT 2 '*In quelle trine morbide*' ('In this gilded cage') Manon complains of being trapped in her luxurious surroundings. Arguably one of Puccini's most lovely **arias**.

'*L'ora o Tirsi,è vaga e bella*' ('These are hours of joy's creating'), A *pianissimo* top C ends this brilliant soprano show-piece.

Intermezzo Stealing a trick from Mascagni's **Cavalleria Rusticana**, Puccini represents the journey from Paris to Le Havre between Acts 2 and 3.

ACT 4 '*Sola, perduta, abbandonata*' ('Alone, lost, deserted') Manon's final, despairing aria in the desert.

RECOMMENDED RECORDING
complete:
Callas/Di Stefano/
Fioravanti/ Calabrese,
La Scala Ch & O, Serafin
EMI CDS7 47393-8 (mono)

THE MARRIAGE OF FIGARO

MOZART

1786

ORIGINAL ITALIAN TITLE: 'LE NOZZE DI FIGARO'
PRONOUNCED: LEH NOT'-ZEH DEE FEE'GAH-ROH
LIBRETTO: LORENZO DA PONTE
AFTER BEAUMARCHAIS'S PLAY OF THE SAME NAME
LENGTH: 2' 45"

After more than two centuries, *Figaro* (as everyone calls it) is still among the most popular and frequently performed of all operas. It is Mozart's comic masterpiece – indeed, one of the greatest masterpieces of comedy in music – but it is not comedy in, say, the more farcical **Offenbach** manner. This is comedy with depth, subtlety and point. It was Mozart's genius to find the substance beneath the glittering superficiality of the story, and he demonstrates here, in a way that few have ever surpassed, the power of music not only to comment on the action, but to add, in the subtlest way, characterization and information that mere words alone cannot convey. And the music he provides is sublime.

BACKGROUND
The story follows the plots and romantic intrigues of the same characters as are found in **Rossini's The Barber of Seville**, *Figaro* being based on the second of Beaumarchais's three plays featuring the rascally Figaro. Rossini's, composed thirty years later, is based on the first. The play was banned in Vienna, as it had been in Paris (where it appeared a decade before the Revolution), for its theme of servants not only plotting against their masters but also outwitting them was considered subversive. However, Emperor Joseph II lifted the ban for Mozart and Da Ponte's opera. It was the first of their collaborations, written in Italian rather than Mozart's native German in order to cater for the taste of the Viennese public.

FIRST PERFORMANCE
Burgtheater, Vienna
1 May 1786
The Irish **tenor** Michael Kelly, who sang Basilio in the first production, recalled the first full band rehearsal. After one particular **aria** 'the effect was electric, for the whole of the performers on stage, and those in the orchestra, as if actuated by one feeling of delight, vociferated, "Bravo! Bravo!

Maestro! *Viva, viva, grande Mozart!*" And Mozart? I never shall forget his little animated countenance, when lighted up with the glowing rays of genius. It is as impossible to describe it as it would be to paint sunbeams.'

The opening night ran twice as long as planned – because everything was encored. So successful were the first performances that the Emperor had to issue a decree banning **encores** of the ensemble numbers, whilst other musicians, jealous of Mozart's popularity, began a cabal against him that eventually led to the work being withdrawn.

STORY

4 acts set in the 18th century at the Count's castle near Seville

PRINCIPAL CHARACTERS
COUNT ALMAVIVA (bar)
FIGARO, his valet (bar)
DOCTOR BARTOLO, formerly the Countess's guardian (b)
DON BASILIO, a music master (t)
CHERUBINO, a page (s)
COUNTESS ALMAVIVA (s)
SUSANNA, her maid, engaged to Figaro (s)
MARCELLINA, Bartolo's former housekeeper (s)

The complicated action takes place in a single day (Beaumarchais' full title for his play was *La Folle Journée, ou Le Mariage de Figaro*). If you know *The Barber of Seville*, you'll remember that Figaro has helped Count Almaviva to marry the lovely Rosina, now Countess Almaviva. Figaro now wants to marry Susanna, but his fickle master is after her himself. An

added complication is that Figaro once promised to marry Marcellina and she, backed by Bartolo – who still bears the erstwhile barber a grudge – appears to claim her due.

Cherubino (a *travesti* role), a young page boy dismissed by the Count for flirting, asks for Susanna's intercession with his master. He hears the Count approaching and hides, only to hear his master making advances to Susanna. Bartolo arrives and, not seeing the Count, talks freely about Cherubino's flirtations with the Countess. Cherubino is then discovered. As he knows all about

the Count's affairs, he's ordered off to join the army. And that's just the *first* act!

The Countess, sad that she is not loved as she once was, is persuaded by Figaro and Susanna to teach her husband a lesson and simultaneously keep him so busy and baffled that he won't have time to stop Susanna and Figaro's wedding. The Count is made to believe that the Countess is to meet a lover and that *he* (the Count) is going to be met by Susanna. Instead of Susanna, though, he will get Cherubino in one of Susanna's dresses; the

Joan Rogers as the Countess and Deborah Pearce as Susanna in The Marriage of Figaro

Countess will then surprise her husband. Just as Cherubino is putting on his disguise, the Count enters. Cherubino hides, but when the suspicious Count is out of the room, he jumps from the window into the garden, to be replaced in the dressing-room by the smiling Susanna. To complicate the situation still further, Marcellina pursues her action against Figaro.

In the third act, there is a revelation: Figaro is discovered to be the son of Bartolo and Marcellina. Clearly he can't wed his mother, so the path to Susanna is conveniently cleared and a double marriage is celebrated. Another attempt to dupe the Count is now made: Susanna is to swap clothes with her mistress. Figaro and Cherubino are not told of the deception, however, the result being that Figaro believes he sees his master making love to his new bride (really the Countess); Cherubino flirts with the Countess (believing her to be Susanna); and the Count gets rid of Cherubino so that he can have 'Susanna' to

himself ... Needless to say, Figaro and Susanna are reconciled and the Count, presented with incontrovertible proof of his erring ways, begs his wife for forgiveness in front of all his retainers and dependents. The noble Countess grants him his wish.

HIGHLIGHTS

Overture Together with the last part of the Overture to Rossini's *William Tell*, one of the most popular of all operatic openers. It's a sparkling mood-setter.

ACT 1 '*Non so più*' ('I know not what I am') Cherubino has been sacked for flirting and sings of the love he has for every woman in the place.

'*Non più andrai*' ('No more games') Figaro prepares Cherubino for his life as a soldier.

ACT 2 '*Porgi amor*' ('Grant O love') The first of two poignant arias for the Countess, incomparable examples of Mozart's ability to mix tears and laughter.

'*Voi che sapete*' ('You who understand') Cherubino has written this song which he sings before trying on the dress and being interrupted by the Count. Why, he asks the Countess and Susanna, does he feel so fluttered by the presence of women? Certainly one of the most famous airs in all opera.

ACT 3 '*Dove sono*' ('I remember days long departed') In her second exquisite aria, the Countess looks back to happier days – before planning her husband's come-uppance.

'*Che soave zeffiretto*' ('Gentle zephyr, softly breathing') Known as the Letter Duet. Mozart, in a stroke of genius, has the Countess dictate a letter to the Count, which Susanna takes down and then 'sings back' with her mistress.

RECOMMENDED RECORDINGS

complete: Sciutti/Jurinac/ Bruscantini/ Stevens, Glyndebourne Festival Ch & O, Gui
CFP CD-CFPD 4724
highlights: Janowitz/Mathis/ Troyanos/Prey, German Opera Ch & O, Boehm
DG 429 822
video: Sylvan/Ommerle, VSO, Smith
DECCA 071 412-3DH

DIE MEISTERSINGER VON NÜRNBERG
WAGNER
1868
PRONOUNCED: DIH MY¹-STER-ZING-ER
LITERALLY: 'THE MASTERSINGERS OF NUREMBERG'
LIBRETTO: WAGNER
BASED ON HISTORICAL FACT

3 ACTS SET IN NUREMBERG IN THE MIDDLE OF THE 16TH CENTURY

You'll find learned opera tomes describe *Die Meistersinger* as 'Wagner's comic masterpiece', one of the 'greatest comic operas ever written', etc. Beware. This is comedy as Wagner understood the term. Certainly when compared with the rest of his output it is his lightest in terms of both music and subject matter, but you will not be rolling in the aisles, clutching your sides helpless with laughter.

It is a lengthy allegory of Wagner's own artistic philosophy which, although undeniably valuable, as expressed here is pompous, long-winded, self-regarding and earnest beyond measure. The basic story is so slight that it wouldn't provide enough meat for the average two-act operetta. Having said that, along the way there are some truly wonderful passages of great power and beauty with, if you are a musician, sufficient evidence of musical genius to provoke dozens of essays and analyses. There are few set-piece arias, for the writing is 'through-composed', seamless orchestral writing, with the vocal line apparently supplying the accompaniment. Technically, the music is a feat of extraordinary virtuosity, 'a monument of knowledge and of musical doctrine,

*Wieland Wagner (in collar and tie)
directing the 1964 Bayreuth
production of* Die Meistersinger.

a tribute of homage to the highest
tradition of German art', one critic
wrote. To the casual listener, that
won't mean a thing. Despite
maintaining its place as one of
Wagner's most popular operas, to
the average customer it's a long
haul.

❖

Hans Sachs (*b*), a cobbler, and
Veit Pogner (*b*), a goldsmith, are
Mastersingers (see box) and
Pogner has declared that his only
daughter Eva (*s*) should marry a
fellow Mastersinger. Eva falls in
love with Walther von Stolzing (*t*),
a young Franconian knight, who
realizes that he must become one
of this company if he is ever to
wed Eva. Pogner announces that
when the Nuremberg singing
contest is held, the winner will
receive his daughter's hand in
marriage. To win the competition
involves singing a song written in
a certain way, laid down by strict
rules and regulations. Walther (for
which read Wagner) disdains this
course, preferring to express his
thoughts freely and rely on
inspiration.

Against him in the contest is the
pedantic critic Sixtus Beckmesser (*b*),
the mean-spirited town clerk who
opposes anything new artistically
and who has his own marriage
designs on Eva. Between them – and
at the heart of the work – stands the
liberal-minded and enlightened
Hans Sachs. He respects the values
of the past while welcoming
justifiable and valuable innovations.
Though he too has thoughts of
marrying Eva, he selflessly advises
Walther how to qualify, for he sees
in him latent genius.

Beckmesser plagiarizes a song,
believing it to be by Sachs. In fact,
it's by Walther. It's not difficult to

The idea for Die Meistersinger
*came shortly after the completion
of* **Tannhäuser** *in 1845. Having
written of the aristocratic medieval
minnesingers (groups of nobles who
sang of love), Wagner took as his
contrasting subject the later middle-
class trade guilds who modelled
themselves on the minnesingers and
called themselves Mastersingers. The
most famous Mastersinger was the*

*shoemaker, poet and dramatist Hans
Sachs, who lived in Nuremberg
(1494–1576).*

*The character of Beckmesser is based
on the eminent critic and Wagner-hater
Eduard Hanslick (indeed, in the first
draft the character was named Hans
Lick). For his review of the Munich
première, Hanslick wrote: 'The only
thing which prevents me from declaring*

[the Overture to Die Meistersinger]
*to be the world's most unpleasant
overture is the even more horrible
Prelude to* Tristan and Isolde. *The
latter reminds me of the old Italian
painting of that martyr whose
intestines were slowly unwound
from his body on to a reel. The
Prelude to* Die Meistersinger, *at
best, goes about it quickly, with
spirit and a club.'*

guess the outcome. Beckmesser makes a fool of himself in the contest, Walther surpasses himself, wins, becomes a Mastersinger and gets the girl.

HIGHLIGHTS

Overture. Whatever longueurs the opera has, here is a masterly piece of writing. Wagner uses many of the principal themes of the work – the Mastersingers' motif, the love motif of Walther and Eva, and the March motif of the tradesmen-musicians – until, at the climax, all three are combined simultaneously with tremendous skill. It has an overwhelming effect in or out of the opera house.

ACT 2 *'Jerum! Jerum!'* (the Cobbler's Song) Sachs sings as he works, to the annoyance of Beckmesser.

'Selig wie die Sonne' ('Blessed as the sun') A celebrated quintet in which Walther and Eva, Sach's apprentice David (*t*), and his sweetheart Magdalena (*s*), celebrate with Hans Sachs the birth of the song that has come to Walther in a dream.

ACT 3 *Walther's Prize Song* With which our knight wins the contest, the acclaim of the Mastersingers and the fair Eva. Wagner had to come up with a good one and he did.

RECOMMENDED RECORDINGS
complete:
Ligendza/Domingo/Fischer-Dieskau
German Opera Ch & O, Jochum
DG 415 278
or: Schwarzkopf/Hopf/
Edelmann/Kunz
Bayreuth Fest Ch & O, Karajan
EMI CHS7 63500 2 (mono)
highlights: Donath/Kollo/Adam/
Evans, Dresden State Opera Ch &
O Karajan
EMI CDM7 63455 2

THE MERRY WIDOW

FRANZ LEHÁR

1905

ORIGINAL GERMAN TITLE: 'DIE LUSTIGE WITWE'
PRONOUNCED: DIH LOOS' TIGGER VITT-VER
LIBRETTO: VIKTOR LEON AND LEO STEIN
AFTER 'L'ATTACHÉ', A COMEDY BY HENRI MEILHAC
LENGTH: 2' 15"

You could do a lot worse than start your opera-going with a visit to *The Merry Widow* – whether sung in English or German. It's in the same league – and the same mould – as **Die Fledermaus**. The complicated story, lifted from a French farce by one of the co-librettists of **Carmen**, is a light-hearted confection of flirtatious intrigue. You can swot up on it beforehand if you feel like it, but the score is so jammed full of hummable (and famous) tunes, that what with the Viennese waltzes, the glamorous costumes and the heady romance of it all ... a good production should sweep you off your feet, whether or not you care to follow the plot.

BACKGROUND

Lehár was definitely second choice as composer. Richard Heuberger, another Viennese composer, had already turned down the libretto when the two writers reluctantly handed it to Lehár, expecting another moderately-successful-without-being-a-hit score from him. Lehár was so inspired by what he read that he wrote the first song on the same evening. The directors

of the Theater an der Wien pronounced the finished score 'tuneless and unmusical' and would only agree to a low budget production without full scenery, costumes or even rehearsals.

FIRST PERFORMANCE

*Theater an der Wien, Vienna
30 December 1905*
The Merry Widow was an immediate hit and had an initial run of 483 performances. When it opened in London eighteen months later, it notched up 778 performances, a success repeated in Paris and New York where it set a new fashion style for women and Merry Widow hats and dresses became the rage. It's been filmed on a number of occasions with varying degrees of success, most bizarrely in 1925 in a *silent* film directed by Erich von Stroheim.

STORY

3 acts set in Paris at
the turn of the century

PRINCIPAL CHARACTERS
HANNA GLAWARI, the Merry
Widow (s)

BARON ZETA, the Pontevedrian
ambassador (bar)
VALENCIENNE, his wife (s)
CAMILLE DE ROSILLON, her
admirer (t)
COUNT DANILO DANILOWITSCH,
an attaché (bar)

In the Pontevedrian Embassy
in Paris, a party is in progress
where the principal guest is
the lovely Hanna Glawari,
widow of a banker and one of
Pontevedria's wealthiest citizens.
The ambassador, anxious that his
impoverished country does not
lose her assets should she choose a
foreigner for her next husband,
suggests to his attaché Danilo that
he woo her. We discover that at
one time Hanna and Danilo had
hoped to marry. Hanna still loves
Danilo and tells him that when
men say they love her, they mean
they love her money – to which
Danilo vows he will never say he
loves her. Though he now prefers

the pleasures of the *grisettes* at
Maxim's, Danilo promises Baron
Zeta to keep other suitors away.
Later, in Hanna's garden, Camille,
on the brink of being caught with
Valencienne in the pavilion, is
saved by Danilo, who substitutes
Hanna for the ambassador's wife.
Camille, in the presence of the
suspicious ambassador, is forced
to pretend his overwhelming love
for Hanna, and does this so
convincingly that he arouses
Danilo's jealousy. He stomps
off to Maxim's. Next, Hanna
decorates her house to resemble
Maxim's and invites all the
dancing girls to provide the
entertainment, during which she
admits to Danilo that she has no
intention of marrying Camille.
The principled Danilo is
overjoyed, but still won't propose
to her. When she tells him that
under the terms of her late
husband's will she loses all her
inheritance if she remarries,

RECOMMENDED RECORDINGS

complete:
Schwarzkopf/
Steffek/Gedda
Philh. Ch
&O, Matacic
EMI CDS7 47178
highlights:
Rothenberger/Gedda,
SO Graunke, Mattes
EMI CDM7 69090 2
video:
Sydney Opera, Bonynge
MCEG VVD828

Danilo declares his love for her
and immediately proposes. Her
money, it turns out, will go to
her second husband ... Thus her
enormous wealth will remain
in Pontevedrian hands. Danilo
accepts his delicious fate.

HIGHLIGHTS

ACT 2 *'Vilja, oh Vilja'* ('Vilia, oh
Vilia, the witch of the woods') –
Hanna entertains her guests with
this enchanting song about a
faithless nymph. Away from the
opera-house, it's among the most
popular of **soprano** requests.
*'Ja, das Studium der Weiber ist
Schwer'* ('Who knows women?')
The catchy chorus in which Danilo
and Hanna's admirers confess
how they are bemused by women.
ACT 3 *'Lippen schweigen'* 'Silent
love' One of the loveliest of all
waltz tunes, to which Danilo
declares his love for Hanna, it's
known as the Waltz Song.

*Danilo admits he loves Hanna
in Act 3 of Welsh National
Opera's 1984 production of
The Merry Widow*

THE MIKADO
GILBERT AND SULLIVAN
1885

THE MIKADO OR THE TOWN OF TITIPU
LENGTH: 2' 30"

'The cleverest comic opera in the English language'; 'the brightest jewel in the Savoy casket'. Certainly *The Mikado* was (and still is) the most popular and frequently performed of all the Gilbert and Sullivan operas. It has more 'hits' per scene than any of the others and is Sullivan's most richly inventive score. But how close it came to never being written.

BACKGROUND

After nearly a decade of untrammelled success, the famous partners had their first serious row (in future years these would become increasingly bitter). After the comparative failure of *Princess Ida* (in their terms a nine-month run was a failure!) they could not agree about the subject for their next collaboration. Sullivan said he wanted something less frivolous and 'topsy-turvy', Gilbert took exception, and the two were at an angry impasse when Fate took a hand. Gilbert was walking up and down the library in his new house in Harrington Gardens, London when an enormous Japanese executioner's sword he had hung on the wall suddenly fell to the floor. It gave him the germ of an idea. Japan and the Orient were fashionable at the time – and the subject appealed to Sullivan. They were off again.

FIRST PERFORMANCE

Savoy Theatre, London
14 March 1885
From inception to first night took just nine months. There was much press speculation as to whether the partnership was played out after *Princess Ida*. Gilbert was more than usually anxious as the first night approached and left Sullivan to conduct the work while he nervously walked the streets of London. The whole cast was almost sick with fright as a result of the gruelling rehearsals. They needn't have worried. Rutland Barrington, who played Pooh-Bah, recorded: 'Never in the whole of my experience have I assisted at such an enthusiastic first night as greeted this delightful work. From the moment the curtain rose ... to its final fall it was one long succession of uproarious laughter at the libretto and overwhelming applause for the music ... "Three Little Maids" was received with such enthusiasm and insistent encores as no musical number in my experience, or I believe anyone else's, has ever equalled.'

The Mikado ran for nearly two years at the Savoy. In the States it was so popular that on one evening in 1886 it is said that there were no less than 170 separate performances being given. America

has since given us *The Swing Mikado* (1938), *The Hot Mikado* (1939) and *The Black Mikado* (1975). It was the first Savoy Opera to be filmed (1939), remade in 1962 as *Cool Mikado* (with Frankie Howerd).

STORY

2 acts set in the town of
Titipu, Japan

PRINCIPAL CHARACTERS
THE MIKADO OF JAPAN (b)
NANKI-POO, his son,
disguised as a minstrel (t)
KO-KO, Lord High
Executioner (bar)
POOH-BAH, Lord High
Everything Else (bar)
PISH-TUSH, a noble (t)
YUM-YUM (s), PITTI-SING (c),
PEEP-BO (c), three little maids
KATISHA, an elderly lady
in love with Nanki-Poo (c)

Nanki-Poo is in love with Yum-Yum, the most desirable of the 'Three Little Maids' (from school). He, however, has submitted to banishment rather than be forced to marry Katisha, a lady of the court and of uncertain age who dotes on him. He has taken to the life of a wandering minstrel and returns to Titipu in disguise only to find his beloved Yum-Yum on the eve of her marriage to Ko-Ko, the Lord High Executioner. Nanki-Poo reveals his true identity to her and and makes it clear how he would woo her if she 'were not to Ko-Ko plighted'.

Ko-Ko, who, we discover, has himself been under sentence of death for flirting, learns that he will lose his job if he doesn't find someone to execute within a month. He persuades Nanki-Poo to offer his own head in exchange for a month of married bliss with

Yum-Yum. This is agreed – Nanki-Poo doesn't want to live without her anyway – but when Yum-Yum discovers that the wife of a beheaded husband must be buried alive, her passion for Nanki-Poo cools somewhat.

The dreaded Mikado arrives – with Katisha 'his daughter-in-law elect'. Ko-Ko, who's found he's too cowardly to execute anyone, presents a false statement to the Mikado saying that the requested execution has already taken place. Katisha makes Nanki-Poo's identity known. Horrors! Ko-Ko has beheaded the heir to

Eric Idle as Ko-ko and Leslie Garrett as Yum-Yum in English National Opera's 1986 production of The Mikado.

the throne and must die. His only hope is to bring Nanki-Poo back to life. He offers himself to Katisha, who accepts him after some persuasion. And Nanki-Poo ends up with his Yum-Yum ... as we knew he would all along.

HIGHLIGHTS

Overture
ACT 1 *'A wandering minstrel I'.*
'As some day it may happen' (*'I've got a little list'*).
'Three little maids from school'.
'I am so proud ... To sit in solemn silence'.
ACT 2 *'Braid the raven hair'.*
'The sun, whose rays are all ablaze'.
'Brightly dawns our wedding day' (Madrigal).
'Here's a how-de-do'.

'A more humane Mikado never did in Japan exist'.
'The flowers that bloom in the spring'.
'Willow, titwillow' (*'On a tree by a river a little tom-tit'*).

RECOMMENDED RECORDINGS

complete: Ayldon/ Wright/J. Reed/ Sandford
D'Oyly Carte, RPO, Nash
DECCA 425 190
(without dialogue)
highlights: as above
DECCA 433 618

NABUCCO
VERDI
1842

PRONOUNCED: NAH-BOOK'-OH
LIBRETTO: TEMISTOCLE SOLERA

4 ACTS SET IN JERUSALEM AND
BABYLON IN THE 6TH CENTURY BC

Originally entitled *Nabuco-donosor* (*Nebuchadnezzar*), *Nabucco* was a turning-point in Verdi's career and thus for Italian opera. He had lost his wife and two children and, after the failure of *Un giorno di regno* (1840), had determined to write no more operas. Fortunately, he changed his mind and, although influenced by **Rossini's** later operas and **Donizetti**, Verdi here nevertheless found a tremendous individual voice of his own, and when *Nabucco* proved to be an instant success, his fame spread throughout Italy.

❖

Nabucco (*bar*), the King of Babylon, has, with the ambitious slave-girl Abigaille (*s*), defeated the Hebrews, although the High Priest Zaccaria (*b*) reveals that he has captured Nabucco's daughter Fenena (*c*). Ismaele (*t*), Prince of Jerusalem, has fallen in love with her, however, and returns her to

*The Chorus of Opera North
in* Nabucco

Solera, the librettist, deserves a book to himself: Italian poet, librettist, composer, theatre manager, editor of a religious magazine, Queen Isabella's lover and secret courier between Napoleon III and the Khedive of Egypt.

her father. Abigaille, taking advantage of Nabucco's temporary absence (Fenena is acting as regent), plots to usurp the throne. Fenena, meanwhile, converts to Judaism. Suddenly Nabucco returns and proclaims himself God, whereupon he loses his mind. Abigaille is now absolute ruler and plans to kill Fenena and all the Hebrews, but Nabucco regains his reason and his throne in the nick of time. Abigaille takes the traditional operatic exit by drinking poison and all the Hebrews are freed.

HIGHLIGHT

ACT 3 '*Va, pensiero, sull' ali dorate*' ('Let my thoughts fly back to Jordan') The Chorus of the Hebrew Slaves. This must be the best known and best loved of all opera choruses, when the Hebrew slaves, in their chains, sing of their homeland. It's not known whether or not Verdi wrote this aching hymn in the knowledge that parallels would be drawn between the plight of the Hebrews and that of the Italians under their Austrian oppressors. Whatever, '*Va pensiero*' became a national anthem for Italian independence; and Verdi himself became a symbol of the resistance.

RECOMMENDED RECORDINGS
complete:
Suliotis/Gobbi/Cava/Previdi
Vienna State Opera Ch & O,
Gardelli
DECCA 417 407
highlights: as above
DECCA 421 867

NORMA
BELLINI
1831
LIBRETTO: FELICE ROMANI
BASED ON ALEXANDRE SOUMET'S
TRAGEDY OF THE SAME NAME

2 ACTS SET IN GAUL DURING THE
ROMAN OCCUPATION, ABOUT 50BC

'Those who weary of declamatory modern opera, in which the music is constantly changing in agreement with the most swift and subtle moods that emotion throws upon the stage, at the expense of clearly defined melody, will have no quarrel with the simplicity of *Norma*.' That was the opinion of an earlier opera guide. Despite having a theme with which it is difficult to become emotionally involved, Bellini's masterpiece is a musical feast – powerful choruses and a great (and very difficult) title role that so many of the great *coloratura* sopranos have relished. Its many passages of passion and poetry make an unforgettable impact. 'A great score that speaks to the heart,' wrote **Wagner**, 'a work of genius.' The first night was a disastrous failure, however. Bellini was seen to shed tears after the performance.

❖

Norma (*s*), High Priestess of the Druids, has forgotten her sacred vows of chastity, fallen in love with the Roman Pro-Consul, Pollione (*t*), one of the hated occupiers of her people's land, and borne him two sons. In modern terms, she has a conflict of interests. She restrains the Druids from revolt so as to protect him and prays for her return to his affections, for she has discovered that he loves another. When she discovers it's Adalgisa (*s*), a young priestess devoted to Norma and whom Pollione has persuaded to return to Rome with him, Norma is enraged. Her impulse is to kill her children, but, restraining herself, she instead calls on the Druids to rise against the Romans. Pollione has been captured trying to abduct Adalgisa from the sacred temple, and is brought before Norma for judgement (the penalty for intrusion: death). Her love rekindled, Norma hopes to save her former lover by offering the Gauls an alternative victim – herself. She

admits breaking her vows and, after entrusting the care of her children to her father, the Chief Druid Oroveso (*b*), she mounts the sacrificial pyre. Pollione, recognizing the greatness of her love, joins her in atonement.

HIGHLIGHTS
ACT 1 *'Casta diva'* ('Chaste goddess') In this justly famous aria (an exacting one to sing well because of its long phrases), Norma and the priestesses of the temple pray to the Moon for peace on earth.
'Va crudele' ('Oh cruel woman') An impressive duet in which Adalgisa, having begged Pollione to leave her, is persuaded to yield and find true happiness with him.
ACT 2 *'Mira, O Norma'* ('Hear me, Norma') One of the greatest duets in Italian opera. Norma instructs Adalgisa to take her children and leave with Pollione. Aldagisa refuses and in the duet undertakes to persuade Pollione to return to Norma.
Finale *'Deh, non volerli vittime'* ('Ah, let them not be victims') A trio that will make your hair stand on end. As the crowd curses its Priestess and Oroveso bids his disgraced daughter farewell, Norma and Pollione prepare to throw themselves on to the pyre.

RECOMMENDED RECORDINGS
complete:
Sutherland/Horne/Alexander/Cross
LSO Ch & O, Bonynge
DECCA 425 488
highlights:
Callas/Ludwig/Corelli/Zaccaria
La Scala Ch & O, Serafin
EMI CMD7 64419 2

Orpheus – the Serious and the Send-up

The Greek legend of Orpheus, the poet and singer whose music could charm wild animals and cause trees to uproot themselves and follow him, has attracted literally dozens of composers. The two most popular versions couldn't provide a greater contrast for an evening at the opera and both, for different reasons, are a treat for the ear and eye.

Calzabigi's version of the legend

The son of Apollo, god of music, and Calliope, muse of epic poetry, has lost the love of his life, Eurydice. She's been bitten by a snake and Orpheus, inconsolable with grief, weeps at her tomb. Amor, the god of love, is so touched that Orpheus is allowed to descend into Hades, to the dark kingdom of Pluto, in order to find and win her back. There is one condition: he must not look at her until he's recrossed the River Styx. Orpheus' music calms the Furies he encounters en route. He meets Eurydice in the Elysian Fields and together they climb upwards, back towards the land of the living. Ever more fretful that Orpheus does not look at her and seems to love her no more, Eurydice at last cries out with such passion that Orpheus can resist no longer and turns to look at her, whereupon she promptly dies. Orpheus cannot live without her and is about to kill himself when Amor, again seeing the depth of his feelings, intervenes and brings Eurydice to life once more.

Orpheus and Eurydice
Gluck
1762

Original Italian title: 'Orfeo ed Euridice'

Pronounced: or-feh'-oh ayd ay-oo-ree-dee'-cheh

Libretto: Ranieri de' Calzabigi

3 acts set in Greece in ancient times

One of the earliest operas still in the repertoire, *Orfeo* is not just a great work of the human imagination but important in the development of opera. Not that you need know this to enjoy the sublime music (the two most famous bits listed below are *very* famous). The part of Orfeo was written originally for a **castrato**; today it is usually sung by a **contralto**, although in a later version Gluck cast it for a **tenor**. 'Here for the first time', wrote Alfred Einstein, 'was a work so closely grown together with its text that it was unique and could not be composed again.'

Kathleen Ferrier as Orpheus in the Royal Opera House's 1951 production of Orfeus and Eurydice

Highlights

Act 2 *Dance of the Blessed Spirits* Orfeo (*c*) enters the Valley of the Blessed in Hades. The beautiful flute solo epitomizes the rapt simplicity of Gluck's music.

'Che puro ciel' ('What pure light') Orfeo gazes at the wondrous sight of Elysium.

Act 3 *'Che farò senza Euridice'* ('What can I do without Eurydice') This immortal **aria** (captured most memorably in an evergreen recording by **Kathleen Ferrier**) is sung by Orfeo after he has held Eurydice (*s*) in his arms, forgetting that he must not look at her. One writer has said of *'Che farò'*: 'All forms of language have been exhausted to praise the stupor of grief, the passion, the despair expressed in this sublime number.'

Recommended Recording

complete:
Hendricks/Von Otter
Monteverdi Ch, Lyon Opera O
Gardiner
EMI CDS7 49834 2

Orpheus in the Underworld
Jacques Offenbach
1858

Original French title 'Orphée aux Enfers'

Pronounced: or'-phay oze aun-fair'

Libretto: Hector Crémieux and Ludovic Halévy

4 acts set in Greece in ancient times

This joyously irreverent satire on Orpheus was something of a *succès de scandale* when first produced, and was really the first operetta: an opera that didn't (couldn't) take itself seriously. It set

out to poke fun at the great Gluck, the current government, the solemn Greek legend and anything else that came in sight. It still works a treat.

❖

Here, Orpheus (*t*) is a violinist. He can't stand his wife, Eurydice (*s*), and she can't stand his violin playing. One of her admirers is Aristeus (*t*), a shepherd (in reality Pluto, god of the Underworld in disguise). Another is Jupiter (*bar*), king of the gods, who changes into a fly in order to squeeze through a keyhole to be near her. Orpheus couldn't be more pleased when his wife is bitten by the snake and dies, but is then compelled by public opinion to retrieve her from the Underworld under the same condition as in the legend (see p.80). He manages not to look at her, but Jupiter intervenes by giving him a good kick that *makes* him turn round! To his delight, she returns for ever to the Underworld, welcomed back by a wild bacchanalian party.

HIGHLIGHTS

Overture A real winner, and very popular, but not by Offenbach. It was added later by one Carl Binder for the 1860 Vienna production.
ACT 3 *'Bel insecte à l'aile dorée'* ('Beautiful insect with gilded wings') Known as the Fly Duet, as silly (and as endearing) a number as you'll come across. The flighty Eurydice and the Fly (Jupiter disguised) buzz their feelings for one another.
ACT 4 *Can-can*. The Can-Can danced by the happy inhabitants of the Underworld.

RECOMMENDED RECORDING
complete:
Mesplé/ Senechal/ Burles
Toulouse Capitole Ch & O
Plasson
EMI CDS7 49647 2

OTELLO
VERDI
1887
LIBRETTO: ARRIGO BOITO
AFTER SHAKESPEARE'S PLAY

4 ACTS SET IN CYPRUS AT THE END OF THE 15TH CENTURY

A powerful and moving opera, Otello is thought by many to be the most perfect ever written – but it is not the Verdi of *La traviata* or *Rigoletto*. This is Verdi writing with his head more than his heart (not that such a big heart could be silenced).

The premiere of *Otello* was eagerly awaited, more so than most because it had been sixteen years since the most experienced, the most famous, the most successful of living opera composers had produced an opera – *Aida*. *Otello* was a major critical success and quickly joined the international repertoire, though the public took longer. This was still Verdi the Great Italian, although now there was also the unmistakable influence of **Wagner**: there were few set **arias**

Placido Domingo as Otello in the 1989 Lisbon production

Placido Domingo as Otello mourns his innocent wife in Zeffirelli's 1986 film

or ensembles, for example, and the action fused scene to scene without a pause. Apart from all this, though, was the fact that here was a musical work, using a vastly cut version of the play, that was worthy to stand by Shakespeare's mighty original. Quite an achievement for a man of seventy-four.

❖

Otello the Moor (*t*), a victorious general in the Venetian Army, lands in Cyprus having defeated the Turks. As the new Governor, he brings with him his beautiful young wife, Desdemona (*s*), and appoints Cassio (*t*) his second-in-command. His aide, Iago (*bar*), is incensed at having been passed over by his confidant and friend and finds an ally in Rodrigo (*t*), who loves Desdemona. Iago and Rodrigo ply Cassio with wine and when Cassio fights with and wounds the former Governor, Montano (*b*), Iago fans the incident into a small riot. Otello appears and relieves Cassio of his office.

Iago's plan having worked, his next act is to poison Otello's mind against his wife, and he begins making insinuations about her. The presence of a favourite handkerchief found, says 'Honest Iago', in

Cassio's room is sufficient proof for Otello that his wife has been unfaithful and that the wretched Cassio must be punished. The innocent Cassio laughingly brings the handkerchief into Otello's presence, wondering how it got there, and is induced by Iago to speak of the affair he's having with Bianca, a lady of the town. Otello, only half-hearing, half-understanding the conversation, believes that Cassio is talking about Desdemona.

Now insane with jealousy and rage, Otello determines to poison Desdemona. Iago declares he will take care of Cassio. Otello is then informed that he has been recalled to Venice and that Cassio is to be Governor of Cyprus in his place. Desdemona, weeping at the change in her husband's attitude towards her, is accused by Otello of weeping because of her imminent separation from Cassio. The final scene takes place in Desdemona's bedroom. Otello enters in a fury, making accusation after accusation against her before finally smothering her with a pillow. The alarm is

sounded. Otello learns at once of his former friend's duplicity and his wife's innocence. With dreadful remorse, he kisses his dead wife, draws his dagger and stabs himself.

HIGHLIGHTS

ACT 1 *'Esultate!'* ('Rejoice') Otello's entrance, celebrating his victory over the Turks. Short the aria may be, but it is thrilling, and never more so than when heard sung by Francesco Tamagno, Verdi's original Otello, who, remarkably, lived to record this and *'Niun mi tema'* ('Do not fear me') – the death of Otello.

'Inaffia l'ugola!' ('Quench your thirst') Iago's *Brindisi* (drinking-song), when he is set on making young Cassio drunk.

'Già nella notte' ('Hidden in the night') Arguably Verdi's most beautiful love duet, encompassing in its sublime music the two characters of Otello and Desdemona.

ACT 2 *'Credo in un Dio crudel'* ('I believe in a cruel God') Known as Iago's Creed, in which he glorifies in evil.

ACT 4 *'Salce, salce, salce'* ('Oh willow, willow, willow') The Willow Song. Desdemona movingly recalls a tale of a girl deserted by her lover in this haunting aria capped by her heart-wrenching cry of farewell.

'Ave Maria' Desdemona kneels in prayer before Otello's entrance.

RECOMMENDED RECORDINGS
complete:
Vickers/Rysanek/Gobbi
Rome Opera Ch & O, Serafin
BMG/RCA GD81969
highlights:
Vickers/Freni/Glossop
German Opera Ch, BPO, Karajan
EMI CMD7 63454 2

PAGLIACCI

LEONCAVALLO

1892

PRONOUNCED: PAHL-YAT'-CHEE
USUALLY TRANSLATED AS 'THE STROLLING PLAYERS'
LIBRETTO: LEONCAVALLO
LENGTH: 1' 10"

Leoncavallo wrote a good many operas both before and (especially) after his one major success in 1892. All save one of these were either fiascos or unenthusiastically received; most have vanished without trace. How strange, then, that the one work of his that has survived in the repertoire is, without doubt, a work of genius. *Pag*, as it's referred to – as in *Cav* (*Cavalleria Rusticana*) and *Pag* – has one act divided into two scenes, and is almost universally given as the second part of the evening following *Cavalleria Rusticana*. Both are prime examples of **verismo** operas.

The correct title, incidentally, is as above and not *I Pagliacci*, as is often given. The title-page of the original manuscript has no definite article '*I*'.

BACKGROUND

Enraged at the lack of interest shown in his work, Leoncavallo eventually approached the same publisher who had organized the competition won by Mascagni's *Cavalleria Rusticana*. In a deliberate attempt to emulate the success of *Cav*, and writing in the same realistic vein, Leoncavallo completed the entire work from start to finish in four months – story, libretto, music and orchestration. He based it on a true-life incident with which he had some connection: during his childhood in Calabria, a jealous actor had killed his wife after a performance; Leoncavallo's father, a magistrate, had tried the case.

FIRST PERFORMANCE

Teatro dal Verme, Milan
21 May 1892

The premiere was conducted by the young Arturo Toscanini and was an immediate success, even greater than *Cavalleria* had been two years earlier. Edoardo Sonzogno, the publisher, now had under his control the two most popular one-act operas ever written. He sent *Pagliacci* around the world and

Canio announces the start of his show in the Metropolitan Opera's production of Pagliacci

within a few months it had been produced in Vienna, Berlin, London, New York, Moscow, Buenos Aires, Stockholm and Mexico. Its popularity with both audiences or singers shows no sign of waning.

STORY

1 act set in Calabria, near Montalto on the Feast of the Assumption, about 1865

PRINCIPAL CHARACTERS

CANIO, ('Pagliaccio' in the play), head of the troupe (t)
NEDDA, ('Columbine' in the play), his wife (s)
TONIO, ('Taddeo' in the play), a clown (bar)
SILVIO, a villager (bar)
BEPPE, ('Harlequin' in the play), (t)

In a Prologue, Tonio announces to the audience that the performance is about to begin, that the drama, though performed by actors, is about real people and real feelings. This sets up the old but effective device of a play within a play, perhaps the most famous example of which is in *Hamlet*.

The curtain rises as a troupe of *commedia dell' arte* players arrives in a village to prepare for a performance, one of the stock Harlequin comedies acted for centuries in Italy by strolling players. In this one, the villagers are told they will see the troubles of poor Pagliaccio and the vengeance he wreaks on the treacherous clown.

Canio then announces that the play will commence at seven o' clock. Tonio helps the lovely Nedda from her gaudily painted cart, at which Canio pushes him roughly away. No one is allowed near his wife. The troupe goes off to the inn, leaving Tonio alone with Nedda. Tonio protests his love for her but when he forces himself on her she strikes him across the face with a whip. The humiliated Tonio slinks off, vowing revenge. He spies a villager, Silvio, talking to Nedda. It transpires that they are in love and she promises to run away with him after the performance. Tonio alerts Canio to this. Silvio makes his escape before Canio returns with drawn dagger, demanding to know the name of his wife's lover. She will not tell him. The performance is about to begin; costume and make-up must be put on.

The second scene is the *commedia dell' arte* play in which Beppe (as Harlequin) appears on stage to meet his lover, Nedda

(Columbine). Canio (Pagliaccio) bursts in and Harlequin runs away. Pagliaccio asks Columbine the name of her lover, to which she replies 'Taddeo'. Suddenly, Canio is aware he is playing his real-life situation. Confused, and with lines no longer from the rehearsed play, he again demands to know the name of her lover. When she refuses to tell him, he stabs her. Nedda cries out for Silvio, who rushes on to the stage to help her, and Canio, realizing this is his wife's lover, kills him, too. Stupefied, he lets the knife fall from his hand and addresses the

Everyone knows Canio's 'Vesti la giubba' ('On with the motley') at the end of Act 1. But what's he singing about? No one in or out of the theatre has used the term 'motley' since God was a boy. The dictionary defines it as 'particoloured garb such as a jester wore, obsolete'. Yet on the radio, record sleeves, whenever this, the

most famous of arias is announced, Canio has to 'put on his motley', completely baffling most people. The original English translation of this and Cavalleria (still used today) were by the barrister and prolific lyricist (1,500 songs to his credit) Fred E. Weatherly, the man who also wrote the words of 'Danny Boy', 'Roses of Picardy' and 'The Holy City'.

Caruso's famous recording of 'Vesti la giubba' (see page 000) became his calling card. In 1904 he followed it with Mattinata, Leoncavallo's popular ballad, accompanied on the piano by the composer. In a 1907 recording conducted by Leoncavallo, Pagliacci became the first complete opera to be issued on record in the UK.

audience: *'La commedia è finita!'* –
'The comedy is ended!'

HIGHLIGHTS

Prologue *'Si può ... Un nido di memorie'* ('May I have your attention ... A song of tender memories') A famous old warhorse for **baritones** written at the request of the original Tonio, Victor Maurel, who complained to Leoncavallo that he didn't have enough solo opportunities in the opera.

'Un tal gioco' ('Such a game') Canio warns that the stage is not the same as real life.

'Qual fiamma avea nel guardo' ('How fiercely he watches me') Nedda reflects on the husband she secretly hates and fears.

'Che volo d'augelli ... Stridono lassù' ('Oh you beautiful birds ... Forever flying') Known as the *Ballatella*, in which Nedda returns to her childhood and envies the freedom of the birds.

'Vesti la giubba' ('Put on the costume') Always translated as 'On with the motley' (see p84). Before *Nessun Dorma* hit the charts, this was arguably the most famous **tenor aria** in all opera. Canio knows the young wife he adores has a lover, yet he must put his misery aside, dress in his ridiculous costume and make people laugh.

'Ridi Pagliaccio' ('Laugh then Pagliaccio') he sings with heartbreaking effect to a phrase the orchestra plays at the end of the opera – Leoncavallo had not studied Wagner's work for nothing.

'O Colombina, il tenero fido Arlecchino' ('O Columbine, your loving and faithful Harlequin') Known as Harlequin's Serenade.

'No, Pagliaccio non son!' ('No, Pagliaccio, no more') Canio cries out that he is no longer an actor but a man.

THE PEARL FISHERS
BIZET
1863
ORIGINAL FRENCH TITLE:
'LES PÊCHEURS DE PERLES',
PRONOUNCED: LEH PEH' SHER
DE PEHRL
LIBRETTO: EUGENE CORMON AND
MICHEL CARRE

3 ACTS SET IN CEYLON
DURING ANCIENT TIMES

*Edmund Barham as Nadir,
Anthony Michaels-Moore as Zurga
in Opera North's The Pearl Fishers*

Not in the main opera repertoire, *The Pearl Fishers* has better music than it has libretto, one *very* popular duet, and the unreserved praise of no less a figure than Berlioz. Productions are scarce, but in any case, it is perhaps one to savour in an armchair.

❖

Zurga (*bar*) is the chief of a tribe of Singalese pearl fishermen. He and his friend Nadir (*t*) once swore an oath never to woo Leïla, the beautiful High Priestess of the Brahmin temple. After many years, Nadir has returned to the fishing village. The friends recall their mutual love for Leïla, who is under a vow of chastity, bound under pain of death to remain from human gaze. Nadir later hears her singing, recognizes her voice and all his old feelings return. The feeling is mutual. Nourabad (*b*), the High

Priest, discovers them together and demands their death. Zurga intervenes and pardons them, but becomes consumed with jealousy and anger at his friend's duplicity when he discovers that the veiled Leïla is the girl in question. The death sentence is upheld. Leïla, however, produces a gold necklace, which Zurga recognises as the token he once gave a little girl who saved his life. He determines to save her from the funeral pyre by setting the village on fire, thereby allowing her to escape with Nadir. The pearl fishermen return and Zurga is the one who dies on the pyre.

HIGHLIGHTS

ACT 1 *'Au fond du temple saint'* ('In the depths of the temple') Nadir and Zurga sing this most famous of operatic duets, recalling the time when they both fell in love with Leïla, the kind of love that would have proved fatal to their friendship. They believe themselves cured of the infatuation and swear eternal friendship.

'Je crois entendre encore' ('I still seem to hear') At the sound of Leïla's voice Nadir realizes he is still in love with her.

ACT 2 *'Comme autrefois dans la nuit sombre'* ('As once upon a time in the dark of the night') Nourabad warns Leïla to be faithful to her vows; when he leaves she sings in the ruined temple of her love.

RECOMMENDED RECORDING

complete:
Hendricks/Aler/Quilico/Courtis
Toulouse Capitole Ch & O
Plasson
EMI CDS7 49837 2

PETER GRIMES
BRITTEN
1945
LIBRETTO: MONTAGU SLATER
BASED ON GEORGE CRABBE'S
POEM 'THE BOROUGH'

PROLOGUE, 3 ACTS AND EPILOGUE
SET IN THE BOROUGH, A FISHING
VILLAGE IN EAST ANGLIA,
ABOUT 1830

This was the opera that gave the composer an international reputation and re-established English opera on an international level. It reopened the Sadler's Wells Theatre after the Second World War, the enthusiasm with which it was greeted coinciding with the end of the deprivations of the previous six years. *Peter Grimes* has since proved to be the most popular of all modern English operas.

❖

At an inquest into the suspicious death at sea of an apprentice, Swallow (*b*), the coroner, advises Peter Grimes (*t*), a fisherman, to employ no more children and returns a verdict of accidental death. Grimes needs help with his work, however, and supported by Ellen Orford (*s*), a widowed

Jon Vickers as Peter Grimes at the Royal Opera House

schoolmistress, he takes on another boy, an orphan from the workhouse. Grimes is a loner, an outsider, and when the boy arrives at the village inn in the middle of a storm, he at once takes the lad off to his hut on the cliff.

Next Sunday morning, Ellen is alarmed to see the boy has a torn coat and a bruised neck and she confronts Grimes, who in the face of her persistence, knocks her down in an inarticulate fury. The quarrel is overheard, popular feeling rises against the fisherman and the villagers make for Grimes' hut. Grimes hears the mob approaching and the two leave by the back door for the cliff top. The boy trips and falls to his death. Grimes disappears and the villagers are convinced that he has once more gone out to sea and committed murder. Some days later he turns up confused and delirious. Ellen wants to lead him to safety, but Balstrode (*bar*), a retired sea captain, Grimes' only other friend, advises him that the only way to escape the village is to go out in his boat and sink in it. This is the fate Grimes chooses as the villagers, unconcerned, go about their normal lives.

HIGHLIGHTS

Four 'Sea Interludes' – 'Dawn', 'Storm', 'Sunday Morning' and 'Moonlight' A suite made from the preludes and interludes of the opera and which are among the most powerful and effective musical evocations of the sea ever composed, cleverly reflecting the emotions in Grimes' soul.

RECOMMENDED RECORDING

complete:
Watson/Pears/Brannigan
ROHCG Ch & O, Britten
DECCA 414 577

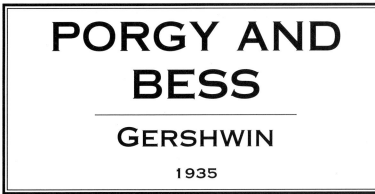

PORGY AND BESS

GERSHWIN

1935

LIBRETTO: IRA GERSHWIN AND [EDWIN] DuBOSE HEYWARD
FROM THE PLAY 'PORGY' BY DuBOSE AND DOROTHY HEYWARD
LENGTH: 3' 20"

This is the first (and still foremost) American opera, a firm departure from the European tradition. The score draws on banjo and percussion, for example, and incorporates indigenous folk-song and speech patterns, popular music idioms, jazz and spirituals. Gershwin was the first composer to combine successfully the popular idiom with the classical. He himself knew that this was his most important work, the first one that had satisfied him completely. After an early rehearsal he told the director: 'I think the music is so marvellous I really don't believe I wrote it.' The 'hits from the show' (or, as we've been brought up to say, 'the famous arias' – there really is no difference) speak for themselves; they are immortal, and the entire work is a high point in twentieth-century music.

BACKGROUND

Opening in 1927, *Porgy* the play had had a run of 367 performances in New York. *Porgy* the musical had begun to germinate in Gershwin's mind soon afterwards

Gershwin with the original cast of
Porgy and Bess

but, involved in a hundred and one other things, he kept putting it off. Finally, in 1933, Heyward rang Gershwin to tell him that Jerome Kern and Oscar Hammerstein (the team responsible for *Show Boat*) had expressed a keen interest in *Porgy*, which they wanted to make into a musical for Al Jolson. Jolson, too, had long been interested in the property. This forced Gershwin's hand. When Heyward intimated that he would rather see a folk opera made from his work than a

money-spinning musical, Gershwin committed himself and began work without delay. It took him more than a year and a half, the composition taking about eleven months, the orchestration about eight finishing in April 1935. The published score runs to 560 pages and it was completed on 3 September 1935.

FIRST PERFORMANCE
Colonial Theatre, Boston
30 September 1935

The premiere was a triumph, with the final ovation lasting over fifteen minutes. High praise was showered on Gershwin from fellow musicians, from the great conductor Serge Koussevitzky to Cole Porter and Irving Berlin. When the opera opened in Broadway's Alvin Theatre, the critics were less impressed – they couldn't decide whether it was a musical, an opera or what. It ran for 124 performances (not good for a musical, incredible for an opera) and lost all the money invested. Later revivals broke all box office records. The Gershwin estate has

decreed (rightly) that English-speaking productions shall use black casts only.

STORY

3 acts set in Catfish Row, Charleston, South Carolina, USA in 'the recent past'

PRINCIPAL CHARACTERS
PORGY, a cripple (b/bar)
BESS, Crown's girl (s)
CROWN, a tough stevedore (bar)
SPORTIN' LIFE, a dope pedlar (t)
ROBBINS, an inhabitant of
Catfish Row (t)
CLARA, (s) wife of Jake, a fisherman

Catfish Row, a former mansion of the aristocracy, is now a negro tenement on the waterfront and the opera begins with some well-drawn and contrasted scenes of night-life in the little backwater – a mother sings a lullaby to her baby, the men play crap. There's a fight and the violent Crown kills his friend Robbins and flees. Bess seeks refuge with the lame beggar, Porgy.

A month later and the fishermen of Catfish Row are going about their business. Porgy and Bess have set up home together and are

The Gershwin brothers played the new score to the man who was to direct the opera, Rouben Mamoulian. He recalled: 'It was rather amusing how all three of us were trying to be nonchalant and poised that evening, yet we were trembling with excitement … It was touching to see how [Ira], while singing, would become so overwhelmed with admiration for his brother, that he would look from him to me with half-open eyes and pantomime with a soft gesture of the hand, as if saying, "He did it. Isn't it wonderful. Isn't he wonderful?" … I shall never forget that evening – the enthusiasm of the two brothers about the music, their anxiety to do it justice, their joy at its being appreciated and with it all their touching devotion to each other. It is one of those rare tender memories one so cherishes in life.'

blissfully contented. Sportin' Life comes round trying to sell drugs and lure Bess away with him. Porgy sees him off. This is the day of the annual picnic on Kittiwah Island and the whole community goes off, leaving Porgy behind. On the island, Crown, who has been hiding there, appears and persuades Bess to go off with him. After some days she returns, terrified and delirious. Porgy promises to protect her from the man she cannot resist but knows is a bad influence on

Porgy and Bess sing their love duet in Act 2 of the Metropolitan Opera's production

RECOMMENDED RECORDINGS

complete:
Haymon/
White/Evans/
Baker
Glyndebourne Festival Ch
LPO, Rattle
EMI CDS7 49568 2
highlights:
L. Price/Warfield/Bubbles/
Boatwright, RCA Victor Ch
& O, Henderson
BMG/RCA GD 85234

her. Bess declares she wants no one but Porgy. There is a violent storm. The men are at sea. Crown has returned and only he has the courage to go with Clara to rescue her husband, which he does after ridiculing Porgy. During the night, Crown reappears and crawls stealthily to Bess's room. Porgy leans out of the window and stabs him to death. The police arrest Porgy and hold him for a week before releasing him for lack of evidence. Meanwhile, Sportin' Life has tempted the confused Bess to try a little dope and run away with him to New York, with empty promises of a better life. Porgy returns from jail in high spirits and calls for Bess. There's no answer. When he learns that she has been seduced by Sportin' Life, he asks how far it is to New York. 'A thousand miles away.' Undiscouraged, the crippled Porgy sets out to search for his Bess.

HIGHLIGHTS

ACT 1 *'Summertime'* Clara sings a lullaby to her baby. This is one of the most popular songs ever written. It's been said that the total accrued royalties on this alone are equivalent to the Argentine national debt. Not true, but you get the point.

ACT 2 *'I got plenty o' nuttin''* Porgy sings of his happiness, his life transformed by his love for Bess.

'Bess, you is my woman now' The ravishing love duet for Porgy and Bess, a real spine-tingler.

'It ain't necessarily so' Sportin' Life entertains everyone at the picnic, with this song, pointing out that not everything 'yo' li'ble to read in the Bible' is *ipso facto* the case.

'There's a boat dat's leaving soon' Sportin' Life tempts Bess to leave with him for New York.

RIGOLETTO

VERDI

1851

LIBRETTO: FRANCESCO MARIA PIAVE
AFTER VICTOR HUGO'S PLAY 'LE ROI S'AMUSE'
LENGTH: 2' 00"

You can put *Rigoletto* near the top of your list if you're just beginning to discover what all this opera fuss is about. It's the first of Verdi's great trilogy, preceding **Il Trovatore** and **La Traviata**, any one of which would have made a mere mortal's reputation. In the *Gazette Musicale de Paris* of 22 May 1853, however, an early critic of the opera wrote: '*Rigoletto* is the weakest work of Verdi ... It lacks melody ... This opera has hardly any chance to be kept in the repertoire'. Thankfully, the rest of us know better and can not only bask in the quite extraordinary procession of glorious melodies, but, unless it is a remarkably dull company, be swept along with the fast-moving drama.

BACKGROUND

Victor Hugo's play was first given in Paris in 1832, but because of its subject was withdrawn after a single performance and banned until fifty years later. What so

Above: The Duke tries to seduce Ceprano's wife in Act 1 of English National Opera's 1982 production of Rigoletto

Ingvar Wixell as Rigoletto in the Royal Opera House's 1989 production

unsettled the censor? Well, the play showed an absolute ruler (Francis I of France) in a highly unflattering light. Verdi wrote to his librettist, Piave: 'Try! The subject is great, immense, and it has a character who is one of the greatest creations that the theatre of all countries and all times can boast. The subject is *Le Roi s'amuse* and the character I'm speaking of is Triboulet.'

The police of Venice – which was then in Austrian hands – had already given Verdi trouble with *Ernani* (also based on a Hugo play). Before Verdi could begin composing, the Austrian-appointed censor insisted that the title be changed and the French king be substituted for the

duke of a small Italian town, along with other alterations. The composer agreed, *Triboulet* became *Rigoletto* and in less than six weeks he had completed the entire score.

FIRST PERFORMANCE

Teatro La Fenice, Venice
11 March 1851

The opening night was a triumph and the work has proved irresistible to audiences and singers alike ever since. In the Duke, there is perhaps the most gracious and rewarding **tenor** part of Verdi's entire work; Rigoletto is as demanding and mellifluous a **baritone** role as any, while Gilda (pronounced *Jeel'-dah*) requires a **soprano** who has both an easy vocal agility and considerable dramatic clout (listen to Act 2!).

STORY

3 acts set in Mantua
in the 16th century

PRINCIPAL CHARACTERS
DUKE OF MANTUA (t)
RIGOLETTO, his jester,
a hunchback (bar)
GILDA, Rigoletto's daughter (s)
SPARAFUCILE, a hired assassin (b)
MADDALENA, his sister (c)
COUNT MONTERONE, a noble (bar)
COUNT CEPRANO, a noble (b)

The licentious Duke seduces any girl who takes his fancy. To the court's amusement, the acid tongue

Many are the stories of mishaps during this oft-performed evergreen: Rigoletto's hump sliding inexorably down his back to produce a bottom of gargantuan proportions; one Duke letting loose in his opening aria ('Questa o quella'), only to find his moustache working loose as well. He continued singing even as it found its way into his mouth reducing his bell-like tones to a soft choking noise. At the conclusion of the aria

he spat out the moustache with such force that it flew across the orchestra pit and, it's said, hit the distinguished conductor in the face. But our favourite Rigoletto story is of the occasion when, at the very end of the opera, the hunchback attempted to lift the sack containing the corpse of his beloved Gilda. The lady in question was no stripling and as Rigoletto struggled under the colossal weight a voice in the audience called out, 'T-A-X-I!'

of his jester mocks his victims. The Count of Monterone, whose daughter has been ravished by the Duke, vents his feelings for the Duke, is arrested for his trouble and puts a curse on Rigoletto. Sparafucile encounters Rigoletto and offers his services should they ever be needed. Another ducal victim is Ceprano, whose wife has also seen action with His Highness. He and some of the other courtiers plan to turn the tables on Rigoletto by abducting the girl he keeps locked up in his house and whom they suppose to be his mistress. The Duke having met a beautiful girl at church, disguises himself as a student and visits her. She falls for his charms. Both Rigoletto's supposed mistress and the Duke's new fancy are in reality Rigoletto's beautiful daughter, Gilda, on whom he dotes. The courtiers trick Rigoletto, blindfolded, into helping abduct his own daughter for the Duke's pleasure.

In Act 2, Rigoletto is searching the palace looking for his daughter but is detained by the courtiers while the Duke seduces her. Rigoletto reveals she is his daughter and, when the girl enters, the abashed courtiers are shamed into leaving. Gilda is distraught when she realizes she has been deceived by the Duke and is not loved by a student; and Rigoletto, learning that the Duke has had his way with his beloved daughter, vows vengeance.

Gilda is now infatuated with the Duke, despite seeing him flirting with Maddalena, Sparafucile's handsome gypsy sister who lures men to an inn to rob or kill them. Gilda has been taken to the inn by her father for him to arrange the assassination of the Duke with Sparafucile who does not know the identity of his victim, only that he is Maddalena's next customer. Maddalena too has fallen for the irresistible Duke (again without realizing his identity) and begs her brother not to murder her new lover. He agrees to substitute another visitor to the inn for the intended victim. Gilda, disguised as a page, overhears this and, determined to save the Duke, later returns to the inn. Here she is stabbed by Sparafucile, who puts her almost lifeless corpse in a sack. Rigoletto returns to savour his revenge. He is amazed to hear the Duke singing outside and knows he's been deceived. Opening the sack, he sees in horror that his own daughter has been killed and collapses over her corpse. Monterone's curse has been fulfilled.

HIGHLIGHTS

ACT 1 *'Questa o quella'* ('This one or that one') The all-powerful Duke boasts of his amorous way of life in one of the tenor repertoire's most popular arias.

'Pari siamo' ('How alike we are') Rigoletto's soliloquy in which he compares himself with Sparafucile. One of the greatest baritone arias.

'Caro nome' ('Dear name') Among the most celebrated (and exacting) of all **coloratura** arias. Not many could tell you that the *'caro nome'* in question is 'Walter Madè', the name used by the Duke, pretending to be a struggling student, when he first visits Gilda. She, poor lamb, is left dreaming of her wonderful lover.

ACT 2 *'Piangi, fanciulla'* ('Weep, my child') Rigoletto tries to comfort his daughter. As touching and poignant a duet as Verdi ever wrote.

ACT 3 *'La donna è mobile'* ('Woman is fickle') Talk about the pot ... The fickle Duke, disguised as

a soldier at the inn, sings of the fickleness of women. This is now such a hackneyed recital number that out of context it is easy to forget just how adroit a piece of writing it is. It has to be a tune that is instantly recognizable for it to make its full dramatic effect at the end of the opera; it also reflects the character of the Duke with its light-headed, buoyant rhythm (and flashy final cadenza). It's said that the tenor who first sang the role was not given the score of this aria until the afternoon of the first performance: Verdi didn't want the tune sung all over town before the first night.

'Bella figlia dell' amore' ('Fairest daughter of the graces') A quartet – *the* great quartet of all opera – between the Duke, who is wooing Maddalena, Maddalena who coquettishly replies, Gilda, who is heartbroken at seeing her love with another, and Rigoletto, who vows revenge on the Duke. You could hear it sung in Eskimo and still marvel at the music.

DER RING DES NIBELUNGEN

WAGNER

1869 ~ 1876

'THE RING OF THE NIBELUNG'
PRONOUNCED: DAIR RING DESS NEEB-ELL-OONG-EN
LIBRETTO: WAGNER
BASED ON THE NIBELUNG SAGA
A STAGE-FESTIVAL PLAY FOR 3 DAYS AND A PRELIMINARY EVENING,
COMPRISING FOUR OPERAS:
DAS RHEINGOLD (PROLOGUE, DAY 1) DIE WALKÜRE (DAY 2)
SIEGFRIED (DAY 3) GÖTTERDÄMMERUNG (DAY 4)

In the whole history of music, let alone the history of opera, there is nothing to compare with Wagner's *Ring* cycle. Its length alone, never mind the musical and dramatic innovations, make it unique. From inception to first performance, it took Wagner nearly thirty years to complete. The result is one of man's greatest creative achievements.

That's not to say that it's an easy ride. Far from it. Many potential opera lovers have been put off the whole thing by unwisely plunging straight into one or all of these without first doing some homework. It's not just the language Wagner uses to express his stories, which are heavy with symbolism, it's the way he uses the music. This can baffle anyone expecting recognizable, four-square tunes, brisk action and a string of memorable arias to hum. *The Ring* is not like that at all. People go around whistling **Verdi's** operas, but they go around talking about Wagner's.

Nevertheless, the star of the evening is the music. The problem to the casual listener is that it cannot be listened to casually; its superficial attractions are many, but the scores have so many ingenious, complex ingredients that a basic route map is needed to appreciate fully the technical wizardry of Wagner's achievement. Each work needs some homework and, for many people, a deal of repetition before its attractions are realised.

There's no doubt that Wagner was a far better composer than he was librettist and the epic poems he provided for his masterpiece are astonishingly poor at times – repetitious, grandiloquent and verbose, barely adequate in their poetry and notably long, making the drama often static and dull. (It was **Rossini** who said, famously, 'Wagner has lovely moments but awful quarters of an hour.') It is Wagner the symphonist (the voices are treated as additional orchestral instruments) who saves the work

from being commonplace, for there's no doubt that the overall effect *can* be totally and uniquely overpowering.

WHAT'S DIFFERENT ABOUT THE RING?

In the late 1840s Wagner invented a new concept of music-drama, that would unify all the muses into a single great art form. Myths, gods and goddesses and ancient legends – these were the proper concerns of the creative spirit. He found his own way of expressing them in words, and adopted radical forms of musical expression. The music, he decided, must grow from the libretto; there must be no display pieces for their own sake, no showy arias inserted just to please the public, and the music, like the story, *must never cease*, for the music *is* the story and comments on the action and the characters just as much as the words of the libretto. **Leitmotivs**, short descriptive tunes associated with different moods and characters, underpin and bind the entire score. You will hear, for instance, material familiar from *Das Rheingold* echoed in *Götter-dämmerung* to stunning effect. (When Sir Thomas Beecham was rehearsing *Götterdämmerung*, he was quoted as saying: 'We've been rehearsing for two hours, and we're still playing the same bloody tune!')

More noticeably, perhaps, it is Wagner's use of the orchestra as an equal partner in the drama that marks a conscious break from the past. His masterly scoring characterizes the action of the story, and singers had to learn to make

Opposite: Madame Kalne as Brünnhilde in Die Walküre *– an early performer of the role*

PRINCIPAL CHARACTERS OF THE RING

GODS

WOTAN (*Vo'-tahn*) (b-bar),
king of the gods, married to Fricka
DONNER (*Dohn'-er*) (b),
god of thunder, brother of Freia
FROH (*Froh*) (t),
god of Spring, brother of Freia
LOGE (*Loh'-ga*) (t) god of fire

GODDESSES

FRICKA (*Frik'-ah*) (s), wife of Wotan
FREIA (*Fry'-ah*) (s), goddess of youth
ERDA (*Air'-dah*) (c), earth goddess

NIBELUNGS (DWARFS)

ALBERICH (*Ahl'-ber-ich*) (bar), lord of
the Nibelungs who inhabit Nibelheim,
the underworld of the old sagas
MIME (*Mee'-ma*) (t), his brother, a smith

GIANTS

FASOLT (*Fah'-zolt*) (b)
FAFNER (*Fahf'-ner*) (b)

RHINE MAIDENS

WOGLINDE (*Vog-lin'-da*) (s)
WELLGUNDE (*Vell-goon'-da*)(s)
FLOSSHILDE (*Floss-hill'-da*) (c)

VALKYRIES

GERHILDE (s), HELMWIGE (s),
ORTLINDE (s), WALTRAUTE (ms),
ROSSWEISSE (ms), SIEGRUNE (ms),
GRIMWERDE (ms), SCHWERTLEITE (ms)
BRÜNNHILDE (*Bruen-hill'-da*) (s),
a Valkyrie, Wotan's favourite
daughter

SIEGLINDE (*Zeeg-lin'-da*) (s),
a Volsung, daughter of Wotan
SIEGMUND (*Zeeg'-moond*) (t),
a Volsung
HUNDING (*Hoond'-ing*) (b),
husband of Sieglinde
SIEGFRIED (*Zeeg'-freed*) (t),
son of Sieglinde and Siegmund

FOREST BIRD (s)

GUNTHER (*Goon'-ter*) (b),
chief of the Gibichungs
HAGEN (*Hah'-gen*) (b),
son of Alberich,
half-brother to Gunther
GUTRUNE (*Goot-troon'-a*) (s),
Gunther's sister
THE THREE NORNS (c, ms & s)

---

themselves heard over the loudest sound yet summoned from the orchestra pit. Wagner even devised a new form of tuba so that his writing for the brass section could reach parts other tubas couldn't reach. He also, of course, had to have a specially built theatre in which to house his gargantuan children. One of Wagner's most intriguing traits is that, somehow, he always got what he wanted – in art and in life.

BACKGROUND

Wagner started work on *The Ring* while exiled in Switzerland for revolutionary activities. The libretti of the four operas were actually written in reverse order. Having become interested in the North European sagas, his first literary text was *Siegfried's Death*, written in 1848 and later to be *Götterdämmerung*. Realizing that this massive canvas needed an introduction, he wrote *Young Siegfried* (1851). This in turn was prefaced by *Die Walküre*, explaining Siegfried's parentage, and finally, as a prologue, he wrote *Das Rheingold*. The whole poem was finished in 1852 and published privately in 1853. Wagner had got as far as composing the second act of *Siegfried* (originally *Young Siegfried*) when even he faltered

and began to wonder if his dream would ever be realized. He set the project aside and, as a little light relief, wrote **Tristan und Isolde** and then **Die Meistersinger**.

In 1862, pardoned for his political activities of the 1840s, Wagner was allowed to return to his native Saxony. Two years later, almost miraculously, the patron he required in order to complete his epic emerged in the form of the young homosexual King of Bavaria, Ludwig II. A strong bond of friendship developed between them (but nothing stronger!) and the regal munificence kept the composer in the lifestyle which he felt was his due, culminating in the building of the theatre he needed to produce his 'stage-festival play'.

FIRST PERFORMANCE
Bayreuth, 13–17 August 1876
The music of *The Ring* was finally completed in 1874, so that when the Bayreuth theatre, built to Wagner's own specifications, was finished, it opened with the first complete performance of all four operas, one on each evening from 13 to 17 August 1876. It was the musical event of the decade. It attracted worldwide attention and some 4,000 visitors descended on the tiny Bavarian town. In the audience were the Emperor of Germany, the King of Bavaria, the Emperor and Empress of Brazil, Grand Duke Vladimir of Russia, Prince George of Prussia and Prince Wilhelm of Hesse, as well as some of the greatest musicians in the world: **Gounod**, Liszt, Tchaikovsky, **Saint-Saëns** and Grieg, among others.

Even such novelties as gas lighting linked to electric projectors and a magic lantern illuminating the 'Ride of the Valkyries' were as nothing compared to the startling originality of what the knowledgeable audience witnessed. Some were baffled; many more were wildly enthusiastic. There were no curtain calls after any of the operas. The reason for so declining was explained by Herr Wagner, who said that 'appearances before the curtain would tend to violate the unity of the representation.'

The festival made a huge deficit. At the closing party, Wagner paid tribute to Liszt. He owed him, he said, everything.

DAS RHEINGOLD

1869

PRONOUNCED:

DASS RINE¹-GOLDT

LITERALLY: 'THE RHINE GOLD'

4 SCENES SET IN LEGENDARY TIMES,
AT THE BOTTOM OF THE RIVER
RHINE, ON A MOUNTAIN NEAR THE
RIVER AND IN THE UNDERGROUND
CAVES OF NIBELHEIM
LENGTH: 2' 30"

The three Rhinemaidens, swimming in the Rhine where the gold they guard is hidden, tell Alberich of their treasure. He is told that anyone who fashions a Ring from it shall be master of the world, on condition that he renounces love. Alberich resolves to steal the gold and pay the price. On a mountaintop, Wotan celebrates the completion of Valhalla, home of the gods. The giants Fasolt and Fafner have built it and their price is Freia. Wotan declines to pay them when Loge tells them of the Rhinegold and its magic powers. The giants offer to accept this instead. Wotan agrees and the giants take Freia as ransom until the gold is delivered. Wotan and Loge plot to steal the gold.

The two gods descend to Nibelheim where, with his magic gold Ring, Alberich lords it over the underworld. His brother Mime has made him a gold helmet (the Tarnhelm), which will enable its wearer to change into any shape he chooses. Wotan and Loge flatter Alberich into changing himself into a toad, whereupon they capture him and take him to Valhalla. The price of his freedom is all the gold and the Ring. Alberich utters a curse on the Ring and its possessors. Wotan can now pay the giants and does so, but the curse begins to work at once for the two giants squabble over the spoil and Fafner kills Fasolt. Thor breaks the clouds and, over a rainbow bridge, the gods enter their new home, Valhalla.

HIGHLIGHTS

Scene 1 *Prelude*
Scene 4 *'The Entry of the Gods into Valhalla'*

DIE WALKÜRE

1870

PRONOUNCED:

DEE VAHL-KUE¹-REH

LITERALLY: 'THE VALKYRIE'

3 ACTS SET IN HUNDING'S HUT,
A WILD, ROCKY PLACE
AND THE SUMMIT OF A MOUNTAIN
LENGTH: 3' 45"

Who and what are the famous Valkyries? They are the nine daughters of Wotan and Erda, wild horsewomen of the air, whose task it is to bear the bodies of dead warriors to Valhalla. Wotan must now retrieve the Ring for without it the race of gods cannot endure, but Fafner, the surviving giant, has transformed himself into a dragon and guards the gold. Wotan has fathered sons by a human woman in the hope that children borne of the earth will regain the gold. These children are called Volsungs. One of them is Siegmund and he seeks shelter from a storm in Hunding and Sieglinde's hut. Unaware that they are brother and sister, Siegmund and Sieglinde fall for each other and when Hunding returns, Sieglinde puts a sleeping potion into her husband's drink, enabling the two to escape. In the tree growing inside the hut is a sword placed there on Sieglinde's wedding-day by a stranger (Wotan), who declared that only a hero could draw it out. No one has been able to remove it, but Siegmund, inspired, wrenches it free and the two, sure of their destiny together, rush out into the night.

Wotan commands Brünnhilde to protect Siegmund against the pursuing Hunding. However, Fricka, on hearing that he has stolen another's wife, demands that Siegmund be slain. Wotan reluctantly agrees and orders Brünnhilde to help Hunding instead. She disobeys and attempts to help Siegmund, but Wotan kills first Siegmund, and then Hunding. Brünnhilde lifts Sieglinde on to her horse and flees to the Valkyries' rock. Wotan pursues them. Sieglinde escapes into the forest, but Brünnhilde's punishment for her disobedience is to be put into a sleeping trance on a rock, surrounded by fire. Only a hero who knows no fear can wake her. Even then, she will wake as an ordinary human and marry the man who finds her. The opera closes as the flames leap around the rock.

HIGHLIGHTS

ACT 3 *'The Ride of the Valkyries'*
Clichéd, hackneyed, almost worn out from overuse, this nevertheless marvellously evokes the neighing and galloping of the horses, the cry of the warrior women and the

sound of the coming storm as the Valkyries ride on magic horses through the clouds to their retreat. *'Wotan's Farewell'* and *'Magic Fire Music'* Wotan bids a regretful farewell to Brünnhilde, 'my brave and beautiful child' once the light and life of his heart. He summons Loge, strikes the rock three times and flames appear.

SIEGFRIED
1876
PRONOUNCED: ZEEG'-FREED

3 ACTS SET IN MIME'S FORGE, THE CAVERN HOME OF FAFNER AT THE FOOT OF THE MOUNTAIN, AND ON BRÜNNHILDE'S ROCK
LENGTH: 4' 00"

Sieglinde has died giving birth to her son, Siegfried, who has been brought up by the crafty dwarf Mime, brother of Alberich. Mime is trying to forge a sword

strong enough for Siegfried (our hero always smashes them up). There is one weapon that Siegfried could not break – the two pieces of Notung, Siegmund's sword, with which Mime hopes Siegfried will slay the giant/dragon Fafner. But Mime can't weld the pieces together. Wotan, in the guise of a Wanderer, arrives and questions Mime, prophesying that the sword will cause his death. Siegfried welds Notung, makes it whole and then fearlessly slays Fafner. A drop of the dragon's blood accidentally touches his lips, enabling him to understand the song of the birds, one of which tells him that the Tarnhelm and the Ring, hidden in Fafner's cave, could make him ruler of the world, and of how Mime plans to kill him. Siegfried retrieves the Tarnhelm and the Ring. He kills Mime and sets off to find Brünnhilde, led by the Woodbird (s).

Wotan realizes that his destiny now cannot be avoided, that

Siegfried and Brünnhilde are the rulers of the future, and that the old gods are facing their twilight. Appearing as the Wanderer, he attempts to block Siegfried's progress with his spear, the same spear that killed Siegmund and the symbol of his authority. Now, however, Siegfried's sword breaks Wotan's spear on whose shaft are engraved the oaths and contracts by which Wotan rules the world. The young hero plunges on into the fire, to awaken Brünnhilde and claim her as his bride. He places on her finger the Ring he has won.

HIGHLIGHT
ACT 2 *'Forest Murmurs'* Wagner's famous portrait of a forest and the sounds of nature.

DIE GÖTTERDÄMMERUNG
1876
PRONOUNCED: DEE GOE-TER-DAYM'-MER-OONG
LITERALLY: 'THE TWILIGHT OF THE GODS'

PRELUDE AND 3 ACTS SET ON THE VALKYRIES' ROCK, THE HALL OF THE GIBICHUNGS BY THE RHINE, BRÜNNHILDE'S ROCK AND A ROCKY VALLEY BY THE RHINE
LENGTH: 4' 15"

The Prelude has the Three Norns predicting the fate of the gods: the curse of the Ring will include the destruction of their home, Valhalla. Brünnhilde sends Siegfried into the world on her horse, Grane, in order to further

The Rhinemaidens try to tease the ring from Siegfried in Act 3 of the 1986 Royal Opera House production of Die Götterdämmerung

prove his love for her. Siegfried leaves the Ring with Brünnhilde and sets off.

Alberich's son Hagen is plotting with his half-brother Gunther to secure the Ring. Gunther has heard of Brünnhilde's beauty and wants her for himself. Siegfried reaches the Hall of the Gibichungs and is given a magic potion that makes him forget his beloved Brünnhilde and fall in love with Gutrune. He asks Gunther for her hand. Gunther agrees as long as Siegfried will fetch Brünnhilde for him. Meanwhile, one of the Valkyrie sisters, Waltraute, tries to persuade Brünnhilde to return the Ring to the Rhinemaidens from whom the gold that made it was stolen. Wotan has told her that the curse of the Ring will be lifted if this is done. However, the faithful Brünnhilde will not part with the Ring Siegfried gave her as a pledge of his love.

Disguised by the Tarnhelm (the magic helmet) as Gunther, Siegfried drags Brünnhilde from her rock to the Hall of the Gibichungs. Alberich, who first stole the gold, encourages Hagen to win back the Ring at any cost. Siegfried, returning to his own self, announces the arrival of Gunther and his bride-to-be, Brünnhilde, while he himself is about to marry Gutrune. Having believed that it was Gunther who took the ring from her Brünnhilde is amazed to see Siegfried wearing it once more. She accuses him of treachery, a charge that he, of course, is unable to understand.

Her love turned to hate, Brünnhilde plots with Hagen to murder Siegfried when he is out hunting. The Rhinemaidens appear to tell Siegfried to give up the Ring or evil will befall him. He refuses and during the hunt, Hagen, having given Siegfried a potion which restores his memory, stabs him.

With his last breath, Siegfried calls upon Brünnhilde. He is borne on shields back to the Gibichung Hall. Hagen demands the Ring as spoil, but when Gunther refuses to hand it over (it is still on Siegfried's hand), Hagen kills him too. The curse of the Ring has worked again. Brünnhilde learns from the Rhinemaidens how Siegfried was deceived and decides to join him on the funeral pyre. Realizing that an act of self-sacrificing love will cleanse the curse of the Ring, she mounts Grane and rides into the heart of the flames. The rising waters of the Rhine engulf the pyre as the Rhinemaidens at last seize the Ring, while Hagen, plunging into the flood to try to retrieve it, is dragged down into the depths. The Hall of the Gibichungs collapses and, in the distance, Valhalla is seen in flames, illuminating the twilight of the gods.

HIGHLIGHTS

Prelude *'Siegfried's Rhine Journey'* The orchestral interlude which, using many of the familiar themes ('Fire Music', the motif from *Rhine Gold* and others from the previous works), paints the hero's journey down the Rhine after parting from Brünnhilde.

ACT 3 *'Siegfried's Funeral March'* Another impressive display of thematic metamorphosis as Siegfried's body is carried solemnly into the Gibichungs' Hall. An orchestra played this as Wagner's own coffin was lowered into the grave.

'Brünnhilde's Immolation' Brünnhilde takes a last look at her beloved Siegfried, places the Ring on her finger and lights the pyre. 'Brünnhilde greets thee in bliss,' she cries, leaping on to Grane's back and riding into the flames.

DER ROSENKAVALIER
RICHARD STRAUSS
1911
LITERALLY: 'THE CAVALIER OF THE ROSE'
LIBRETTO: HUGO VON HOFMANNSTHAL

3 ACTS SET IN 18TH CENTURY VIENNA DURING THE REIGN OF MARIA THERESA

A 'comedy for music' was how the composer described this glorious work, which combines elements of intrigue, farce and satire as well as truly touching pathos, all in the Mozartian style he intended (there's even a *travesti* role). The music, written after *Salome* and *Elektra*, is nowhere near as dissonant as the earlier scores, and the waltz themes that pervade the opera are worthy successors to those written half a century earlier by Johann Strauss II (no relation). It is certainly the most popular German opera written this century and to many is the last great romantic opera.

❖

Thanks to the orchestral introduction, the audience is in no doubt as to what has been going on as soon as the curtain rises. The young Count Octavian (*ms*, the *travesti* role) has been making love to Princess von Werdenberg (*s*) (a role always referred to as the Marschallin, since she is the wife of an Austrian Field Marshal). It is morning, we are in the private apartments of the Princess and it is time for her youthful lover to leave – the Marschallin's elderly cousin, the licentious Baron Ochs (*b*), is demanding to be admitted. There's no escape route, so Octavian slips into an inner room and emerges disguised as a maid. Ochs has come to ask the Marschallin to nominate a 'Knight of the Rose' who, according to an old established custom, will carry an offer of marriage to an intended bride, in this case to Sophie (*s*), the daughter of the *nouveau riche* Faninal (*bar*). Having flirted with the disguised Octavian and invited 'her' to supper, Ochs leaves the Silver Rose with the Marschallin to bestow as she thinks fit. Octavian departs also, and the Marschallin, knowing that one day he will desert her for a younger woman, sends the Silver Rose for Octavian to deliver. 'He will know what to do with it'.

The presentation of the rose in Act 2 of the Royal Opera House's 1925 production of Der Rosenkavalier

The inevitable consequence is that as soon as Octavian claps eyes on Sophie, they fall for each other. Ochs interrupts their lovemaking, makes some highly disparaging remarks about Sophie's upstart family and, having greatly offended her, fights a duel with Octavian in which he (Ochs) is slightly wounded. Sophie refuses to marry the boorish Ochs, but her father, seeing his plans for his family's connection with the aristocracy go out of the window, declares Sophie shall either marry Ochs or take the veil. Octavian dreams up a plan to save her ... The Baron receives a note from the Marschallin's 'maid'.

At a dubious inn, Octavian, in his maid's clothes, makes the promised rendezvous with Ochs but plays such a variety of tricks on him – faces appearing out of trap doors and at windows, paternity suits brought against him – that Ochs believes he's going mad. A brawl ensues, the police arrive to arrest Ochs. The Marschallin is sent for to help him out, whereupon Octavian reveals his true self and the Baron sees he has been throroughly duped. The Marschallin reminds Ochs of his rank, then, with resignation, seeing she must relinquish her young lover, generously gives her blessing to Sophie and Octavian.

HIGHLIGHTS

ACT 1 *'Kann mich auch an ein Mädel erinnern'* ('I too can remember a young girl') Known as the Marschallin's Monologue, in which she acknowledges that a woman of her age, handsome though she still is, cannot hope to keep a young man like Octavian.
ACT 2 *'Mit mir keine Kammer dir zu klein'* ('With me no room is too small') An inspired waltz song sung by Ochs, lustfully assuring Sophie

that no night with him would seem too long.
ACT 3 *'Hab' mir's gelobt'* ('I promised') The first words of the famous trio, which the Marschallin begins, to be joined by Octavian and Sophie. This is among the most ravishing passages in the entire operatic literature.

RECOMMENDED RECORDINGS
complete:
Gueden/Reining/ Jurinac
Vienna State Opera Ch
VPO, E. Kleiber
DECCA 425 950 (mono)
highlights:
Schwarzkopf/Ludwig/Stich-Randall, Philh. Ch & O
Karajan
EMI CDM7 63452 2

SAMSON ET DALILA
SAINT-SAËNS
1877
PRONOUNCED: SAHN-SO'HN AY
DA-LEE'-LA
LIBRETTO: FERDINAND LEMAIRE
AFTER JUDGES 14–16

3 ACTS SET IN GAZA, PALESTINE,
IN PRE-CHRISTIAN TIMES

By far the most popular of Saint-Saëns's twelve operas, and the only one still surviving in the repertoire, the strengths of this biblical epic lie in its music – which is undeniably beautiful and effective throughout – rather than in its characterization or psychological insights.

Inspired by the book of Judges, it had a long gestation period. Saint-Saëns began work on it in 1867 and continued, on and off, for the next ten years. Although one of the most revered composers of the age, he could not get the work produced in France and it

was due to his friend Liszt (how many composers owed the production of their works to him!) that the first performance took place, under Liszt's patronage, in Weimar. *Samson* was not seen in Paris until fifteen years later.

❖

The Israelites are oppressed by the Philistines. Samson (*t*), leader of the Hebrews, rouses his people into action, urging them to pray for deliverance. Abimelech (*b*), the Philistine Satrap of Gaza, appears and taunts the Israelites, blaspheming their God. Samson suddenly leaps forward, snatches a sword and slays Abimelech. The unprepared Philistine soldiers are routed and Samson, with his flowing locks, is the invincible hero of the day. The Philistine maidens, among whom is the beautiful Dalila (*ms*), dance for the Israelites. Samson falls for Dalila's seductive charms.

In Act 2, Dalila, at her home in the Valley of Sorek, has fallen out of love with her strong man. The High Priest of Dagon (*bar*) comes to persuade her to betray Samson into revealing the secret of his great strength. Against his better judgement, Samson returns to her, and is chided for not trusting her when she questions him. After more hesitation, he enters her house. The Philistine soldiers quietly surround it as Dalila cries out that Samson is now harmless: she has discovered his secret to be his hair, and has cut it off. Samson is captured. In prison, shackled and blinded, he prays for forgiveness for having betrayed his people. In the temple of Dagon, Dalila mocks her former lover, now helpless and weak, in front of the High Priest and the Philistine princes. Samson is ordered to sacrifice to Dagon but, standing between the pillars of the temple, he prays to the God of

SANSONE E DALILA. Opera di Saint-Saëns. 6
Vendetta.

Sansone: "Possa o santa vendetta di te Tutti insieme seppellirli con me!" Atto IIIº. sc 3ª

Samson knocks down the temple of Dagon in Act 3 of Samson et Dalila

the Israelites for strength once more, and with a supreme effort pushes the columns apart. The temple collapses, burying him and all his enemies.

HIGHLIGHTS

ACT 1 *'Printemps qui commence'* ('With the coming of spring') The seductive aria in which Dalila captures Samson's heart.
ACT 2 *'Mon coeur s'ouvre à ta voix'* ('My heart opens at the sound of your voice') A heart-melting song of love and passion as the false Dalila coaxes Samson to surrender himself to her. Almost the first thing that Saint-Saëns composed for the opera, it's always been a favourite.
ACT 3 *Bacchanale* The dance, preceding Samson's arrival in the temple, begins slowly with an oriental theme and rises to an abandoned, frenzied climax. A terrific orchestral show-piece.

RECOMMENDED RECORDINGS
complete: Gorr/Vickers/Blanc
Paris Opera O, Prêtre
EMI CDS 47895
highlights: as above
EMI CDM7 63935

THE TALES OF HOFFMANN
JACQUES OFFENBACH
1881
ORIGINAL FRENCH TITLE:
'LES CONTES D'HOFFMANN'
LIBRETTO: JULES BARBIER AND
MICHEL CARRÉ
BASED ON THREE STORIES BY
E. T. A. HOFFMANN

3 ACTS WITH A PROLOGUE AND
EPILOGUE, SET IN NUREMBERG,
MUNICH AND VENICE DURING THE
19TH CENTURY

Offenbach wrote this captivating work – quite different in tone to the rest of his output – using three tales by the extraordinary German writer, music critic, caricaturist and composer Ernst Theodor Amadeus Hoffmann (his third forename was actually Wilhelm, but he replaced it with Amadeus from his love of Mozart), whose fantastic tales influenced the Romantic movement in literature and music.

Offenbach died during rehearsals of the work. The complicated story of its subsequent revisions, cuts, rearrangements and other alterations made by other hands is a tale in itself. You might come across versions with an alternative ending for Act 2 and with Acts 2

and 3 reversed, but given below is the version considered closest to Offenbach's intentions.

❖

Hoffmann (*t*), a poet, is in love with Stella, an opera singer who is appearing in Mozart's **Don Giovanni**. His rival in love is Lindorf (*b-bar*), a Nuremberg councillor, who intercepts a letter in which Stella promises to meet Hoffmann. The poet is seen drinking with students in Martin Luther's Wine Cellar in Nuremberg but he seems despondent. The students tease him, saying that he's in love. No, he replies, he's given up love affairs. The three acts of the opera reveal why.

In them, Lindorf represents all Hoffmann's love rivals, becoming Coppelius (a scientist), Dapertutto (a sorcerer) and Dr Miracle (a doctor), roles usually sung by the same singer. Stella is likewise represented by Olympia (a doll), Giulietta (a courtesan) and Antonia (a singer), although, because of the wide vocal demands of the roles, they are generally sung by three different sopranos. (One of the few singers with sufficient vocal range to tackle all four roles has been Joan Sutherland – and even she found it taxing.)

In Act 1, Spalanzani (*t*), an inventor, has made a wonderful mechanical doll named Olympia (*s*), which he hopes will enable him to make back some of the money he has lost in a banking failure. His rival Coppelius has helped him make her eyes. Hoffmann, thinking Olympia is Spalanzani's daughter, falls in love with her, despite the attempts of his friend (and alter ego) Nicklausse (*ms*) to dissuade him. At a party to introduce Olympia to the public, Hoffmann woos her and dances with her. Meanwhile, Coppelius discovers that the banker's draft Spalanzani used to buy off his contribution to the project is worthless. Coppelius smashes the doll to pieces, leaving Hoffmann heartbroken and ridiculed by all.

In Act 2, Hoffmann is in Munich, where he's fallen in love with the frail soprano Antonia (*s*) against the advice of Nicklausse. She, like her mother before her, is suffering from consumption and has been forbidden to sing again. Her father, Councillor Crespel (*b*), is afraid that she will go the same way as her mother, a famous mezzo-soprano. When Hoffmann and Crespel are out of the room, the evil Dr Miracle brings the mother's portrait to life and forces Antonia to sing. She collapses, exhausted by her efforts, and dies in her father's arms. Hoffmann has again lost his love.

The third act finds our poet-lover in Venice, where, despite Nicklausse's warnings, he allows himself to fall for the beautiful courtesan Giulietta. She is in the power of Dapertutto, who wants her to capture the reflection (i.e. the soul) of Hoffmann. Unable to resist her, Hoffmann then looks into the mirror to find he has no reflection. He attempts to obtain the keys to Giulietta's bedroom from Schlemil (*b*), her current lover, and kills him in a duel. Hoffmann rushes to find his love only to see her float away in a gondola in the arms of Pittichinaccio (*t*) the dwarf – an admirer of Giulietta.

Hoffmann's stories have finished, and back in the tavern, Lindorf has made sure that Hoffmann has had plenty to drink before he leads Stella from the room. Even though she throws the poet a flower from her bouquet, he is too drunk to notice or care.

HIGHLIGHTS

Prologue *'The Legend of Kleinzack'* Hoffmann sings a satirical ballad in answer to the students' request, but soon drifts off into a reverie about his latest love, Stella.

ACT 1 *'Les oiseaux dans la charmille'* ('Songbirds in the bower') Olympia's aria, known as the Doll Song. A tremendously demanding *coloratura* display piece during which the singer has to be wound up.

ACT 3 *'Belle nuit, ô nuit d'amour'* ('Lovely night, oh night of love')

A Barcarole (*the* Barcarole!), one of the world's best-known tunes, a duet sung by Nicklausse and Giulietta. A marvellous evocation of the moonlit canals of Venice with lovers drifting over the waters in swaying gondolas.

RECOMMENDED RECORDINGS
complete:
Sutherland/Domingo/Bacquier
Suisse Romande Ch & O
Bonynge
DECCA 417 363
highlights: as above
DECCA 421 866

TANNHÄUSER
WAGNER
1845
PRONOUNCED: TAHN'-HOY-ZER
LIBRETTO: WAGNER

3 ACTS SET IN THURINGIA, NEAR EISENACH, DURING THE EARLY 13TH CENTURY

Arguably Wagner's most important early work, it is certainly his most popular. The opera's full title is *Tannhäuser und der Sängerkrieg auf dem Wartburg* (Tannhäuser and the Singing Contest on the Wartburg) and its subject is taken from legend and history. Tannhäuser actually existed, as did the singing contests. He was a minnesinger, born around 1205, one of a group of poets and musicians, mainly of noble birth, who sang of love and beauty, frequently holding contests for the purpose (see *Die Meistersinger*, based on a similar idea). With the heroine possibly based on the real-life figure of Princess Elisabeth of Hungary (St Elisabeth, 1207–31), Wagner works his theme: love and redemption, the conflict between good and evil, the victory of the

Elizabeth saves Tannhäuser's life in Act 2 of the 1867 production.

spirit over the senses. The medieval legend he used was of Venus, the goddess of Love, establishing her court near the Wartburg beneath a mountain that came to be known as the Venusberg. Into her court she would tempt the knights of the Wartburg and hold them captive.

The original production in Dresden was given a lukewarm reception. In Paris, the work was whistled off the stage by members of the Jockey Club.

❖

The knight and minstrel Tannhäuser (*t*) has been enjoying the delights of the Venusberg for a year. Satiated with pleasure, he decides to return to the real world and, when he calls the name of the Virgin Mary, the Venusberg disappears. He finds himself in a valley near the castle of Wartburg. A group of noblemen returning from the chase appear, led by Hermann, the Landgrave of Thuringia (*b*). Recognizing Tannhäuser, they invite him to return to the castle, where a fellow knight and minnesinger, Wolfram von Eschenbach (*bar*), tells him that the Landgrave's niece Elisabeth (*s*) pines for him. It's evident that Tannhäuser has been in love with the beautiful and virtuous Elisabeth and regrets his stay in the Venusberg.

In the Hall of the Minstrels, Elisabeth greets her lost love ecstatically, although Tannhäuser will not tell her where he's been. A song contest is announced. The Landgrave is so confident of Tannhäuser winning it that he offers the hand of Elisabeth as the prize. Wolfram, the first contestant, sings of the value of spiritual love. When it's Tannhäuser's turn he cannot resist the temptation to sing a song in praise of Venus and the joys of sensual passion. Everyone is outraged and the knights draw

their swords to kill Tannhäuser. Elisabeth intervenes, begging their forgiveness, and the deeply repentant Tannhäuser agrees to accept the Landgrave's command to seek atonement by joining pilgrims bound for Rome.

Several months later, Tannhäuser has still not returned. He is not among a band of pilgrims who pass by the Wartburg and Elisabeth sadly enters the castle, praying to the Virgin that she might be allowed to take on the sins of Tannhäuser and, by dying, win his salvation. At length, the knight appears in rags, exhausted, and tells Wolfram of his despair when the Pope, instead of absolving him, told him he had as much chance of redemption as the papal staff had of sprouting leaves. Tannhäuser wants to return to the Venusberg when Wolfram invokes the name of Elisabeth. Mention of her gives him strength to reject the temptation just as a funeral procession approaches with Elisabeth's coffin. She has died of a broken heart, and Tannhäuser, embracing her corpse, dies too. More pilgrims from Rome arrive bearing the Pope's staff, which, miraculously, has broken into leaf. Tannhäuser has been forgiven.

HIGHLIGHTS

Overture. One of the finest and most famous of all opera overtures, it presents many of the themes Wagner develops in the course of the work, including the Pilgrims' Chorus. It tells the story of the whole opera – an excellent introduction to Wagner's world.

ACT 1 *Venusberg Music and Bacchanale.*

The Pilgrims' Chorus (repeated in Act 3)

ACT 2 *'Dich teure Halle'* ('This blessed room') Elisabeth's expressive aria at seeing again

her beloved Tannhäuser.

Procession of the Guests and Festal March The dazzling march before the song contest.

ACT 3 *'O du mein holder Abendstern'* ('O star of eve') Wolfram, who also loves Elisabeth, can give her no comfort, and in this touching song of farewell, he prays to the evening star, symbol of his lost love.

RECOMMENDED RECORDING
complete: Dernesch/Ludwig/
Kollo/Braun/Sotin, Vienna State
Opera Ch, VPO, Solti
DECCA 414 581

THE THREEPENNY OPERA
KURT WEILL
1928
ORIGINAL GERMAN TITLE:
'DER DREIGROSCHENOPER'
PRONOUNCED: DEE DRY'-
GROSH-UN-OP-UH
LIBRETTO: BERTOLT BRECHT
FREELY ADAPTED FROM
'THE BEGGAR'S OPERA'
BY JOHN GAY

PROLOGUE AND 3 ACTS
(OR 8 SCENES) SET IN LONDON
AROUND 1900

Its musical bite and stark picture of tawdry, underworld corruption have become a cliché for evoking the Berlin of the Weimar Republic. Brecht wrote better texts than this but it is (once again) the composer who saves the day. Weill's spare, telling score, with its mixture of popular song and dance rhythms, its clever European transmutation of American jazz elements and distinctive instrumental ensemble make it a miniature masterpiece. A sardonic, tongue-in-cheek satire, it received more than 4,000 performances in its first year alone.

❖

The notorious criminal Mack the Knife (*bar*) marries Polly (*s*). She is the daughter of J. J. Peachum (*b*), who runs a begging racket. When he hears that the main attraction of his business (his daughter) has gone, Peachum, hoping to get his hands on his son-in-law's fortune, denounces him to the police. He and Mrs Peachum (*s*) bribe Pirate Jenny (*ms*), Mack's ex-lover, to betray him. Tiger Brown (*b*), the chief of police, reluctant to upset his profitable financial arrangements with Mack, is persuaded to co-operate with the Peachums when they threaten to disrupt the forthcoming coronation of the Queen. In prison, Mack is forced to choose between Tiger Brown's daughter Lucy (*s*), and Polly. He opts for Lucy and is thereby able to escape. He is betrayed again by Jenny, arrested and sentenced to be hanged. The faithful Polly goes to bid farewell to her love but at the last minute a royal messenger arrives on horseback. Mack is pardoned by the Queen, given a castle and a peerage and best wishes are sent to the happy couple. Peachum concludes, 'Unfortunately real life is very different as we know. Messengers rarely arrive on horseback, if the downtrodden dare resist.'

HIGHLIGHTS

Legend of Mackie Messer ('Mack the Knife'), Wedding Song, Pirate Jenny, Soldier Song, Love Duet, Ballad of the Easy Life

RECOMMENDED RECORDING

complete: Lemper/Milva/ Kollo/Adorf, Berlin Radio Sinfonietta, Mauceri

DECCA 430 075

TOSCA

PUCCINI

1900

LIBRETTO: GIUSEPPE GIACOSA AND LUIGI ILLICA
BASED ON THE PLAY BY VICTORIEN SARDOU
LENGTH: 2' 00"

Tosca can be seen as the other side of the coin from Puccini's earlier opera, *La Bohème*. In place of the tender and romantic we have the sombre and tragic, although it is no less ardently lyrical than its predecessor. If you are building a collection of operas and getting to know the repertoire, *Tosca* must surely be one of the first to be sampled in its entirety. Cavaradossi is one of *the* **tenor** roles (a favourite of everyone from **Placido Domingo** down), Tosca one of the most rewarding **soprano** roles (**Maria Callas** was supreme here), and in Scarpia, we have one of the most believable and sadistic of opera villains.

BACKGROUND

Puccini, insecure as he was, never felt happier about his opera plots than when they'd already been successful in another format. He had considered using Sardou's play (a vehicle for Sarah Bernhardt) as

Scarpia (Tito Gobbi) puts his proposition to Tosca (Maria Callas) in the 1964 Royal Opera House production

early as 1889, but it was a rival composer, the wealthy Alberto Franchetti, known as 'the Italian Meyerbeer', who finally inspired Puccini to do something about it. The libretto for an operatic treatment of Sardou's *La Tosca* (1887) had already been written by Luigi Illica for Franchetti's use, but Franchetti wanted changes that Illica refused to make. For an adjudication, the two men went with Franchetti's publisher Ricordi to seek the opinion of the octogenarian **Verdi**. Verdi pronounced it excellent. When Puccini heard this, he anxiously persuaded Ricordi, who was also *his* publisher, to wrest the rights from Franchetti. This he did and the same team that had written *La Bohème* then began work.

FIRST PERFORMANCE
Teatro Costanzi, Rome
14 January 1900
A bomb scare during the performance (the Queen was to be present) did nothing to help first night nerves, but the critics were in any case divided. They have been

ever since – quite in the face of public opinion. Shaw referred to Sardou's melodramas as 'Sardoodledom', describing *La Tosca* itself as 'a cheap shocker', a remark copied by the American critic Joseph Kerman some fifty years later when he described Puccini's work as 'that shabby little shocker'. The opinions of critics, like the diagnoses of doctors, should always be open to question by the rest of us, no matter how inferior we may feel our specialist knowledge to be. Kerman, as a case in point, was talking piffle.

STORY
3 acts set in Rome in June 1800

PRINCIPAL CHARACTERS
FLORIA TOSCA,
a celebrated singer (s)
MARIO CAVARADOSSI, a painter (t)
BARON SCARPIA,
chief of police (bar)
CESARE ANGELOTTI (b),
a political prisoner
SPOLETTA (t), a police agent

The action is set in a specific period

of Italian history when Napoleon's invading army was greeted by Italian patriots as their liberator from oppressive Austrian rule.

Cesare Angelotti, having escaped from prison, finds a hiding-place in the Church of Sant' Andrea della Valle. Cavaradossi returns to the church to resume work on his picture of Mary Magdalen, the model for which is an unknown lady who comes daily to pray in the church (in fact she is Marchesa Attavanti, Angelotti's sister). When Angelotti emerges from his hiding-place, Cavaradossi recognizes him as the consul of the moribund Roman Republic. The voice of Tosca, Cavaradossi's mistress, is heard approaching, forcing Angelotti into hiding again. Jealous of the model in her lover's painting, Tosca goes. Cavaradossi decides to hide Angelotti in his villa and the two leave. Scarpia, the feared and lecherous chief of police, enters looking for the prisoner, and finds not only a fan left by Angelotti's sister but Cavaradossi's empty lunch basket. Scarpia is suspicious; he knows Cavaradossi is a republican. He also knows of his relationship with Tosca, whom he covets. When Tosca returns to alter the plans for the evening, Scarpia suggests that Tosca's painter friend might have left with the owner of the fan. Tosca leaves in a fury to go to Cavaradossi's villa, not realizing that she is being followed by Spoletta. Scarpia plans to execute the painter and seduce the singer.

Scarpia is waiting to have supper with Tosca in his apartment at the Farnese Palace. Cavaradossi has been arrested, under suspicion of helping Angelotti, and he is brought in by Spoletta. Tosca is compelled to hear his cries under torture and promises to reveal Angelotti's hiding-place if her lover is freed. Cavaradossi, confronted with Tosca, spurns her and, hearing that the royal troops have been defeated, defies Scarpia. Scarpia orders him to be shot. He is taken out but Scarpia suggests to Tosca that there may be a way to save him – she is to let him have his way with her. She agrees if he will spare Cavaradossi. The wily Scarpia instructs Spoletta that the execution will be 'simulated – just as in the case of Palmieri'. What Tosca doesn't know is that Palmieri's so-called 'simulated' execution used real bullets. Scarpia turns to embrace his prize. Tosca stabs him with a knife, then, having arranged his body, leaves with a safe conduct pass for herself and Cavaradossi.

At dawn, Cavaradossi is brought from his cell to be executed by a firing squad on the battlements of the Castel Sant' Angelo. His last thoughts are for Tosca, who appears unexpectedly to tell him that his execution is to be faked and that after the dummy bullets have been fired, he is to lie still and pretend to be dead. They look forward to their life together. But the painter is killed, and as the agonized Tosca hears the voices of Spoletta and others mounting the stairs, having discovered Scarpia's corpse, she flings herself over the battlements to her death.

HIGHLIGHTS

ACT 1 *'Recondita armonia'* ('Strange harmony') Cavaradossi takes out the miniature he carries of his adored Tosca (his interest in the unknown lady who is his model for the Madonna is purely artistic) and sings of the beautiful way in which her features blend into a harmonious whole. A popular aria in and out of the opera house.

ACT 2 *'Vissi d'arte'* ('I have lived for art') Cavaradossi has been taken away for execution; Scarpia suggests Tosca surrenders herself to him. In this moving and celebrated aria, the singer wonders, having devoted her life to art and love, gone regularly to church and given freely to charity, what she has done to deserve this cruel fate.

ACT 3 *'E lucevan le stelle'* ('Stars were shining') Cavaradossi has been told he has one hour to live. He sings this touching farewell (a great favourite) recalling his meetings with Tosca on starlit nights in quiet gardens. See below.

*Many are the stories of disaster during performances of **Tosca** – the opera seems to attract mishaps in much the same way as Macbeth does in the theatre. Some of them are apocryphal and a few are amusing, for example the untrained, unrehearsed firing-squad who enter in the final act not knowing which of the two artists they are supposed to shoot. They aim at Tosca, they fire at Tosca. On the opposite side of the stage, Cavaradossi falls dead as Tosca, apparently riddled with bullets, rushes over to him. Following vague instructions about how to make their exit ('Follow the principals!'), the firing squad see Tosca jump over the battlements and, obeying instructions, decide to do the same. Most famously, there is the story of the overweight and unpopular soprano singing Tosca who, instead of falling on to a mattress when she jumped over the battlements, had a trampoline substituted by the stage-crew. Having disappeared from view behind the scenery, she was seen to reappear and disappear some fifteen times before the curtain was lowered to hysterical laughter. Can it be true? One hopes so.*

One Tosca story that is certainly true concerns Cavaradossi's final aria, 'E lucevan le stelle'. Listen to the first eight notes and then, if you can, listen to 'Avalon', a popular song by one Vincent Rose and Al Jolson (no less), which they penned jointly in the 1920s. The eight notes are exactly the same. Puccini's publishers, Ricordi, noticed the similarity and successfully sued Rose and Jolson for breach of copyright. It's said that the royalties from that one song alone made the Puccini estate more money than all his operas.

LA TRAVIATA

VERDI

1853

THE TRANSLATION OF 'LA TRAVIATA' – LITERALLY 'THE FALLEN WOMAN'
OR 'THE WAYWARD WOMAN' – IS, UNUSUALLY, NEVER USED
LIBRETTO: FRANCESCO MARIA PIAVE
BASED ON THE PLAY (DERIVED FROM THE NOVEL)
'LA DAME AUX CAMÉLIAS' BY ALEXANDRE DUMAS FILS
LENGTH: 2' 00"

Its romantic subject, its deliciously tuneful score, its intimacy (this is Verdi's smallest canvas) and its agreeable length have all helped to make this a perennial favourite, although its first performance (see below) was not a success. The last of the three great operas of Verdi's middle period, following **Rigoletto** and **Il Trovatore**.

BACKGROUND

Dumas's original was based on fact. When he was only twenty he fell in love with the legendary Parisian courtesan Marie Duplessis. She died from tuberculosis in 1847, aged twenty-three. In Dumas's novel, she becomes Marguerite Gautier; in the play, Camille; in the opera, Violetta Valéry. The story became more and more romanticized with each successive version, until the figure of the Lady of the Camelias achieved a myth-like status: the fallen woman who sacrifices everything for love and is thereby redeemed.

Cheryl Baker as Violetta and David Maxwell Anderson as Alfredo in Opera North's Production of La Traviata

The subject was fixed on by Verdi after many months of searching. He'd been invited to write an opera for Venice in January 1852 and only started writing it in the following November.

FIRST PERFORMANCE
Teatro La Fenice, Venice
6 March 1853

Another of the world's most durable operas which suffered a painful birth. In the first place it was dressed in contemporary costume and audiences did like their period finery; in the second place, the theme was not at all in line with contemporary morality. Most importantly, the leading tenor was hoarse, the baritone was nearing the end of his career and, in the immortal words of Victor Borge, the prima donna filling the role of Violetta not only filled it but overflowed it. She was a lady of generous proportions and when, in the last act, the doctor declared that the heroine was dying of consumption, the audience, instead of reaching for their handkerchiefs, fell about laughing.

STORY
3 acts set in Paris and its environs about 1850 (sometimes 1700)

PRINCIPAL CHARACTERS
VIOLETTA VALÉRY, a courtesan (s)
FLORA BERVOIX, her friend (ms)
ALFREDO GERMONT, Violetta's lover, a young man about town (t)
GIORGIO GERMONT, his father (bar)
BARON DOUPHOL, a rival of Alfredo's (bar)

Violetta is receiving guests in her house in Paris. Among them is Alfredo, who is introduced as the man who came to enquire after her health every day during her recent illness. The consumptive Violetta collapses in a fit of coughing. She recovers and as the other guests go off to dance Alfredo remains and declares his love for her. She tells him not to be so silly, but his devotion touches her nevertheless and she is left wondering whether perhaps this is the lover for whom she has waited to make her truly happy. In conclusion she decides to forget him and continue her life of pleasure.

Next, however, we find Alfredo and Violetta in a country house outside Paris. He has won her, but his father comes to beg Violetta to give up his son. Her association with him will not only ruin his prospects and his name, but jeopardize the marriage of his innocent sister. With great reluctance Violetta consents, but cannot bear to tell Alfredo the truth and goes away leaving a note telling him that she wants to return to her old life. We next see her at her friend Flora's costume ball in the company of her former protector, Baron Douphol. Alfredo is there and Violetta, true to the promise she gave his father, keeps up the pretence that she left him of her own free will. The young man is tormented with grief and rage, insults her in front of the company, and goes sorrowfully away. In the last act we are in Violetta's bedroom where the doctor tries to cheer her, but Violetta knows that she is dying. A letter from Germont *père* tells her that Alfredo has been wounded in a duel with the Baron but is recovering. Alfredo knows of the sacrifice Violetta made and has come to ask her pardon for his behaviour. The two meet in time to admit their great love for one another before Violetta dies in his arms.

HIGHLIGHTS

ACT 1 *Prelude* The tranquil opening before the gaiety of the first scene, prefiguring Violetta's death.

'Libiamo, libiamo, ne' lieti calici' ('Let's drink') Known as the *Brindisi* (drinking-song). Alfredo has just been introduced to Violetta and toasts her. She takes it up. A rollicking start to the party, it's also the best-known drinking-song in opera.

'Un dì felice' ('Happy one day') Alfredo's confession of love and Violetta's nervous reply – a duet that will haunt her.

'Ah fors' è lui ... Sempre libera' ('The one of whom I dreamed ... Ever free') Violetta left alone in contemplation wonders if Alfredo is for her and then banishes such thoughts with this dazzling *coloratura* aria.

ACT 3 *Prelude*

'Addio del passato' ('Farewell to the past') Old Germont has written to say that he will allow the union with Alfredo to take place. It's too late, though, and Violetta sings farewell to the happiness and peace she knows she will not live to enjoy.

TRISTAN UND ISOLDE
WAGNER
1865

PRONOUNCED: TRISS'-TAN OONT
EE-ZOHL'-DAH
'TRISTAN AND ISOLDE'
LIBRETTO: WAGNER

3 ACTS SET AT SEA,
KING MARK'S CASTLE IN CORNWALL
AND TRISTAN'S CASTLE IN BRITTANY
IN LEGENDARY TIMES

To musicologists and those interested in the history of music and its evolution, *Tristan und Isolde* is a seminal work. Technically, Wagner's use of chromaticism to express the themes of love and death heralded the break up of tonality and pointed the way forward to composers such as Schoenberg. It is the starting point of modern music; its very opening, the famous Prelude, breaks with previous conceptions and is not written in any definable key. The subject Wagner explores in the opera was inspired by a) the philosopher Schopenhauer, whose thoughts were permeated by the idea that in life there is no place for 'will' except in free aesthetic contemplation and that the focal point of existence lies in erotic desires; and b) Wagner's love for Mathilde Wesendonk, with whom he had a passionate affair from 1857 to 1859. He wrote *Tristan* during this period, having broken off the composition of *Siegfried*, the second opera in the *Ring* cycle, after Act 2. (He didn't get round to Act 3 for another twelve years.)

You will gather from all this that *Tristan* is not a light-hearted romp. Neither is there much in the way of dramatic action, for this is psychological music-drama. It's a hugely important and influential work, no question of that, as revolutionary in its day as Gluck's *Orpheus* was in his. The longish three acts might not be to everyone's taste – it's a matter of personal preference – but it's not an opera to be approached casually. Still, you'd have to be pretty hard of heart not to respond to, say, the great love duet in Act 2, or Isolde's final aria known as the *Liebestod*.

The bare outlines of the story reveal nothing of the inner conflicts and obsessions of the characters on stage (see also the *Ring*), but below is Wagner's framework.

❖

On the deck of a ship, Isolde (*s*), an Irish princess, attended by her friend Brangäne (*s*), is voyaging from her home to Cornwall, where she is to become the wife of King Mark (*b*). Mark has sent his nephew Tristan (*t*), a Cornish knight, to escort Isolde. Tristan is accompanied by his servant Kurwenal (*bar*).

The two protagonists have met before. Tristan once killed an Irish knight betrothed to Isolde, and she, as the only person with the remedy to cure Tristan's wounds, had nursed him back to health. Horrified to discover that she was nursing the killer of the man she loved, Isolde had been about to stab Tristan when their eyes met. They fell for each other. Now, on her way back to be the bride of the Cornish King, she realizes she is passionately in love with Tristan – and he with her. They agree that the only remedy for such a passion is poison. Instead, Brangäne gives them a love-philtre that fills them with an irresistible longing for each other.

Having arrived at King Mark's castle, the lovers meet while the King is out hunting. Kurwenal comes to warn them that the jealous courtier Melot (*t*) has spied on them, but it's too late. King Mark discovers the two together. Tristan and Melot fight and Tristan is wounded.

Kurwenal faithfully tends his wounded master and sends for Isolde to come to the castle in Brittany to heal her lover with the magic powers she possesses. At last she arrives, but the delirious Tristan tears the bandage from his wounds and dies in her arms. Brangäne had told King Mark the truth about the love-philtre. With forgiveness in his heart, Mark follows Isolde to Brittany. Kurwenal, however, thinking that the King and his men have come to storm the castle, rallies the defenders, kills Melot and is slain himself. Isolde's heart breaks and she falls lifeless on the body of Tristan.

HIGHLIGHTS
ACT 1 *Prelude*
ACT 2 *'O sink' hernieder, Nacht der Liebe'* ('Descend upon us, O night of love') The rapturous love duet of Tristan and Isolde. They sing of their hatred of day, which means separation, and of the joy of death that would give their love complete freedom.
ACT 3 *Liebestod* ('Love-Death') The name given to Isolde's final impassioned song of lament for Tristan, as ecstatic a declaration of love as has ever been written.

RECOMMENDED RECORDINGS
complete:
Flagstad/Suthaus/Thebom/Greindl
Ch of ROHCG, Philh.O,
Furtwangler
EMI CDS7 47322 8 (mono)
or: Ludwig/Dernesch/Vickers/Berry
German Opera Ch, BPO
Karajan
EMI CMS7 69319 2

IL TROVATORE

VERDI

1853

PRONOUNCED: EEL TROH-VAH-TOH-REH
'THE TROUBADOUR'
LIBRETTO: SALVATORE CAMMARANO, BASED ON THE SPANISH TRAGEDY
'EL TROVADOR' BY ANTONIO GARCIA GUTIÉRREZ
LENGTH: 2' 10"

This middle opera of Verdi's popular trilogy of the early 1850s (*Rigoletto* and *La Traviata* frame it) has a notoriously imponderable plot, and it says something for Verdi's genius as a composer that its narrative weakness has never affected its still enduring hold on audiences. The magical thing about *Il Trovatore* is that you really don't need a full understanding of what is going on in order to have a richly rewarding evening. Even by his own standards, Verdi provides a wonderfully varied musical feast. The fairly absurd (not to say confusing) events of the melodrama didn't stop it from being the most popular opera of the nineteenth century. Today, if well cast, the demanding roles of the four principal characters, provide an encyclopedic reference to the vocal arts of the mid-nineteenth century.

BACKGROUND

Verdi had had the idea of using Gutiérrez's play even before he began work on *Rigoletto*. It had been presented in Madrid for the first time only fifteen years earlier and had already acquired the status of a Spanish masterpiece. Verdi's mistress (and future wife) Giuseppina Strepponi made an Italian translation of it for him and he was immediately captivated by the story of the two lovers and the central villain – more so than by the half-mad gypsy woman, Azucena, who was to become the centre of attention in his opera. Cammarano, who'd provided the libretto for Verdi's *Luisa Miller* and for Donizetti's *Lucia di Lammermoor*, died before completing the versified story (it was completed by Leone Bardare), but in a burst of white-hot inspiration, one of the most remarkable in the history of music when the variety and invention of the score are considered, Verdi completed the piece in the amazingly short time of thirty days, between 1 and 29 November 1852.

FIRST PERFORMANCE

Teatro Apollo, Rome
19 January 1853
The audience had had to wade through water and mud to reach the theatre – the Tiber had burst its banks the same day – yet, despite increased admission prices, the house was full. The weather didn't deter the Romans from giving an immediate thumbs up to the latest Verdi and by the end of the year *Il Trovatore* had been staged in a further thirty opera houses. In Venice, three different theatres had to mount productions simultaneously to meet public demand. You could compare its success with that of an Andrew Lloyd Webber musical nowadays, for in the short period of five years, the opera had been performed on all five continents. Verdi wrote to a friend: 'If you go to the Indies or into deepest Africa you will hear *Il Trovatore*.'

STORY

4 acts set in Spain
in the 15th century

PRINCIPAL CHARACTERS
COUNT DI LUNA, a young
nobleman (bar)
FERRANDO, a captain
of his guard (b)
MANRICO, a young troubador,
supposed son of Azucena (t)
LEONORA, lady-in-waiting to the
Princess of Aragon and loved by Di
Luna and Manrico (s)
INEZ, confidante to Leonora (s)
AZUCENA, a gypsy woman
from Biscay (ms)
RUIZ, a soldier
in Manrico's service (t)

Before the story unfolds, there is a sequence of events we have to know about, and these are explained by Ferrando: the Count di Luna's younger brother was supposed to have been bewitched by an old gypsy woman when he was a baby, for which crime she was burnt alive. Seeking revenge, the gypsy's daughter, Azucena, seized the allegedly bewitched baby, meaning to throw him on the same pyre as her mother; in her confusion, however, she threw her *own* child on the flames.

Placido Domingo as Manrico in the Royal Opera House production

Thereafter, she brought up the Count's young brother as her own. Meanwhile, the old Count, hoping that his younger son was alive somewhere, charged the new Count di Luna with seeking the babe. Clear?

The young, supposedly bewitched son of the old Count, is named Manrico. In reality of course (though neither knows it), he is the Count di Luna's brother. In the gardens of the palace, the fair Leonora tells Inez of her fascination with an unknown knight, the victor of a recent tournament who has since serenaded her. They refer to

him as 'The Troubadour'. Leonora is loved by the Count di Luna. He comes to her but she mistakes him for her unknown troubadour, whose voice she hears singing. The two rivals in love fight a duel and the troubadour escapes, badly wounded.

Recovering in the gypsies' encampment, Manrico is told by

Azucena of her mother's death and is urged to avenge it. He now realizes that Azucena is not his natural mother, added to which we learn that during the duel with the Count, a strange feeling prevented him from killing his opponent when the opportunity arose. A messenger arrives to tell Manrico that by order of the Prince of Biscay, he is to command a fortress, and also that Leonora, believing him to be dead, is about to enter a convent and take the veil. Manrico rushes off to assure her that he is still alive and that he loves her. Outside the convent, he encounters Di Luna and his soldiers attempting to abduct Leonora. Manrico's forces rout Di Luna's and Leonora, on being reunited with her troubadour, decides to take the bride's veil instead of the nun's.

Believing Azucena to be a spy, Ferrando captures the gypsy woman, then recognizes her as the woman who (so all believe) cast the baby brother of the Count into the flames all those years ago. Azucena denies it and calls upon her son Manrico to help her. Manrico? The Count is delighted to have such a victim and throws her into the

torture chamber. Manrico and Leonora are about to be married in a nearby chapel when Ruiz rushes in with the news that Azucena is to be burned. Manrico hurries from the celebrations with some men to rescue her.

The rescue attempt fails. The Count condemns Manrico to death. Leonora tries to find him, hears the death knell and the voice of Manrico fron his prison cell and promises the Count that she will give herself to him if he will free Manrico. The Count is only too pleased to accept. Privately she vows to die rather than live without Manrico and she presses a poisoned ring to her lips. Manrico and Azucena comfort each other before their execution. Leonora enters, wild-eyed and dying, to tell her lover he is to be freed. When Manrico learns the terms his joy turns to frenzy, thinking that Leonora loves him no longer. The poison takes its effect and Leonora collapses in her death throes. He realizes the full extent of her sacrifice and begs her forgiveness. The Count has appeared on the threshold just in time to hear Leonora confess that she has preferred, rather than live for him, to die for Manrico. She dies and the Count orders Manrico's immediate execution, compelling Azucena to witness it from the prison window. Manrico is put to death. The half-crazed woman shrieks, 'He was your brother!' and with a last cry of 'Thou art avenged, O mother!', she sinks to the ground, leaving the Count to realize with horror what he has done.

HIGHLIGHTS

ACT 1 *'Tacea la notte placida'* ('Peaceful was the night') Leonora tells Inez of her gallant knight at the tournament.

ACT 2 *'La Zingarella'*.('The gypsy girl') This is the famous Anvil Chorus, one of the best of the whole genre. What are the gypsies singing about? Not one in a thousand could tell you, yet this is an evergreen 'pop classic'. In fact, the gypsies are forging weapons on their anvil, thinking of all those gypsy girls who cheer their ceaseless hard work.

'Stride la vampa!' ('The flames are roaring') Azucena tells the story of her mother's terrible execution.

ACT 3 *'Ah, sì, ben mio coll' essere'* ('Ah, yes, you're mine') Leonora and Manrico, waiting to be married, sing this love duet.

'Di quella pira' ('From that dread pyre') The thrilling aria in which Manrico vents his rage and horror before the attempted rescue of his mother. A favourite *tour de force* of all tenors, ending with a long top C (which Verdi didn't write, but so what – it's just what's needed before one rescues one's mother).

ACT 4 *'D'amor sull' ali rosee'* ('On the rosy wings of love') Leonora sings outside the prison where, unknown to her, Manrico is held. It's followed immediately by ...

Miserere At one time this was the most popular tune from any opera. A chorus from within the prison chants the doleful theme, against which are set Leonora's heart-broken cries and Manrico's voice from his cell. Old hat it may be, but it works every time.

'Ai nostri monti' ('Home to our mountains') In their prison cell, mother and son sing this duet, another one of opera's 'top hits', in which the fierce old gypsy dreams of the happy days and the mountains where she brought up Manrico.

TURANDOT
PUCCINI
1926

PRONOUNCED: TOO'-RAN-DOT
LIBRETTO: GIUSEPPE ADAMI AND
RENATO SIMONI
BASED ON THE FAIRY TALE BY
CARLO GOZZI

3 ACTS SET IN PEKING
IN LEGENDARY TIMES

*Dame Eva Turner as Turandot –
One of her most famous roles*

Despite its ubiquitous hit aria, *Turandot* is by no means as accessible as Puccini's earlier operas. Of its composition, Puccini confessed to Adami while he was writing the work that 'All the music I have written before seems a joke and is no longer to my taste', and those expecting the sounds of **Tosca** or **La Bohème** are in for a surprise. He uses more features from contemporary music than any of his other works, including extreme dissonance, polytonal vocal and orchestral passages, and incorporates a number of authentic Chinese motifs into the score. It is not all pretty arias. That said, it provides one of the most powerful and effective evenings you can spend in an opera house. Just as Massenet's success with the story of **Manon** had not dissuaded him from producing his own version, so Busoni's 1917 *Turandot*, using the same fairy tale, did not stop him from creating this exotic and original work. (There had been at least ten other operas on the same subject written over the previous century, none of which made an impression.)

❖

Turandot (*s*) is the bewitching daughter of Altoum (*t*), the Emperor of China. She will marry any man of royal blood who can answer three riddles, but he who fails to answer correctly will have to suffer the penalty – and the penalty is death. The latest suitor, a Persian prince, has failed and his execution is announced to a large crowd. In the crowd are Timur (*b*), the exiled blind King of Tartary, and the slave girl Liù (*s*) who helped him to escape. There, too, is Calaf (*t*), Timur's son, believed to have died in battle. Liù is secretly in love with Calaf (he smiled at her one day in the palace), but when Calaf sees Turandot appear to sanction the present execution, he is immediately smitten and sets out to win her. Three courtiers, Ping (*bar*), Pang (*t*) and Pong (*t*), try in vain to dissuade him – so do his father and Liù – but Calaf sounds the gong, the signal that another suitor has arrived.

Ping, Pang and Pong reflect on the state of China under the cruel Turandot, while, in the next scene, the Princess herself tells the court the reason for her vow: thousands of years previously an ancestress was dishonoured and killed by a barbarian king and this is her revenge. Calaf answers the riddles correctly, one by one. Turandot is humiliated at the prospect of having to marry the son of a foreign slave and begs her father to

Puccini died before he could finish Turandot. It was the conductor Arturo Toscanini who suggested that the score be completed by Franco Alfano (1876–1954) and it is Alfano's work (based on Puccini's notes) we hear after Liù's funeral music dies away and the crowd leaves. This is the version that was played at La Scala for the dress rehearsal. At the premiere on 25 April 1926, however, Toscanini, in a famous gesture, came to the end of the score Puccini had been able to complete himself, put down his baton and turned to the audience. 'At this point death forced Giacomo Puccini to break off this work.' The audience left in silence.

After the first night, cuts sanctioned by Toscanini were introduced and it was not until a concert performance at London's Barbican in 1982 that the full Alfano ending was heard again.

The premiere of Turandot nearly didn't happen at all. Mussolini was in Milan for a Fascist rally and let it be known that he would attend the La Scala premiere if the Fascist hymn 'Giovinezza' preceded the performance. Toscanini's reply was brief: either Turandot would be performed without the Fascist hymn, or they could look for another conductor. Il Duce stayed away.

be released from the vow. Her father replies that it is sacred, but Calaf offers to withdraw, as though he had not answered correctly, even forfeiting his life, *if* she can discover his name by the morning.

Turandot decrees no one shall sleep until the unknown prince's name is known, while Calaf, confident of winning her, imagines his first kisses with Turandot. Timur and Liù are brought before Turandot and Liù declares that she alone knows the Prince's name. She is tortured but still refuses to tell. Turandot demands to know what gives her the courage not to betray the name. 'Princess,' she replies, 'it is love.' Unable to take more torture, Liù seizes a dagger and stabs herself. Calaf reproaches Turandot for her cruelty and then kisses her passionately. The ice maiden melts and confesses that she's loved him from the start. Calaf likewise throws caution to the wind, says he will die for her and – tells her his name. He is Calaf, the son of Timur. The cold-blooded Princess seems to have returned for she cries from her throne that she has won. She has discovered the stranger's name. To the assembled court she announces it. His name is Love.

HIGHLIGHTS

ACT 2 *'In questa reggia'* ('In this same palace') In this spine-tingling aria of thrilling effect, Turandot describes how one of her forebears was cruelly abducted. The historic recording of this made by Eva Turner in 1929 is among the finest of all opera recordings.

ACT 3 *'Nessun dorma'* ('None shall sleep') At night, in the garden of the palace, Calaf relishes the moment when he will tell Turandot his secret. The penultimate note, a high B natural, which Pavarotti *et*

al. take delight in holding for as long as they can, with undeniable effect (*'vin*-cer'*-o!'*), was not written by Puccini. He wrote the penultimate note as a short semi-quaver. Whatever, every composer since then wishes he'd written this (justly) favourite aria.

RECOMMENDED RECORDINGS

complete: Nilsson/Corelli /Scotto
Rome Opera Ch & O
Molinari-Pradelli
EMI CMS7 69327
highlights: Caballé/Carreras/Freni
Rhine Opera Ch, Strasbourg PO
Lombard
EMI CDM7 63410
or: (excerpts)
Turner/Martinelli/Albanese
ROHCH Ch, LPO, Barbirolli
EMI CDH7 61074 (mono)

WERTHER
JULES MASSENET
1892
PRONOUNCED: VAIR'-TUH
LIBRETTO: EDOUARD BLAU, PAUL MILLIET AND GEORGES HARTMANN
BASED ON 'DIE LEIDEN DES JUNGEN WERTHERS' ('THE SORROWS OF YOUNG WERTHER') BY GOETHE

3 ACTS SET IN WETZLAR NEAR FRANKFURT IN 1780

A 'sugary cake', said one critic, 'but baked by a high-class confectioner.' *Werther* was a huge success for the composer in its day, and though its hyper-romantic theme may be too much for today's cynical age, it is Massenet's most melodic score.

❖

The story takes place just before Christmas. The young poet Werther (*t*) is enchanted with Charlotte (*ms*):

the vision of her dispensing a supper of bread and butter to her brothers and sisters captivates him. She returns his love but tells him that she is betrothed to Albert (*bar*). He leaves in despair, returning months later to find Charlotte married. Again he declares his love for her. She tries to persuade him to forget her and never return again; he writes a note asking for Albert's pistols, saying he wants them 'for a long journey'. The gloomily jealous Albert insists that Charlotte hands over the pistols to Werther's servant. Charlotte runs to Werther's room, but is too late: he lies mortally wounded. Just as he dies, Charlotte, now an accomplice in his suicide, confesses she has loved him from the start. In the distance, children are singing Christmas carols …

HIGHLIGHT

ACT 3 *'Pourquoi me réveiller'* ('Why awaken me') Known as Ossian's Song, Werther reads one of the famous poet's verses and in doing so realizes they reflect his own despairing love.

RECOMMENDED RECORDINGS

complete: Domingo/ Obraztsova
RSO, Chailly
DG 403 304
highlights: Kraus/Troyanos
LPO, Plasson
EMI CDM7 63936

Thackeray sent up Goethe's virtuous Charlotte with:

Charlotte, having seen his body
Borne before her on a shutter,
Like a well-conducted person,
Went on cutting bread and butter.

THE COMPOSERS

*'If an opera cannot be played by an
organ grinder – as Puccini and Verdi's
melodies were played – then that opera
is not going to achieve immortality'*

SIR THOMAS BEECHAM, 1879 ~ 1961

AUBER
DANIEL FRANÇOIS ESPRIT
1782 ~ 1871
FRENCH COMPOSER

Fabulously successful during his lifetime but now almost entirely forgotten except for the jolly overtures to some of his operas – which is how he justifies his place here.

He wrote some forty operas, mostly *opéras comiques*, many of them with Eugène Scribe, a partnership which was as fruitful as that of **Gilbert and Sullivan**. He was a kind of French **Rossini**, much admired by contemporaries, including **Wagner**. Though Wagner later compared Auber's lighter vein to 'the work of a barber who lathers but forgets to shave', his *Lohengrin* was influenced by Auber's most enduring work *La Muette de Portici* (The Dumb Girl of Portici) otherwise known as *Masaniello*, the first French **grand opera**. With its political libretto, the 1830 Brussels première of *La Muette* sparked off the revolt against the Dutch that eventually led to Belgium's independence from Holland.

Strangely, Auber never listened to performances of his own work. Even so ...

THE BEST OF AUBER'S OPERAS AND WHAT TO LISTEN TO

Fra Diavolo Overture and the Serenade from Act 3, '*Pour toujours*'.
Le Cheval de Bronze Overture.
Les Diamants de la Couronne Overture.
Le Domino Noir Overture.
La Muette de Portici Overture and the *Barcarole* from Act 2.

BEETHOVEN
LUDWIG VAN
1770 ~ 1827
GERMAN COMPOSER

Although he made sketches for other operas, the only one Beethoven completed was *Fidelio*. For one of the giants of music to have contributed but a single work to the genre is explained by the fact that he found it difficult – difficult to find the right libretto (not for him the fashionable *buffo* stories, magic plots or social satires), difficult to compose (the number of different versions of *Fidelio* confirms that), and difficult to find the right way of expressing himself (the introduction to Florestan's **aria** at the beginning of Act 2, for example, was changed eighteen times before he settled on its final form). Compared to some of the Italians, Beethoven was not a natural opera writer and *Fidelio*, with all its strengths, is as much a staged celebration of the ideals of heroism and political liberation as it is an opera.

VINCENZO
BELLINI

B. CATANIA, 3 NOV. 1801~ D. PUTEAUX, 23 SEPT. 1835

'Long, long melodies, such as no one has ever written before'
VERDI

In his short life and career, Bellini changed the face of Italian opera and laid the foundations for the later work of **Verdi** and **Puccini**, who, for many, represent the high points of the art. Before Bellini, Italian opera composers put vocal display first and dramatic content a very definite second. Bellini didn't exactly give his singers enormous acting challenges, but he did for the first time match the emotion in the music to the moments when the characters and the story development required it. Singers were now asked to act in character *and* sing like birds, not that the vocal lines he gave them were less ornate – far from it. Few have ever composed such brilliant, agile music for the voice, nor such long-breathed, decorated phrases. Bellini's writing epitomizes the Italian *bel canto* style of singing and it had a strong influence on both Berlioz and Chopin, who was his close friend. (Some of Chopin's writing for the piano – the slow movements of his Sonatas and some of his Nocturnes for example – are Bellini arias for the keyboard.)

Like Chopin, Bellini was slim and aristocratic-looking, suffered from the same fashionable disease of tuberculosis and died young (of dysentery). He wrote only ten operas of which *Norma* and *La Sonnambula* are generally agreed to be his greatest works, though *I Capuleti e i Montecchi* has some of his most beautiful music and *I Puritani* his most brilliant vocal demands.

THE BEST OF BELLINI'S OPERAS AND WHAT TO LISTEN TO

I Capuleti e i Montecchi (1830).
La Sonnambula (1830).
Norma (1831).
Beatrice di Tenda (1833).
I Puritani (1835).

GEORGES
BIZET

B. PARIS, 25 OCTOBER 1838 ~ D. BOUGIVAL, 3 JUNE 1875

'I would go to the ends of the earth to embrace the composer of Carmen*'*
BRAHMS

Bizet (whose baptismal name was Alexandre-César-Léopold – a good trick question for any opera buff) was the son of professional musicians, his father a singing teacher, his mother a fine pianist. Remembered today solely as the composer of *Carmen*, one of the greatest of all operas, it's usually forgotten that he began his musical career as a child prodigy on the piano, entering the Paris Conservatoire when he was only nine. (His *Jeux d'Enfants* is probably still the most popular suite for piano duet ever written.) His first symphony was written at the age of seventeen and when it was unearthed in 1933, it proved to be as joyfully vivacious and captivating as any other seventeen-year-old's (**Mozart's**, for instance, or Mendelssohn's). With his natural talent, he soon attracted attention.

Bizet was a plump young man with a short temper and an addiction to chocolate, cakes and *petits fours*, always elegantly dressed, and always nibbling. In 1869 he married the daughter of Halévy, composer of *La Juive*, an immensely popular opera at the time, and his old professor at the Conservatoire. (Geneviève Bizet was later the model for Proust's Princesse de Guermantes.)

At a superficial glance, it might seem that Bizet's short career (he died from heart failure at the age of thirty-six) did not produce the number of masterpieces that might have been expected from someone with his gifts and auspicious beginning. None of his operas was a huge success while he was alive and he was easily discouraged. With the notable exception of *Carmen*, they all suffer from poor libretti and are rarely produced, although, because of Bizet's melodic power, individual numbers are still popular. It was cruel that he should die so soon after completing the first work of his maturity, a work that showed the way forward for French opera and included many diverse, original touches. In *Carmen*, Bizet attempted what **Mussorgsky** was seeking to do in his own Russian way: the portrayal of real life on the stage, tackling complex emotions and powerful action with truth and passion. Indeed, many see *Carmen* as the first *verismo* opera. A longer life might have led Bizet to revolutionize opera in France; it has

It's unusual for other composers to come out in force in praise of one of their number, but Bizet's gifts were commented on favourably by three geniuses who rarely agreed about anything. Bizet united Wagner ('Here, thank God, at last for a change, is somebody with ideas in his head'), Tchaikovsky (who adored the opera) and Brahms.

been said that his early death was the biggest blow to French music in the whole of the nineteenth century.

THE BEST OF BIZET'S OPERAS AND WHAT TO LISTEN TO

Les Pêcheurs de Perles (1863). *'Au fond du temple saint'* ('In the depths of the temple') from Act 1 is the famous **tenor–baritone** duet in which Nadir and Zurga recall the love they both once had for the beautiful Leïla. (See **Björling**.)
La Jolie Fille de Perth (1867). Loosely based on the novel by Sir Walter Scott, it contains the popular *Serenade* (Act 2), long a concert favourite with tenors.
Djamileh (1872). A favourite work of Mahler's.
Carmen (1873–4) (see p31)
Also *Orchestral Suites 1 and 2*

BOITO, ARRIGO
1842 ~ 1918
ITALIAN COMPOSER
AND LIBRETTIST.

In an art form where the name of the person who wrote the words and/or book of an opera is always forgotten (Gilbert and Sullivan being the exception), the name of Boito looms large. He wrote the libretti for **Verdi's Otello** and *Falstaff* and **Ponchielli's** *La Gioconda*, as well as translating

other people's operas – *Der Freischütz*, *Rienzi*, **Tristan und Isolde** and *Russlan and Ludmilla*, for example. He was also a composer in his own right and his *Mefistofele* held its own in the repertoire for some time.

BORODIN
ALEXANDER
1833 ~ 1887
RUSSIAN COMPOSER

The illegitimate son of a Georgian prince, Borodin spoke several languages fluently, played the flute and piano proficiently and became a doctor of

---

BRITTEN, BENJAMIN
1913 ~ 1976
ENGLISH COMPOSER

The most important and original contribution to opera by a British composer this century was made by Britten. He chose his texts well with Maupassant, Melville, Shakespeare, Henry James and Thomas Mann providing a basis for five of the collaborations he made with such librettists as Eric Crozier, Ronald Duncan and Myfanwy Piper. He was as successful at tragedy (**Peter Grimes**, *Billy Budd* and *Death in Venice*) as he was at comedy (*Albert Herring*) and the supernatural (*The Turn of the Screw*). Of necessity he scored sparingly, as few as twelve performers on occasion, thus enabling small groups to perform his work outside the confines of the opera house. However, his inventive orchestration put no limits on the rich variety of texture he achieved and one characteristic of Britten's operas are the orchestral interludes that form part of the entertainment.

chemistry. He also found time to compose music. He was one of the protagonists of the new nationalistic Russian school, making particularly effective use of the exotic oriental influences popular at the time, which came from Asiatic Russian folk music. These can be heard to great effect in his unfinished masterpiece *Prince Igor* written between 1869–70 and 1874–87 – Borodin composed slowly. His friends Glazunov and Rimsky-Korsakov finished the work. The musical *Kismet* features songs – 'Baubles, Bangles and Beads', 'This is my beloved', 'Stranger in Paradise' – using themes borrowed from Borodin.

In 1948 Britten, with his partner the tenor **Peter Pears**, founded in his own home town the Aldeburgh Festival, still an important contribution to the nation's cultural life. He was only fifty-two when he was awarded the Order of Merit, Britain's highest (and rarely given) civilian honour; when he was created Lord Britten of Aldeburgh in June 1976, just six months before he died at the age of sixty-three, he was the first composer to be elevated to the peerage.

GAETANO
DONIZETTI

B. BERGAMO, 29 NOVEMBER 1797 ~ D. BERGAMO, 8 APRIL 1848

'When he chose to take the trouble, he was capable of attaining remarkable heights'
CECIL GRAY

An amazingly prolific composer, Donizetti produced twelve string quartets, and seven masses, as well as motets, psalm settings, cantatas, songs, piano music – and seventy operas. Such a facility was both a strength and a weakness; the music simply poured out but too often uncritically. Sometimes he would write three or four operas a year and was said to have sketched and written the last act of *La Favorita* in a few hours. The titles of some, unperformed for years, certainly intrigue: *Alfredo il Grande*; *Alina, Regina di Golconda*; *Elisabetta o Il castello di Kenilworth*; *Imelda de' Lambertazzi*; *Rosmonda d'Inghilterra*. To say nothing of the (since revived) *Emilia di Liverpool*.

The son of a weaver turned pawnbroker, he determined, at an early age, that he would write opera, and his first success was in 1818, when he was twenty-one years old, with *Enrico di Borgogna*. This first period, while he was still finding his own voice, was dedicated to comedies in the Rossini manner. With *Anna Bolena* (1830) he found his own style and wrote a string of successes, some sentimental and tragic, others witty and subtle, three of which remain among the most popular of all

operas still performed today: *Lucia di Lammermoor, Don Pasquale* and *L'Elisir d'amore*. Thanks to the championing of such singers as **Joan Sutherland**, **Maria Callas** and **Montserrat Caballé**, others have returned to the repertoire after some years of neglect: *La*

Favorita, Anna Bolena and *La Fille du Régiment*.

Donizetti understood what makes good theatre, he knew what appealed to audiences and he was also a practical musician. He appreciated the benefits of writing for the particular talents of certain singers and it was the vocal opportunities he gave them (especially his **sopranos**) that helped keep his work so popular: Donizetti's **arias** make a singer look good. Some critics emphasize the uncritical fecundity of his output instead of acknowledging the works of a true genius; for only a genius in complete control of his craft could have written the sextet from *Lucia* and more memorable tunes in a lifetime than is one man's right. Even more than his two contemporaries, Bellini and Rossini, Donizetti exerted a profound influence on other composers, especially the young Verdi.

Donizetti was one of those rare individuals who seems to have been well liked by all who came into contact with him, a man without, it is said, the least trace of jealousy or viciousness. He never got over the death in 1837 of his adored wife.

Sir Charles Hallé (1819–95), the German-born conductor and founder of the Manchester orchestra, met Donizetti in Paris now and then in 1840 and 1841 and found him 'A most distinguished, amiable, and fashionable gentleman, as elegant as most of his music. He was young still, but such a prolific composer that at the time he had already written

*upwards of forty operas. I remember talking to him about Rossini, and asking if he had really written **Barbiere** in a fortnight. "Oh, I quite believe it," said he, "he has always been such a lazy fellow!" I confess that I looked with wonder and admiration at a man who considered that to spend a whole fortnight over the composition of an opera was a waste of time.'*

In 1845, after periodic bouts of violent headaches, depressions and hallucinations, he suffered a paralytic stroke and, suffering from syphilis, slowly went insane.

THE BEST OF DONIZETTI'S OPERAS AND WHAT TO LISTEN TO

Emilia di Liverpool (1824).
Anna Bolena (1830).
L'Elisir d'amore (1832) (see p41).
Lucrezia Borgia (1833).
Maria Stuarda (1834).
Lucia di Lammermoor (1835) (see p56).
Roberto Devereux (1837).
La Fille du Régiment (1840).
La Favorita (1840) (see p44).
Linda di Chamounix (1842) Includes the soprano show-piece, 'O, luce di quest' anima' ('O guiding star of love') from Act 1.
Don Pasquale (1843) (see p40).

GERSHWIN GEORGE
1898 ~ 1937
AMERICAN COMPOSER

'I have more tunes in my head than I can write down in a lifetime'
GERSHWIN

The composer of *Rhapsody in Blue* and some of the finest popular songs ever written wrote one opera. *Porgy and Bess* is a masterpiece.

Gershwin, born Jacob Gershvin in Brooklyn, had his first hit when he was twenty – 'Swanee' sold over 2,250,000 copies. By the time he started writing *Porgy* in 1933 he was among the most successful and prolific of popular songwriters ('I Got Rhythm', 'Someone To Watch Over Me', 'The Man I Love', 'Fascinating Rhythm', ' 'S Wonderful', 'A Foggy Day', 'Love Is Here To Stay' and dozens of other standards), as well as attracting attention from the serious musical establishment for such works as *An American in Paris* and his Piano Concerto in F (still the most performed American concerto).

Gershwin's musical growth throughout his tragically short career is inspiring. His earliest pieces rely on ragtime and jazz; these he combined with his increasing interest in the blues, charged with his rhythmic vitality, melodic genius and, later, with a thorough understanding of classical orchestration, harmony and counterpoint. Had he lived, there's no doubt that Gershwin, more than any other composer working at the time, could have achieved that (still) unattained fusion of classical and popular music in an ideal marriage.

He was working in Hollywood on the score of *Goldwyn Follies* when he began experiencing blackouts and excruciating headaches. A brain tumour was detected too late to be operable and he died at the age of thirty-eight.

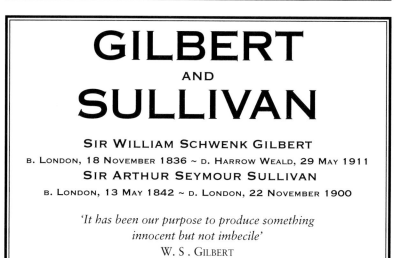

GILBERT
AND
SULLIVAN

SIR WILLIAM SCHWENK GILBERT
B. LONDON, 18 NOVEMBER 1836 ~ D. HARROW WEALD, 29 MAY 1911
SIR ARTHUR SEYMOUR SULLIVAN
B. LONDON, 13 MAY 1842 ~ D. LONDON, 22 NOVEMBER 1900

'It has been our purpose to produce something innocent but not imbecile'
W. S . GILBERT

The only partnership in the history of opera and operetta in which the librettist's name is mentioned in the same breath as the composer's. Not only that, but the librettist is always billed *before* the composer! To the average music lover, who can name any number of opera *composers*, W. S. Gilbert is the only librettist they can readily recall.

Gilbert and Sullivan worked together like a horse and carriage, though they were like chalk and cheese, the classic balance of a creative partnership. Although he had the (mis)fortune of writing a popular hit, 'The Lost Chord', and also the tune of 'Onward, Christian Soldiers', Sullivan – 'Queen Victoria's favourite composer' – was a serious musician who enjoyed a frivolous social life. Gilbert was frivolous in his art but was immensely serious in his social life.

The two first collaborated in 1871 on the operetta *Thespis* (now lost), but it was not until three years later that the impresario Richard D'Oyly Carte persuaded them to work together again. The result was *Trial by Jury*, a one-acter written to precede **Offenbach's** *La*

Périchole. In 1881, after the successes of *The Sorcerer, HMS Pinafore* and *The Pirates of Penzance,* D'Oyly Carte built the Savoy Theatre specially to stage their works, and the three of them began the series of operettas which became known as the *Savoy Operas.* (Why they are not known as the *Savoy Operettas* is a moot point.) The stars who played in them, often for many years, were known as Savoyards.

Gilbert's lyrics are still among the most brilliant and inventive of any ever written and later writers from Noël Coward downwards have acknowledged Gilbert's influence on their work. His patter songs, comic verse, ingenious plots and razor-sharp targets have rarely been equalled. Sullivan, though he hated to admit it, was never so inspired as when working with Gilbert's material. He himself was an immensely gifted musician of no great originality but his ability to parody or extract the essence of another's style for his own ends made him the perfect match for his partner. He also happened to be one of music's greatest melodists. Like **Rossini, Johann Strauss II** and **Offenbach,** whose musical styles he plundered mercilessly, Sullivan could not help but write hummable tunes. Everyone, whether in the opera house or the bath, likes singing them.

THE COMPLETE OPERAS OF GILBERT AND SULLIVAN AND WHAT TO LISTEN TO

Thespis (1871).
Trial by Jury (1875)
'When I, good friends, was called to the Bar'. Sullivan was so amused by Gilbert's courtroom satire that he set to work immediately and finished the score in three weeks.

The Sorcerer (1877)
'Time was when love and I were well acquainted'; 'My name is John Wellington Wells'. The first full-length G & S introduced the character of John Wellington Wells, the sorcerer of the title and the prototype of many similar characters to come. He administers a love potion to the villagers of Ploverleigh that makes them fall in love with the first person they see after they next awake.
HMS Pinafore (1878)
'I'm called Little Buttercup'; 'I am the Captain of the Pinafore*'; 'I am the monarch of the sea'; 'When I was a lad I served a term'; 'Never mind the why and wherefore'.* One of the strongest Sullivan scores with a story revolving around Captain Corcoran's daughter Josephine, who refuses to marry Sir Joseph Porter, First Lord of the Admiralty, because she is in love with humble sailor Ralph Rackstraw. Unusually, this was premièred in New York, not London.
The Pirates of Penzance (1879)
'Poor Wand'ring One'; 'I am the

very model of a modern Major-General'; 'When a felon's not engaged in his employment'; 'With cat-like tread'; 'Come friends, who plough the seas'. Most people know this last tune with different words: in 1908, someone in America pinched it and gave it the title 'Hail! Hail! the gang's all here'. Among the best of the series. G & S had been suffering from pirated versions of their work in the United States and so, having finished the work in America, *The Pirates* was first produced at the Royal Bijou Theatre, Paignton in Devon. This gave it UK copyright protection and prevented *The Pirates* from being pirated. It was then given in New York, four months before its London première.
Patience (1881)
'Twenty lovesick maidens we'; 'If you want a receipt for that popular mystery', one of Gilbert's most elaborate patter songs; *'When I first put this uniform on'; 'If you're anxious for to shine'; 'Prithee pretty maiden'; 'A magnet hung in a hardware shop'; 'A Waterloo House young man'.* A send-up of the aesthetic movement of the day as personified by Oscar Wilde, but it still works on its own terms. Well worth a listen.
Iolanthe (1882)
Overture – perhaps Sullivan's best; *'When I went to the Bar'; 'When all night long a chap remains'; 'When Britain really ruled the waves'; 'When you're lying awake with a dismal headache'* – the patter song known as *The Nightmare Song.* Gilbert's targets here are the House of Lords and the Lord Chancellor, who opposes the marriage of his ward Phyllis to Strephon, son of Iolanthe, who is a fairy who's fallen for Private Wills of the Grenadier Guards … It all gets sorted out in the end.

Princess Ida (1884)
A rather ponderous satire on the feminist movement. Not one of their best.

The Mikado (1885) (see p 76).

Ruddigore (1887) *'Happily coupled are we'*; *'My eyes are fully open ... It doesn't matter, matter, matter, matter, matter!'* Subtitled 'The Witch's Curse', this was G & S's crack at the supernatural. Originally entitled *Ruddygore* (considered a trifle coarse), it was a relative failure.

The Yeomen of the Guard (1888) *Overture*; *'I have a song to sing-o'*; *'Oh! a private buffoon is a light-hearted loon'*; *'A man who would woo a fair young maid'*; *'When a wooer goes a-wooing'*. This is the most serious of the collaborations and was hailed as 'a genuine English opera' after its triumphant opening. Still mightily popular with amateur companies, its plot rivals any of the Italian operas for complexity. Set in Elizabethan England, it concerns Colonel Fairfax, under sentence of death in the Tower, and his search for a sorceress bride who will save him from execution. Jack Point and Elsie Maynard, two strolling players, save the day.

The Gondoliers (1889) (see p51).

Utopia Limited (1893)
Not a good one. *'Utopia'* is Britain run as a British limited liability company.

The Grand Duke (1896)
The last of the line and a failure. The Duke loses his title through a type of duel with playing-cards.

GLASS, PHILIP
B. 1937
AMERICAN COMPOSER

A minimalist.

GLUCK
CHRISTOPH WILLIBALD VON
1714 ~ 1787
GERMAN COMPOSER

'There is no musical rule that I have not willingly sacrificed to dramatic effect'
GLUCK

'Gluck'. Such an unmusical sound and a name that inevitably leads to mention of (oh no) 'opera history'. But his music is far from dry and academic. His most famous opera (in fact the only one out of roughly fifty that still receives regular productions) is **Orfeo ed Euridice**, the mythological story of Orpheus and Eurydice. In terms of the development of opera as an art form, *Orfeo* is important as the first of Gluck's six so-called 'reform operas'. 'Reform' because Gluck, having had a successful and steady career as a composer and conductor, was inspired by the poet and librettist Ranieri Calzabigi to make radical changes in the presentation of opera (see p.80).

Gluck had the right temperament for the job. Short and stocky, he was tough, grasping, dictatorial (he could have been a model for the Italian conductor Arturo Toscanini as far as his treatment of musicians was concerned) and enjoyed the same gruff, independent spirit as **Beethoven**. Tact was not his strong point and he had an explosive temper. If he upset people, no matter; he knew what he wanted and was determined to get his own way.

Gluck's music is chaste, elegant and pure – a perfect counterpoint to the classical themes he set to music.

THE BEST OF GLUCK'S OPERAS AND WHAT TO LISTEN TO

Orfeo ed Euridice (1762) (see p80).

Alceste (1767) *'Divinités du Styx'* ('Gods of the Styx') Alcestis has chosen to die in the place of her husband, Admetus, and sings this aria defying the powers of death.

Paride ed Elena (1770) *'O del mio dolce ardor'* ('O thou belov'd') This ravishingly lovely aria (originally written for a **castrato**) is sung by Paris as he arrives in Greece, happy in the knowledge that he will soon be with his Helen.

GOUNOD
CHARLES FRANÇOIS
1818 ~ 1893
FRENCH COMPOSER

To opera buffs, Gounod means *Faust* and *Roméo et Juliette* (one of several operatic encounters with the tragic couple); to those who think they don't know a note of Gounod, it comes as a surprise to find that he wrote (or at least co-wrote!) one of the most frequently requested classical 'pops'. He took the first prelude from J. S. Bach's *The Well-tempered Clavier* (a collection of forty-eight preludes and fugues) and added a tune for solo violin (1853). Six years later someone set the words of the *Ave Maria* to it.

The son of an unsuccessful artist who died when Gounod was four, he picked up draftsmanship and music from his talented mother. Later, after studying at the Paris Conservatoire and winning the prestigious *Prix de Rome*, he became fascinated by theology and more than once thought of entering the Church. (He never did, though, like Liszt, he affected semi-clerical garb at times and called himself '*Abbé*'.) His marriage to the daughter of one of the piano teachers at the Conservatoire effectively ended his dreams of the priesthood and, in a later tussle with flesh and the devil (Gounod was known in some quarters as 'the philandering monk'), he seduced the wife of Captain Weldon, in whose London house he was staying. (He lived in England for the duration of the Franco–Prussian War, from 1870 to 1875.) He eventually tired of her, returned to Paris and was billed $50,000 by Mrs Weldon for three years' board and lodging.

Gounod wrote thirteen operas in all. Before *Faust* (1859) he had only failures; after *Faust* he was the most famous composer in France and spent the rest of his life trying to write another to equal it. He never did, despite his own favourite, *La Reine de Saba* (1862), *Mireille* (1864) and the relative success of *Roméo et Juliette* (1867). His *Messe Solonelle Sainte-Cécile* is worth a listen, but otherwise Gounod after 1870 was rather as Tennyson described himself: 'The greatest master of English living with nothing to say'.

HANDEL
GEORGE FRIDERIC
1685 ~ 1759
GERMAN-ENGLISH COMPOSER

The *Water Music*, the *Royal Fireworks* and *Messiah* – these are the popular works of Handel regularly heard today in their entirety. He also wrote about forty-six operas. Very few are given performances now, although he has recently enjoyed a revival, notably with productions of *Julius Caesar* and *Xerxes* by the English National Opera. However, the stumbling blocks for a first-time listener are the acres of **recitative** giving the plot and story-line (often pretty silly at that). They are worth discovering, however, for the **arias**, which are usually of quite ravishing beauty. As Handel wrote most of his male roles for **castrati**, they are sung today by women in trousers or by **counter-tenors**.

THE BEST OF HANDEL'S OPERAS AND WHAT TO LISTEN TO

Acis and Galatea (1720) *Overture*; *'Love in her eyes sits playing'*; *'Ruddier than the cherry'*; *'As when the dove'*. Strictly speaking a 'masque'.
Rodelinda (1725) *'Dove sei'* ('Art thou troubled?') especially sung by Kathleen Ferrier.
Ptolemy (1728) *'Non lo dirò col labbro'* ('Silent Worship') Among the most touching of all lovers' arias.
Atalanta (1736) *'Care selve'* ('Come beloved').
Berenice (1737) *Minuet*.
Xerxes (1738) *'Ombra mai fu'*. A favourite classical pop known universally as 'Handel's Largo' – though the music says *'larghetto'*!

HUMPERDINCK
ENGELBERT
1854 ~ 1921
GERMAN COMPOSER

He really didn't deserve to have his unlikely name usurped by the sentimental pop singer Gerry Dorsey. The original Mr Humperdinck was a prodigiously talented student famous now for just one work. In fact he hadn't written very much before **Hänsel und Gretel** and was never able to repeat its success.

JANÁČEK, LEOŠ
PRONOUNCED: YAN'-ER-CHECK
1854 ~ 1928
CZECH COMPOSER

To most people the name of Janáček doesn't mean a thing; it's not one up there in the immortal pantheon alongside Beethoven, Brahms *et al*. Yet the sound world he created in his music is as individual in its way as that of Debussy or Stravinsky. He used folk music and the inspiration of Nature, but most importantly, he adapted the abrupt speech patterns of his native Lachian dialect into musical phrases. There is much declaiming rather than singing, with the orchestra taking what melody there is. He invented his own harmonies and worked out an unconventional style of composition that really is completely original. He is both a romantic of the last century and a modernist of the twentieth.

The extraordinary thing about Janáček is that he wrote no music of any significance until he was forty and remained in Brno in complete obscurity until he was over sixty. A chance visit to the town by a music lover led to his opera *Jenůfa* being performed in Prague – twelve years after it was first produced in Brno. Overnight, Janáček found himself famous.

THE BEST OF JANÁČEK'S OPERAS AND WHAT TO LISTEN TO

Jenůfa (1904).
The Excursions of Mr Brouček (1920).
Katya Kabanova (1921).
The Cunning Little Vixen (1924).
The Makropoulos Affair (1926).
From the House of the Dead (1930).

LEHÁR, FRANZ
1870 ~ 1948
AUSTRO-HUNGARIAN COMPOSER

Johann Strauss II's musical heir, Lehár took the Viennese operetta into the twentieth century, giving it a blend of nostalgia and sophisticated humour, wit and irony that perfectly suited the audiences of turn-of-the-century Europe. And, like his predecessor, the tunes came tumbling out. One of these was a waltz he wrote

Franz Lehár

early in his career (1899), the 'Gold and Silver' waltz. Today it is invariably included in 'Your Hundred Best Tunes' compilations, and is just one of the large output of songs and orchestral pieces he wrote before the theatre came to dominate his life. Although he had some operatic success as early as 1896, it was his greatest and most enduring triumph, *The Merry Widow* (1905), that made him internationally famous.

After the First World War, when the pretty, privileged society of Vienna disappeared for ever, Lehár's popularity declined, but was revived partly by the championship of the tenor **Richard Tauber**. Lehár subsequently wrote his works with his principal singer in mind. Though no less melodic, his later plots tended to end unhappily.

THE BEST OF LEHÁR'S OPERETTAS AND WHAT TO LISTEN TO

The Merry Widow (*DIE LUSTIGE WITWE*, 1905) (see p70).
Der Graf von Luxembourg ('THE COUNT OF LUXEMBOURG', 1909) *'Love breaks every bond'*; *'A carnival for life'*; *'Say not love is a dream'*.
Frasquita (1922) *'Farewell, my love, farewell'* (Serenade).
Paganini (1925) *'Girls were made to love and kiss'*.
Friederike (1928) *'O maiden, my maiden'*.
Das Land des Lächelns ('THE LAND OF SMILES', 1929) *'Patiently smiling'*; *'Love, what has given you this magic power?'*; *'You are my heart's delight'*. This last is inseparable from Richard Tauber, who was said to have sung it 3,000 times; there's a famous record of

him singing it, conducted by the composer. The two collaborated on a number of recordings, in fact, all of which capture the flavour like no others, despite the rather faded sound.
Giuditta (1934) Lehár considered this to be his best work – more of an opera than an operetta (5 acts and a tragic love story).

LEONCAVALLO, RUGGIERO
1858 ~ 1919
ITALIAN COMPOSER

Leoncavallo wrote his first opera at the age of twenty-one on the curious subject of Thomas Chatterton, the young English poet who poisoned himself in 1770. He wrote a good many other operas both before and (especially) after his one major success in 1892, *Pagliacci*. All were either fiascos or received with indifference; all have vanished without trace.

MASCAGNI, PIETRO
1863 ~ 1945
ITALIAN COMPOSER

A one-hit wonder with *Cavalleria Rusticana*, Mascagni wrote a further sixteen operas without coming remotely near the success of his first triumph. Among his later works, *L'amico Fritz* (1891) was fairly popular and is sometimes still revived in Italy; *Iris* (1898), *Isabeau* (1911), based on the story of Lady Godiva, and *Il Piccolo Marat* (1921) have their moments; while *Le Maschere* (*The Masks*, 1901) was hissed in Milan, Venice, Turin and Verona, and in Genoa they didn't even let them get to the end of it.

Mascagni ended his life in disgrace. After allowing himself to become Mussolini's musical mouthpiece most of his friends deserted him, he was stripped of all his honours and spent the last years of his life in comparative poverty in a small hotel room in Rome.

MASSENET, JULES
1842 ~ 1912
FRENCH COMPOSER

The most successful French composer of opera in the last part of the nineteenth century (he wrote twenty-seven), Massenet is remembered today for just two – *Manon* and *Werther* – and for one brief instrumental piece beloved of violin players, the 'Meditation' from his 1894 opera *Thaïs*.

Manon is Massenet's masterpiece, but he is one of those composers whose popularity is not maintained after their deaths. Works such as *Le Cid*, *Le Jongleur de Notre-Dame*, *Don Quichotte* and *Hérodiade*, written with an unusual variety of style and subject, were immensely successful for him but were no longer performed regularly after the 1920s.

He was a businessman-musician who gave the public what they wanted. His fondness for fashionable quasi-religious themes suited his frequently saccharine music, but he was disliked by his colleagues who viewed him as an ambitious opportunist and smug cynic. 'I don't believe in all that creeping Jesus stuff,' he told the composer Vincent d'Indy, 'but the public likes it, and we must always agree with the public.'

In life as in art, he was an old charmer, elegant-looking, romantic and courtly. He made enormous amounts of money, which he invested with appropriate acumen.

MEYERBEER
GIACOMO
1791 ~ 1864
GERMAN COMPOSER

Fabulously successful during his lifetime but now out of fashion and forgotten save for the occasional revival of *Les Huguenots* or *L'Africaine*, Meyerbeer had a colossal influence on opera.

He was born Jakob Liebmann Beer into a prosperous Jewish family. Clementi, a frequent guest in the Beer house, gave him piano lessons. One of his fellow pupils when he studied at Darmstadt was **Weber**. Meyerbeer wrote his first opera when he was nineteen. Perhaps the biggest influence came when as a young man he met Salieri in Vienna (yes, the Salieri who, so the ridiculous legend had it, poisoned Mozart). He advised Meyerbeer to infuse his heavy German contrapuntal style with enlivening Italian melodic invention. He did so and, with Rossini no longer writing, Meyerbeer rapidly assumed a position as the most important active composer of opera in France.

(He moved to Paris in 1834, having begun his long and fruitful association with the librettist and writer Eugène Scribe in 1827.)

The overriding features of Meyerbeer's operas are their spectacle, their huge epic tales, melodramatic effects and effective, rather than memorable scores. In many ways, he was the Andrew Lloyd Webber of his day: he had an enormous influence on his contemporaries, gave the public what it wanted and made pots of money. Musically he was fairly vapid; melodically, apart from the occasional **aria** and balletic interlude, he was second-rate. **Wagner**, **Verdi**, **Gounod** and **Massenet** were all to a greater or lesser extent influenced by Meyerbeer, and Wagner was helped financially by him, for which he was repaid by Wagner's venomous attack on him as a bad musical influence and as a Jew.

THE BEST OF MEYERBEER'S OPERAS AND WHAT TO LISTEN TO

Robert le Diable (1831).
Les Huguenots (1836).
Le Prophète (1849).
L'Etoile du Nord (1854).
Dinorah (1859) (see p124).
L'Africaine (1865) (see p20).

Berlioz described Meyerbeer's operas as consisting of 'high Cs from every type of chest, bass drums, snare drums, organs, military bands, antique trumpets, tubas as big as locomotive smokestacks, bells, cannon, horses, cardinals under a canopy, emperors, queens in tiaras, funerals, fêtes, weddings ... jugglers, skaters, choirboys, censers, monstrances, crosses, taverns, processions, orgies of priests and naked women, the bull Apis and massive oxen, screech-owls, bats, the five hundred fiends of hell and what have you – the rocking of the heavens and the end of the world interspersed with a few dull cavatinas and a large claque thrown in.'

WOLFGANG AMADEUS
MOZART

B. SALZBURG, 27 JANUARY 1756
D. VIENNA, 5 DECEMBER 1791

*'When the angels sing for God, they sing Bach; when they sing
en famille they sing Mozart – and God eavesdrops'*
KARL BARTH (adapted)

The most awesome child prodigy in the history of music, Mozart went on to become the greatest composer of his day. The fact is that during his lifetime there was nothing in the world of music that anybody did better. Not only was he the finest pianist, organist and conductor in Europe (and at that time, for Europe read the world), he was a perfect master of every form of music – operas, symphonies, choral works, chamber music, concertos, and instrumental works. He had one of those brains able to cope with musical organization in a way given to very few. He was able to hear lengthy works and write them down note for note immediately afterwards, and he could write out one complicated piece of music while planning another in his head – extraordinary gifts quite beyond the capabilities of most human beings.

Mozart's father Leopold was a composer and violinist. Mozart (actually christened Johannes Chrystostamus Wolfgangus Theophilus) and his sister Anna Maria (nicknamed Nannerl) were the only two of Leopold's seven children to survive infancy. There's no doubt that Leopold had a responsible attitude to the nurturing of his children's musical gifts, but also that he exploited these gifts to the full. Both children were hardened touring professionals by their early teens. After hearing the young Mozart improvise, sight read and play, the writer Grimm recorded, 'I cannot be sure that this child will not turn my head if I go on hearing him often; he makes me realize that it is difficult to guard against madness on seeing prodigies. I am no longer surprised that St Paul should have lost his head after his strange vision.'

Mozart began composing early – his first works were published in Paris when he was seven. He wrote his first opera (*La Finta Semplice*) when he was thirteen. By the time of his first major success in this field (*Idomeneo*) in 1781, he was considered a great master. Opera was just one area in which he not only made a significant contribution but pointed the way forward.

Mozart was the first composer

For a musician whose work is often described as 'divine', Mozart was a reassuringly fallible human being with a tactless, arrogant, impulsive streak that made him few friends and many enemies. (It's difficult when you know you're the best!)

He was not a glamorous figure physically – his head was too big for his body, he had protruding blue eyes, a large nose, a yellowish complexion and was very short in stature. Like many great keyboard players he had plump hands. His face was pitted from smallpox scars.

His death at thirty-five, caused by a combination of many bodily failures, was noted by his elder son, Carl Thomas: 'Particularly remarkable is in my opinion the fact that a few days before [my father] died, his whole body became so swollen that the patient was unable to make the smallest movement, moreover there was a stench, which reflected the internal disintegration and after death increased to the extent that an autopsy was rendered impossible. The corpse did not become stiff and cold but ... remained soft and elastic' (this was probably the result of a terminal collapse of the kidneys).

DA PONTE, LORENZO
1749 ~ 1838
ITALIAN LIBRETTIST

Indelibly associated with Mozart as the librettist for The Marriage of Figaro, Don Giovanni *and* Così fan tutte. *From 1793 he worked in London but spent the last thirty-three years of his life in New York. In an adventurous life, Da Ponte's other noteworthy achievement was to introduce Italian opera to American audiences.*

of opera to write about the individual, to apply psychology. Here for the first time we meet *real* people expressing recognizable emotions which touch us, set to music that evokes and comments upon what we see. It is this rare combination that makes Mozart's operas appeal equally to both opera-goer and general music lover. Before him, comic operas had been mere entertainments. Mozart wrote music that was at once superior in melodic beauty and originality *and* able to depict mood and character beneath the surface artificiality of the stage situations.

THE BEST OF MOZART'S OPERAS
AND WHAT TO LISTEN TO

Idomeneo (1781).
Il Seraglio (*DIE ENTFÜHRUNG AUS DEM SERAIL*) ('The Abduction from the Seraglio') (1782).
The Marriage of Figaro (1786) (see p 68).
Don Giovanni (1787) (see p39).
Così fan tutte (1790) (see p36).
La Clemenza di Tito (1791).
The Magic Flute (1791) (see p66).

MUSSORGSKY
MODEST
1839 ~ 1881
RUSSIAN COMPOSER

From the ranks of the wealthy aristocracy, Mussorgsky began his career as an ensign in the élite Preobrajensky regiment, described by a friend as 'an impeccably dressed, heel-clicking society man, scented, dainty, fastidious'. Yet the indelible picture we have is of the frightening, dissolute, tousle-headed mess with a toper's red nose depicted by his artist friend Ilya Repin just a few weeks before Mussorgsky's death from alcohol poisoning at the age of forty-two.

What happened? The hard-drinking life of the regiment led to alcoholism by the age of nineteen; his parents went bankrupt six years later and for the rest of his life Mussorgsky struggled to get down on paper his musical thoughts while enduring abject poverty. Of his four operas, the only one he lived to complete was **Boris Godunov**, and that is now usually heard in the reorchestrated version by his friend Rimsky-Korsakov. Yet from this and two other popular masterpieces, *Night on the Bare Mountain* (again, best known in Rimsky's orchestration) and

Pictures at an Exhibition (best known in the orchestration by Ravel!), Mussorgsky is considered a cornerstone, the most original of all the new Russian school of composers flourishing in the last half of the nineteenth century.

OFFENBACH
JACQUES
1819 ~ 1880
GERMAN-FRENCH COMPOSER

Rossini christened him 'the Mozart of the Champs-Elysées'; his music is the epitome of 'Gay Paris'. Yet the King of the Paris Boulevards was German, born Jakob Eberst in Cologne, the son of a Jewish cantor (Offenbach was the name of the town where his father lived). He entered the Paris Conservatoire at the age of fourteen – his instrument was the cello – and Paris became his home. An eccentric-, wiry-looking man with a head like a mangy parrot in glasses, he had little success as a composer until his forties, when he opened his own theatre in order to mount the work that had been consistently rejected by others. The Bouffes-Parisiens became *the* fashionable place and remained so

for the next decade, during which time Offenbach elevated burlesque opera into an art form all his own. His melodic invention, his skill as a composer and his love of satirizing other composers, the government of the day, Greek legends, the social order, pomposity, the army – you name it – made him incredibly popular. **Wagner** wrote that 'Offenbach's music was a dung heap on which all the swine of Europe wallowed', which confirms its jolly, catchy, frivolous, hummable inconsequentiality.

By the 1870s, the public had begun to tire of Offenbach. He spent some time in America in 1876 and when he returned began to write *Les Contes d'Hoffmann*, different to his previous work, showing a more serious side. He never lived to finish it, dying in October 1880. It was his 102nd piece of work for the stage.

THE BEST OF OFFENBACH AND WHAT TO LISTEN TO:

Orphée aux Enfers (1858) (see p80).
La Belle Hélène (1864).
La Vie Parisienne (1866).
La Grande Duchesse de Gérolstein (1867).
La Périchole (1868). It was the 1875 London production of this for which Richard D'Oyly Carte needed a one-act curtain raiser. He asked **W. S. Gilbert** to provide it and suggested **Arthur Sullivan** write the music. The result, *Trial by Jury*, was the beginning of the Gilbert and Sullivan partnership.
Les Brigands (1869). How well Sullivan knew this and other Offenbach works you can judge for yourself when you hear this.
Les Contes d'Hoffmann (1881) (see p100).

GIACOMO PUCCINI

b. LUCCA, 22 DECEMBER 1858
d. BRUSSELS, 29 NOVEMBER 1924

'While the ground-bass of Verdi's operas is a battle cry, of Puccini's it is a mating call'
MOSCO CARNER, PUCCINI'S BIOGRAPHER

'Almighty God touched me with his little finger and said "Write for the theatre – mind, only the theatre." And I have obeyed the supreme command,' wrote Puccini. On another occasion: 'Just think of it! If I hadn't hit on music I should never have been able to do anything in the world.'

Puccini's musical life was predestined. Christened Giacomo Antonio Domenico Michele Secondo Maria, he was the fifth generation (and, as it turned out, the last in the line) of a family of professional musicians: his great-great-grandfather Giacomo, his great-grandfather Antonio, his grandfather Domenico and his father Michele all had some official positions in the musical world of Italy.

He trained at the Milan Conservatory where his chief teacher was the composer of *La Gioconda*, Amilcare Ponchielli. His first opera, the one-act *Le Villi*, appeared when he was twenty-six, and with the exception of his next work, *Edgar*, and the later *La Rondine*, everything he wrote was a success. He was not a fast-working composer and it is remarkable that his reputation rests on so few works (Verdi had to write a great deal more to achieve the same number of 'hits'). Today, three of the world's most popular operas are by Puccini. When he died his wealth was estimated at $4 million. *Turandot*, completed after his death, was the last opera to be written that has entered today's standard repertoire, beloved by the public at large.

As a composer, Puccini belonged to no particular school and led to no others. Although he was obviously aware of current musical trends (**Verdi** and **Wagner**, early on, then Debussy), his music is always recognizably Puccinian and the development of polytonality, Futurism, Neo-classicism and the other musical movements crashing around him left him untouched. It's hardly surprising, then, that the more intellectual of musicians and critics have derided his work with its dramatic clarity and musical accessibility. To them, Puccini appeals to the listener's basic instincts in too obvious and sentimental a way. The fact is that Puccini was a master musical dramatist (he drove his librettists frantic changing, cutting and reworking material) who knew exactly how to achieve the effects he sought. He spent huge amounts of time seeking out the right libretto, researching and checking every aspect of its authenticity, its psychological and historical accuracy. His music is highly charged and as a manipulator of the audience's emotions, he is second to none. And that is a large part of what theatre is about. Many composers die without realizing it.

Apart from his gift for melody, Puccini was an inspired craftsman both as a composer and an orchestrator (not the same thing), who was also adventurous and skilful enough not to stand still but to seek fresh challenges in every new work. He was shrewd enough

to take his public with him, whatever harmonic or orchestral novelties he introduced. Two years before he died of throat cancer he wrote of the then current state of opera in words that may find some sympathy today: 'By now [1922] the public for new music has lost its palate. It loves or puts up with illogical music devoid of all sense. Melody is no longer practised – or if it is, it is vulgar. People believe the symphonic element must rule, and I, instead, believe this is the end of opera.'

PUCCINI'S COMPLETE OPERAS AND WHAT TO LISTEN TO

Le Villi (1883) (1 act).
Edgar (1889) Leave this one till last. It was Puccini's only real failure (mainly due to its libretto), but it has its moments.
Manon Lescaut (1883) (see p63).
La Bohème (1896) (see p27).
Tosca (1900) (see p103).
Madam Butterfly (1904) (see p60)
La Fanciulla del West ('The Golden Girl of the West') (1910). This is Puccini at home on the range, set in California in the days of the Gold

Rush. *'Ch' ella mi creda'* ('Let her believe me free'), sung by Dick Johnson in Act 3, is a winner though.
La Rondine ('The Swallow') (1917).
Il Trittico ('The Triptych') (1918) Three one-act operas, *Il Tabarro* ('The Cloak'), *Suor Angelica* ('Sister Angelica') and *Gianni Schicchi*, all thematically unconnected. *Gianni Schicchi* is by far the best, and the most popular – deservedly so (see p50).
Turandot (1926) .(see p114).

PURCELL, HENRY
1659 ~ 1695
ENGLISH COMPOSER

T he double tragedy of Purcell, the only truly great home-grown composer for two centuries, was that he died aged only thirty-six and, prolific though he was, lived to complete only one opera. *Dido and Aeneas* is a flawed masterpiece, way ahead of its time in terms of musical and dramatic expression and the first work in English that can truly be called an opera.

He wrote important works in every other field of musical activity, an innovator in every one of them: odes for various occasions, anthems, songs, sonatas for strings, for keyboard, for organ (he was organist of Westminster Abbey) and the incidental music for forty-four plays. Five days after he died in November 1695, he was buried in Westminster Abbey. So unique was his contribution that there were no musical successors and when, fifteen years later, Handel arrived on the scene, the idea of an English national opera was already forgotten. The Italian style soon reigned supreme.

He once described himself as 'a mighty hunter of wild fowl, opera librettos and attractive women' (he was addicted to shooting ducks and other game birds on his estate at Torre del Lago near Florence). He had any number of affairs. One relationship ended in tragedy. Elvira Gemignani had been Puccini's mistress for years. Following her husband's death, she and Puccini were married in 1904, but what had been a passionate relationship soured to one of frequent and violent quarrels. The

couple employed a servant girl at the villa, Doria Manfredi. Elvira became convinced that her husband was having an affair with Doria and, wildly jealous, made the matter public, accusing her of all sorts of things until the poor girl was driven to commit suicide by taking poison. The autopsy revealed she was still a virgin.

Puccini fled to a hotel in Rome and remained there for days, weeping. Elvira was sentenced to five months in prison.

GIOACCHINO
ROSSINI

B. PESARO, 29 FEB. 1792 ~ D. PARIS, 13 NOV. 1868

'Rossini, in music, is the genius of sheer animal spirits'
LEIGH HUNT

Both Rossini's parents were musicians – his mother was a singer and his father played the trumpet – and by his early teens he could play the piano, the viola and the horn proficiently, as well as being much in demand as a boy soprano. He entered the Liceo Musicale in Bologna when he was fifteen and by the time he left three years later he had composed a great deal of music including five accomplished string quartets.

Following a commission to write a one-act opera for Venice (*La Cambiale di Matrimonio*), Rossini produced another thirty-eight over the next nineteen years – as well as chamber music, cantatas and other vocal music – by which time he was the most famous opera composer in

the world, and the most successful. 'The glory of the man', wrote his biographer Stendhal, 'is only limited by the limits of civilization, and he is not yet thirty-two.' However, when he was only thirty-seven, and at the height of his powers, Rossini abandoned opera composition, and although he lived for another thirty-nine years, he

wrote very little else in any form. Not that he needed the money: at his death, his estate was valued at about $1,420,000.

Rossini's contribution to the development of opera was immense, as a composer of both *opera buffa* and *opera seria*. Pure melody, immense vitality and rhythmic verve were his hallmarks. He extended the range of both instrumental textures and lyric ornamentation. Among his innovations were the writing out of all ornaments and cadenzas instead of leaving it to the whims (and dubious tastes) of the singers, as was normal practice before that time (*c*..1815). In *Tancredi* he introduced an unusually large number of ensembles and in *Otello* he had all the **recitatives** accompanied by the orchestra, not by continuo. There was also the 'Rossini crescendo', an orchestral device using many repetitions of the same passage so that each time it is played, it is presented at a higher pitch and with fuller orchestration, the effect being one of mounting excitement. (Listen to '*La calunnia*' in Act 1 of **The Barber**.) He was also the first to introduce a military band on stage (*Semiramide*), an

*A charming and affable host who entertained on a lavish scale, **Rossini** was also a great gourmet and inventor of recipes, including Tournedos Rossini. Though for twenty years he suffered from depression he was celebrated as a great wit (see **The Ring**, p92). After hearing the Symphonie Fantastique by Berlioz he commented, 'What a good thing it isn't music.' Le cygne de Pesaro ('The swan of*

Pesaro'), as Rossini was known, was to have a statue erected in his honour by the burghers of his native town. They approached the maestro, informing him that although they had sufficient money to pay for the pedestal, they couldn't raise enough for the statue itself. Would Signor Rossini care to donate 10,000 francs towards the project? 'For 10,000 francs,' replied Rossini, 'I'd stand on the pedestal myself.'

Like many Italians, he was uncommonly superstitious; he died on Friday 13 November 1868. Nearly twenty years later his remains were transferred for reburial in Florence. There were over 6,000 mourners in the procession, four military bands and a chorus of 300 which sang the Prayer from Rossini's Mosè in Egitto. The crowd outside the church was so enthusiastic that the service could not continue until an encore was given.

idea that subsequently was frequently copied by other Italian composers.

Few have managed to reach the heights of sparkling comic writing (as in *The Barber*) whilst being equally successful with the dramatic and dignified (*William Tell*). While he was active, Rossini's work was the one against which others were judged. Though sometimes shallow and written to captivate by its own brilliance, it is difficult not to succumb to the life-enhancing *joie de vivre* of his music. Thomas Pynchon in *Gravity's Rainbow* (1973) wrote: 'The point is ... a person feels *good* listening to Rossini. All you feel like listening to Beethoven is going out and invading Poland ... there is more of the sublime in the snare-drum part of *La Gazza Ladra* than in the whole of the Ninth Symphony.'

THE BEST OF ROSSINI'S OPERAS AND WHAT TO LISTEN TO

La Scala di Seta (1812) *Overture*.
Il Signor Bruschino (1812) *Overture*. This is the one where the violins play with the wood of their bows (*col legno*) instead of the hair.
Tancredi (1812–13) '*Di tanti palpiti*' from Act 1. Possibly the most famous **aria** of its day, it was a huge hit all over Europe. Rossini was said to have composed it in four minutes while waiting for his rice to cook, and although both are impossible, it still became known as the '*aria dei risi*' (The Rice Aria). Said to have been adopted as a favourite melody by the Venetian gondoliers.
L'Italiana in Algeri (1813) *Overture*.
Il Barbiere di Siviglia (1816) (see p24).
Otello (1816).

La Cenerentola (1816–17) (see p36).
La Gazza Ladra (1817) *Overture*.
Mosè in Egitto (1818) '*Dal tuo stellato soglio*' ('From your starry throne'), which was added for the 1819 revival, was sung at Rossini's funeral.
Semiramide (1822–23) *Overture* and '*Bel raggio lusinghier*', a much-favoured **coloratura** work-out. One of Rossini's longest and most ambitious works.
Le Comte Ory (1828).
William Tell (1828–29) *Overture*. Alpine bells, thunder storm, The Lone Ranger.

SAINT-SAËNS
CAMILLE
1835 ~ 1921
FRENCH COMPOSER

Saint-Saëns was an astounding musical prodigy, with one of the most fertile and precocious minds of the last century. He could read and write before the age of three, composed his first piece of music at the same age and gave his first public recital, as a pianist, at the age of five. Apart from becoming one of the most important pianists and organists of his day (Liszt hailed him as the greatest organist in the world), he was also a fine conductor, composer and musicologist, as well as a respected critic. His music reading was phenomenal – Wagner was roused to admiration when Saint-Saëns played at first sight Wagner's entire opera scores at the piano. He also dabbled in poetry, astronomy, archaeology, the occult and science in general.

As a musician, quipped his friend Bizet, the one thing that Saint-Saëns lacked was inexperience. 'I produce music', said Saint-Saens, 'like an apple tree produces apples.' His instrumental music especially is a joy, full of melodic invention, grace and skill ('The Swan' from the *Carnival of the Animals* is his most famous piece), but his twelve operas were less successful. These included *Le timbre d'Argent*, *Henry VIII*, *Proserpine*, and *Ascanio*. After the première of *Ascanio*, George Bernard Shaw wrote, 'I can recall no alleviation of my prodigious boredom.' *Samson et Dalila* is the only one still in the repertoire.

Saint-Saëns's life, curiously at odds with his sunny music, was marked by resentment of his rivals, arch-conservatism in later years (he hated Debussy) and bitterness over his slow acceptance as a composer. His marriage foundered after six years: both his infant sons died accidental deaths within months of each other; he left his wife one day while on holiday and never saw her again. She died as recently as 1950.

SMETANA
BEDŘICH
(1824 ~ 1884)
CZECH COMPOSER

Smetana, the founding father of Czech music, was almost as formidable a prodigy as **Saint-Saëns**, but because of parental opposition, he did not flourish in the same way. Still, he was good enough to play the violin in a Haydn quartet at the age of five, and played in public as a pianist aged six. His early struggles as a pianist and composer were alleviated by Liszt (another example of his generosity) when the latter helped him open a piano school of his own. Bohemia, then a province of the Austrian Empire, was the subject of much unrest in the 1840s and Smetana, by then fiercely partisan, joined the movement. When it was crushed he moved to Sweden.

By the 1860s, the political situation in his homeland had changed and Smetana returned. He knew Glinka's nationalistic operas, with their Russian librettos and Russian melodies and determined to do the same for Bohemia. He was given the important job of music director of the Prague Provisional Theatre and his first opera, *The Brandenburgers in Bohemia* (1863), made use of his ideas. Three years later he wrote *The Bartered Bride*. Most of his other six operas are still performed in Prague, but this is the only one to remain in the international repertoire.

As a composer, he influenced Dvořák, Janáček, Martinů and others; as a teacher, conductor and propagandist he inspired his country to a new musical heritage.

Towards the end of his life he, like Beethoven, went deaf. Eventually, he lost his memory and speech and, like Schumann, went insane.

STRAUSS II, JOHANN
1825 ~ 1899
AUSTRIAN COMPOSER AND CONDUCTOR

Johann Strauss II was 'The Waltz King', the composer of *The Blue Danube* and *Die Fledermaus*. No relation of **Richard Strauss**, but the son of Johann I ('The Father of the Waltz') and the brother of Josef (a conductor, poet, painter, inventor and also composer in his own right – 283 pieces in all) and Eduard (another conductor and composer of 318 works who, in 1901, dissolved the orchestra his father had founded in 1826).

Johann II, by far the most gifted composer of the family, wrote 400 waltzes, 300 polkas, galops, marches, etc., as well as sixteen operettas, of which *Der Zigeunerbaron* ('The Gypsy Baron') of 1885 is the only one apart from *Die Fledermaus* regularly revived today. The others, despite sections of ravishing music, suffer from impossible librettos; indeed, Strauss composed at least one (*Eine Nacht in Venedig*) without knowing the plot. 'I never saw the dialogue but only the words of the songs. Consequently I put too much nobility into some parts of it that did not suit the work as a whole ... At the final rehearsal, when I learned the complete story in its correct sequence, I was horrified,' he wrote. If **Offenbach** gave to the operetta a satirical wit and bite, Strauss invented that peculiarly sweet never-never land of Viennese hedonism – sentimental, exuberant and ultimately care-free.

STRAUSS, RICHARD
1864 ~ 1949
GERMAN COMPOSER AND CONDUCTOR

Richard enjoyed a parallel career of composing and conducting all his life; at only twenty-two he was one of Germany's busiest conductors, music director of the Munich Opera and assistant at Bayreuth, no less. The works that made him internationally famous were his tone poems, among them *Don Juan* and *Till Eulenspiegel*.

Turning next to larger scale orchestral works (*Symphonia Domestica* and *The Alpine Symphony*, for example), he also tackled opera. *Salome* and *Elektra* created a furore, not just because of the dissonant language of the music but because of their (as some saw it) dissolute subject matter, *Salome* with its erotic, sensuous overtones, *Elektra* with its powerful depiction of matricide ('Pornographic rubbish,' was the opinion of the composer Sir Charles Stanford). With *Der Rosenkavalier* Strauss abandoned such excesses, adopting a mellifluously melodic style, a sort of Johann Strauss-ified **Wagner** ('Cheap and poor,' said Stravinsky).

A succession of operas followed, created in collaboration with the poet Hugo von Hofmannsthal (also the librettist of *Elektra* and *Der Rosenkavalier*) and others. None came anywhere near capturing the public affection engendered by *Der Rosenkavalier*. Nevertheless, theirs was a historic collaboration, akin to that of Mozart and Da Ponte, if rather formal and one-sided. Hofmannsthal, one of Germany's most distinguished men of letters, knew that Strauss was a genius and stood in awe of him. 'I consider Dr Strauss entirely as the principal partner, and the music as the dominant one of the elements joined together.' It's interesting then, that Strauss, practical man that he was, should once have admitted that he would be happy if only forty per cent of the words of his operas were distinguishable above the orchestra. (Indeed, *Capriccio*, his last opera, dramatizes the old argument as to whether words or music should have priority in opera.)

Materialistic, opportunistic and apolitical, he stayed on in Nazi Germany, although he openly spoke out against the regime and used a Jewish librettist, Stefan Zweig, for *Die schweigsame Frau*. When asked why he had not left the country, Strauss reportedly replied:

'Germany had fifty-six opera houses, the United States had two. It would have reduced my income.'

THE BEST OF RICHARD STRAUSS'S OPERAS AND WHAT TO LISTEN TO

Salome (1905).
Elektra (1909).
Der Rosenkavalier (1911) (see p98).
Ariadne auf Naxos (1912).
Die Frau ohne Schatten (1919).
Intermezzo (1924).
Die schweigsame Frau (1935).
Capriccio (1942).

TCHAIKOVSKY
PIOTR ILYICH
1840 ~ 1893
RUSSIAN COMPOSER

It's often forgotten that the composer of the world's most popular piano concerto (No. 1 in B flat), overture (1812), and ballet (Swan Lake) was also a composer of operas, ten in all. Of these, **Eugene Onegin** is the only undisputed masterpiece, but The Maid of Orleans (much influenced by **Meyerbeer**) has some spectacular choruses and sumptuous arias, as you would expect from one of music's supreme melodists. The Queen of Spades, much influenced by **Carmen** with its theme of love and cruel fate, is second best, though, and contains some of Tchaikovsky's finest vocal writing.

THE BEST OF TCHAIKOVSKY'S OPERAS AND WHAT TO LISTEN TO:

Eugene Onegin (1879) See p. 42
The Maid of Orleans (1881)
Mazeppa (1884)
The Queen of Spades (1890)
Iclanta (1892)

GIUSEPPE VERDI

B. LE RONCOLE, 10 OCTOBER 1813 ~ D. MILAN, 27 JANUARY 1901

'He wept and loved for all of us'
GABRIELE D'ANNUNZIO

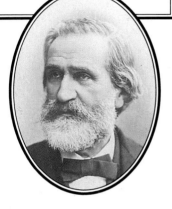

Verdi is said to be the last great hero of Italian opera, the end of a line that started with Monteverdi. Others testify that he was the greatest Italian composer of the nineteenth century. Indeed he was, but he was also more than that, not only one of his country's most notable citizens, but a symbol of Italian liberty. His star has never faltered and his works, diverse as they are in character and content, reveal a musician constantly developing his art, producing a treasure-chest of masterpieces.

Verdi, although he described himself as a peasant, was in fact from a modest bourgeois background – his parents kept the local inn, which doubled as a wine shop and grocery store. In his teens he became an organist and composer, but was rejected by the Milan Conservatoire as being 'over age and insufficiently gifted'. His piano playing was weak, he knew little of musical theory, but he persevered with private studies, a short, pale, pock-marked young man, taciturn, moody and intense.

His first opera, *Oberto*, was produced in 1839 at La Scala when he was twenty-seven; his last, *Falstaff*, at the same theatre in 1893, when he was eighty. By the time he was forty, he had written *Rigoletto* (1851), *La Traviata* (1853) and *Il Trovatore* (1853), three works that made him the most acclaimed opera composer of the day, eclipsing even the fabulous success of **Meyerbeer**, and which alone would have guaranteed him a place among the immortals.

Verdi was as pro-Italian as

The first operatic disc recording in the US was made in 1896. Ferruccio Giannini sang 'La donna è mobile' from Rigoletto.

The first complete opera recording was another first for Verdi: in 1902 the Italian Gramophone Co. issued the whole of Ernani *on forty single-sided discs!*

Wagner was pro-German. He hoped fervently for the Risorgimento, the reorganization of the numerous small Italian states into one country. His patriotism paid off handsomely. The theme of resurgent nationalism in his early operas, the frequent clashes with the censor, who suspected him of revolutionary tendencies, his political career in the 1860s when he sat as a deputy in that part of Italy already unified, the anti-monarchist sentiments in some of his operas – all these things endeared him to the general public. But they also loved the red-blooded, spontaneous warmth of his lyricism, the directness of his melodic gift, the perfect dramatic timing and the infinite variety of orchestral colour he brought to his work, the high point of the Italian school of opera.

'The theatre yesterday evening was filled to bursting; that's the only gauge to success,' wrote Verdi. He was as unlike Wagner, the other great figure of nineteenth-century opera (born just five months earlier), as was possible. The Italian was never a theoretician. 'There is hardly any music in my house,' he wrote in a letter in 1869. 'I have never gone to a music library, never to a publisher to examine a piece. I keep abreast of some of the better contemporary work not by studying them but through hearing them occasionally at the theatre ... I repeat, I am the least erudite among past and present composers.' He was a simple man who wanted his music to speak to the masses, not to an intellectual élite. 'Io son un paesano,' he told King Victor Emmanuel when the latter wished to ennoble him. When he died at the age of eighty-eight, he was a national hero.

THE BEST OF VERDI'S OPERAS AND WHAT TO LISTEN TO

Nabucodonosor known as **Nabucco** (1842) (see p78).
I Lombardi alla Prima Crociata (1843), revised as JÉRUSALEM (1847).
Ernani (1844).
I Due Foscari (1844)
Giovanna d'Arco (1845).
Attila (1846).
Macbeth (1847; revised and translated into French, 1865).
La Battaglia di Legnano (1849).
Luisa Miller (1849).

Rigoletto (1851) (see p89).
Il Trovatore (1853;.revised 1857) (see p111).
La Traviata (1853) (see p108).
Les Vêpres Siciliennes (1855).
Simone Boccanegra (1857; revised 1881).
Un Ballo in Maschera (1859) (see p23).
La Forza del Destino (1862; revised 1869) (see p48).
Don Carlos (1867; revised 1884) (see p38).
Aida (1871) (see p21).
Otello (1887) (see p81).
Falstaff (1893).

RICHARD
WAGNER

B. LEIPZIG, 22 MAY 1813 ~ D. VENICE, 13 FEBRUARY 1883

'The whole Ring will then become – out with it! I am not ashamed to say so – the greatest work of poetry ever written'
RICHARD WAGNER

No composer has had so much written about him and none thought quite so much of himself as Richard Wagner. Arguably, though, no single composer before or since has ever had so deep an influence on the course of his art. His admirers have risen to heights of ecstasy – 'I can only adore you ... an earthly being cannot requite a divine spirit,' wrote Ludwig II of Bavaria – as frequently as his detractors have sought new metaphors with which to castigate him. 'I love Wagner,' wrote Baudelaire, 'but the music I prefer is that of a cat hung up by its tail outside a window, and trying to stick to the panes of glass with its claws.'

But while it is easy to admire his achievements, it is far harder to admire the man and his methods, although both continue, more than a century after his death, to exercise a fascination. His egocentricity was of Napoleonic proportions. Without it, of course, he would never have done what he did, but in the end, the only thing that Wagner revered and could be true to was his art. 'The world owes me what I need,' he declared and he did not hesitate to lie, cheat, borrow money without any intention of repaying it, use people quite unscrupulously and regard with contempt anyone who did not adore him. He was as indifferent to the pain he caused others as he was neurotically concerned with the pain anyone caused *him*.

Wagner's background was entirely unmusical and far from affluent. His first love was literature. His stepfather (see below) had planted the seeds of this and when he was only eleven Wagner wrote a drama, drawn from Shakespeare and the Greeks, in which forty-two characters died in the first four acts, some of whom appeared as ghosts in the fifth. Brevity and wit were never Wagnerian hallmarks. A performance of **Weber's *Der Freischütz*** first aroused his interest in music; after hearing **Beethoven's** symphonies and *Fidelio* in Leipzig it became an obsession.

By the time he was twenty-two Wagner was the conductor of a small opera house and had written two unproduced operas. He purchased a notebook in which he jotted down every detail of his life, specifically to use when writing his future autobiography. Even then, he sensed he would become one of the immortals of music, although his first opera, *Das Liebesverbot*, produced in 1836, was such a fiasco that the theatre in Magdeburg was empty when it was repeated. It was not until *Rienzi* in

1842 that he had his first success. He and Minna Planer, his actress wife, whom he married in 1836, were often near starvation and besieged by debts as they moved from Riga to Paris to Dresden. After ***The Flying Dutchman*** and ***Tannhäuser***, Wagner fled to Zürich, exiled from his home country after siding with the revolutionaries.

While he was in exile, Wagner formulated his ideas about opera, rejecting accepted traditions and evolving the concept of 'music drama' involving a synthesis of all the arts. ***The Ring, Tristan und Isolde*** and ***Die Meistersinger*** were all written according to these principles over the following two decades. *Tristan* was, at the time of its composition (1859), the most revolutionary piece of music ever composed. Inspired by his passionate affair with Mathilde Wesendonk, the wife of the rich merchant with whom he was staying in Switzerland, it pushed his new 'symphonic' ideas to the limit. With it, he made use of harmonic innovations that paved the way for Mahler and Schoenberg and made many people think that perhaps Wagner's opinion of himself was justified.

Soon after his return from exile (he was pardoned in 1860), Wagner met King Ludwig II of Bavaria, who not only financed his regal lifestyle and paid off his debts, but finally enabled his operas to be produced. After a number of affairs, Wagner finally left Minna in 1862 (she died four years later) for the love of his life. Being Wagner, this was a far from straightforward matter. The woman in question was Liszt's daughter, Cosima, who was married to Wagner's intimate

friend, the conductor and pianist Hans von Bülow. Despite Wagner seducing and having two children (Isolde and Eva) by his wife, poor von Bülow remained devoted to Wagner and accepted the situation. 'You have prefered to devote your life and the treasures of your mind to one who is my superior,' he wrote to Cosima. 'Far from blaming you I *approve* your action from every point of view and admit you are perfectly right.' Another child, Siegfried, was born in 1869. Cosima and Wagner married the following year. After *The Ring* was completed in 1873 with *Götterdämmerung*, Wagner wrote only one more music drama, *Parsifal*, which, although begun in 1857, he only finished in 1882, the year before he died of a heart attack in Venice. He was buried in the garden of his house in Bayreuth.

THE BEST OF WAGNER'S OPERAS AND MUSIC DRAMAS
(Dates given are those of composition)

Rienzi (1837–40).
Der fliegende Holländer (*The Flying Dutchman*) (1841).(see p47).
Tannhäuser (1842–5) Final version 1865 (see p101).
Lohengrin (1845–8) (see p54).
Tristan und Isolde (1856–9) (see p110).
Die Meistersinger von Nurnberg (1845, and 1861–7) (see p74).
DER RING DES NIBELUNGEN (1848–74) (p92), comprising:
Das Rheingold (1851–4) (see p95).
Die Walküre (1851–56) (see p95).
Siegfried (1851–2, 1857, 1864–5 and 1869) (see p96).
Götterdämmerung (1848–52 and 1869–74) (see p96).
Parsifal (1857, 1865 and 1877–82).

VON **WEBER**
CARL MARIA
1786 ~ 1826
GERMAN COMPOSER

Weber, a sickly, consumptive man, who was born with a diseased hip and who walked with a limp all his life, was just forty when he died in London (his remains were transferred to Dresden in 1844), a year before **Beethoven** and two years before Schubert. His genius often goes unacknowledged and it is only the cruelty of history that has robbed him of his place alongside his two immortal contemporaries, for he was to the development of opera what Beethoven was to the symphony and what Schubert was to song: he showed the way forward. But whereas most people could tell you something about Beethoven or Schubert, they would be hard pressed to come up with anything about Weber.

Although he was a slim, weak man, he had enormous hands and was one of the great pianists of his day. Much of his keyboard music is beyond the average player because of the enormous stretches he wrote, natural to him – he could stretch the interval of a twelfth – but impossible for others. His most famous piano composition is the *Invitation to the Dance*, usually heard today in an orchestral version by Berlioz. Weber dabbled in lithography, was a virtuoso on the guitar, and a good singer until 1806, when he ruined his voice by accidentally drinking a glass of nitric acid.

He was a precocious talent as a composer and conductor. At the age of eighteen he was chief conductor of the opera-house at Breslau; in 1812 he was director of the one in Prague and five years later the King of Saxony summoned him to Dresden specifically to found a German opera-house as a reaction to the Italian-dominated opera craze. Like Gluck, Weber had the right sort of single-minded personality and supreme musicianship to get what he wanted, ordering German translations of all the major works, correcting errors in scores and being fiercely demanding of his musicians and singers.

Before him, there was very little German opera. *The Magic Flute* was Mozart's only major success in German (all his others were in Italian), and just as Beethoven's *Fidelio* and the handful of (still unknown) operas by Schubert had failed to do, it had not led to any new German school. With one opera, *Der Freischütz*, Weber founded one. Many of his ideas anticipate Wagner's by thirty years or more: listen to Weber's overture to his 1823 opera *Euryanthe* – its strange harmonies can be heard in parts of the **Ring** cycle; he toyed with the idea of writing an opera based on the Tannhäuser legend as early as 1813; he was one of the first to insist on total control of all aspects of the production of his work; in 1817 he wrote of wanting to create works that would take from every individual art form and be fused into one great *new* form. This was Wagner anticipated by *forty* years.

Der Freischütz can be said to have established the Romantic movement in music. Its highly dramatic, poetic subject, concerned with a Germanic fairy-tale, legends, the supernatural and the symbolic, made a great appeal. Weber's melodic genius and mastery of his craft made it possible to break with the traditions of the past. As with Mozart and Schubert, one wonders what more he would have achieved had he lived longer.

THE BEST OF WEBER'S OPERAS AND WHAT TO LISTEN TO

Abu Hassan (1811) *Overture*.
Preciosa (1821) *Overture*.
Der Freischütz (1821) (see p49).
Die drei Pintos (1821) Completed by Gustav Mahler.
Euryanthe (1823).
Oberon (1826).

WEILL, **KURT**
1900 ~ 1950
GERMAN COMPOSER

He studied with Humperdinck for one term at the Berlin Hochschule für Musik. What a world of difference there is between the masterpieces of master and pupil (*Hänsel und Gretel* was written thirty-five years before *The Threepenny Opera*). Weill began by composing pieces in the contemporary idiom, but then he became drawn to the new German cult of *Zeitkunst* (music for the people). Influenced by the left-wing writer Bertold Brecht, he began producing operas using popular-music techniques. *The Threepenny Opera* was his most successful (extraordinarily so) and, despite the reputations of *Mahagonny*, *Happy End* and other works, he never quite achieved the same level of invention. The individual sound of his instantly recognizable music is haunting, and partly because of his political and social alliegiances, has become associated with the decadence of the Weimar Republic. In 1933, Weill and his wife, the actress Lotte Lenya, left Nazi Berlin and went to America. Apart from a few mediocre attempts at an equivalent 'American opera', the rest of Weill's story belongs to Broadway, where he achieved a different kind of success.

AMELIA
BELINDA
CAROLINE
DIANA
ELIZA
FANNY
GEORGIANA
HARRIET
JENNY
KATE
LUCY
MARY
NANCY
OLIVIA
PATTY
QUINTILIA
RACHEL
SALLY
THOMASINA
URANIA
VALERIA
WILHELMINA
XANTIPPE
YOLANTE
ZOAMIRA

Woolnoth sc.

THE ARTISTS

*'I do not mind what language
an opera is sung in as long as it is a
language I don't understand'*

Sir Edward Appleton, 1892 ~ 1965

ALLEN, THOMAS
B. 1944
BRITISH BARITONE

A world-class voice and a commanding stage presence has made Allen one of Britain's most sought-after artists. A versatile actor, he is equally at home in Mozart, Britten, Puccini or the French repertoire.

ANDERSON, JUNE
B. 1952
AMERICAN SOPRANO

Her technique in terms of agility is awesome: many see her as the successor to **Joan Sutherland** in the *coloratura* and *bel canto* repertoire.

ANGELES, VICTORIA DE LOS
B. 1923
SPANISH SOPRANO

One of the most beautiful voices of the post-war era. Her looks and radiant stage presence helped her to become, for many people, the perfect Mimi (*La Bohème*), Butterfly and Manon of the age. She has appeared less and less in operas since the mid-1960s, recital and concerts becoming her main sphere of activity.

BAILEY, NORMAN
B. 1933
BRITISH BASS BARITONE

Having made his debut in Rossini and achieving immense success in such roles as **Rigoletto**, the Count in *Il Trovatore* and Scarpia in *Tosca*, Bailey was among the pre-eminent Wagnerian singers of the day. His Wotan with the English National Opera, and Hans Sachs (*Die Meistersinger*) brought him international acclaim. A master, too, of the intimate song repertoire from German *lieder* to drawing-room ballads.

BAKER, DAME JANET
B. 1933
ENGLISH MEZZO-SOPRANO

Among the great British artists of the century and as successful in *lieder* and recital as in opera. She had a broad repertoire (Purcell to Britten, Berlioz to Richard Strauss) and a wide range, as comfortable in the mezzo repertoire as that for contralto, but it was with the music of Monteverdi, Handel and Gluck that she had a special affinity. Created Dame in 1976, she gave her last operatic appearance in 1982.

BERGANZA, TERESA
B. 1935
SPANISH MEZZO-SOPRANO

After her 1955 début in Madrid, she quickly made a name for herself in roles such as Dorabella (*Così fan tutte*) and Neris (*Medea*) which she sang with **Callas**. But it was her superb *coloratura* singing, especially in Rossini, which brought her international success.

BERGONZI, CARLO
B. 1924
ITALIAN TENOR

Began his career as a baritone but after a second début as a tenor (in 1951 in *Andrea Chénier*) his rise to the front rank was rapid. A stylish and unusually elegant singer with an individual tibre, he was at his best in lyrico-dramatic roles.

BJÖRLING, JUSSI
1911 ~ 1960
SWEDISH TENOR

Among the supreme lyric tenors of the century, perhaps even the greatest, Björling is unsurpassable in Gounod, Verdi and, most famously, Puccini (Rodolfo in *La Bohème*; Pinkerton in *Madame Butterfly*). The record he made with Robert Merrill of the duet from Bizet's *The Pearl Fishers* ('Au fond du temple saint') has been voted by listeners the most popular record of classical music (BBC Radio 2 poll 'Your Hundred Best Tunes').

CABALLÉ, MONTSERRAT
B. 1933
SPANISH SOPRANO

A great exponent of *bel canto* and the Italian lyrical roles. She can outsing most of her rivals in the Bellini–Donizetti repertoire. Listen to her in *Lucrezia Borgia*, *Il Pirata* and *Anna Bolena*. An influence on the career of José Carreras, she made a chart-topping crossover disc with the late Freddie Mercury of Queen.

CALLAS, MARIA
1923 ~ 1977
GREEK SOPRANO

Y ou either love her or loathe her. The fact is her vocal technique was far from perfect. Cognoscenti will tell you that her voice was never the same after she drastically lost weight in 1954. By then she had irreversibly damaged her vocal muscles by forcing and overworking her voice. Her off-stage life did nothing to help (see below). And yet ... Her gifts as an actress, the extraordinary power, range and beauty of her voice, her intensity and forceful intelligence have made her among the most important (and influential) singers in history.

Born Maria Anna Cecilia Sofia Kalogeropoulou, she made her debut as Santuzza (*Cavalleria Rusticana*) in 1938. Few sopranos have been able to encompass the heavyweight German soprano roles (Isolde, Brünnhilde) with as much

success as they have the dramatic Italian heroines (Violetta, Lucia). The famous record producer Walter Legge, who produced her EMI/Angel recordings, said: 'There is hardly a bar in the whole range of nineteenth-century music for

high soprano that seriously tested her powers.' It was thanks to her that many neglected *bel canto* operas were restored to the repertoire (*Medea*, *Beatrice di Tenda*, *I Capuleti e i Montecchi* and *La Straniera* among them), while the careers of **Montserrat Caballé**, **Beverly Sills** and **Joan Sutherland** would have been very different had it not been for the influence of Maria Callas.

CARRERAS, JOSÉ
B. 1946
SPANISH TENOR

S eeded number three in the world at the moment. Among the most gifted of present-day artists, with an ardently lyrical voice, he is best known for being one of the Three Tenors (the whole thing was his idea) and for being torn off a strip by Leonard Bernstein in a documentary made during the recording of *West Side Story*. He has made a courageous fight against leukaemia and subsequently a triumphant come-back. Listen to his Rodolfo (*La Bohème*), Don José (*Carmen*) and Nemorino (*L'Elisir d'amore*).

*Callas's first husband was Giovanni Meneghini, a Veronese millionaire twice her age whom she married in 1949. Her well-publicised reputation as a tough and temperamental **diva** made her many enemies in the opera world, and relations with her own family were unhappy. When her mother once begged her for $100 'for my daily bread', Callas is said to have replied, 'If you can't make enough money to live on, you can jump out of the window or drown yourself.' She was at the height of her fame when she became the mistress of the Greek shipping millionaire Aristotle Onassis, a relationship that to all intents and purposes finished her voice and career. When, after a decade, he suddenly abandoned her to marry Jacqueline Kennedy, widow of the assassinated American president, Callas was devastated. She was only fifty-one when she sang for the last time, her voice by then badly impaired. She died alone in her Paris flat three years later from a heart attack. It was whispered that she had killed herself. Her estate was valued at $12 million, and she left it all to her butler and maid. However, her will was never signed and, after a court battle, her mother and Giovanni Meneghini split everything between them.*

CARUSO, ENRICO
1873 ~ 1921
ITALIAN TENOR

Though he died more than seventy years ago, there are few people, music-lovers or not, who have not heard of Caruso. Until the emergence of Pavarotti, no tenor apart from Gigli had quite achieved that reputation which made his name a synonym for his art. Indeed, many people hold the view that, all in all, Caruso's voice is still the most beautiful tenor voice the world has known.

Born in Naples, he was the eighteenth child of a poor machinist. All seventeen of his brothers and sisters died in infancy; two born after him survived. He made his debut in his home town in 1894. We can hear how he sounded just eight years later when he made his first recording. (Every single one of his discs is available on CD, incidentally, and many of them have never been out of the catalogue since being issued.)

After his American debut in *Rigoletto* at the Metropolitan in New York (1903), he went on to notch up more than 600 performances in forty operas there, idolised by the Americans for nearly two decades, despite the scandals of his private life. Unlike so many of his profession, Caruso was a convincing and impressive actor, and his most successful roles were in the *verismo* Italian operas, for example Cavaradossi in *Tosca* and Canio in *Pagliacci*. Wagner and the German repertoire did not interest him, but the range of his work in the Italian and French operas was extraordinary, taking in both lyric and dramatic roles in the standard works as well as the new roles from Puccini, Giordano *et al*.

What was it that made his voice so exceptional? In his youth he was taken for a baritone, so strong and mellow was the tone produced by his middle and lower voice; his *bel canto* phrasing and style allowed him to excel in lyrical parts; and there was also the 'Caruso sob', which he used to great dramatic effect. Size, brilliance and warmth combined with ringing, resonant, velvety smoothness.

Caruso's fees rose from $2 as a boy in 1891 to $15,000 for a single night's work in Mexico City in 1920. He was the first star to make a fortune from the 'gramophone'. His annual income from royalties alone was $115,000 at his peak, while the total royalties earned by all his discs during his lifetime and since his death had reached $3,500,000 by the 1950s. The collective sales of his recording of 'Vesti la giubba' ('Put on the costume' from *Pagliacci*), which he first recorded in 1902, made him the earliest recorded artist to sell more than a million copies.

He sang for the last time on 24 December 1920, only a fortnight after suffering a throat haemorrhage during a performance at the Brooklyn Academy. After several operations to arrest a pleurisy, he died in Naples the following August.

Chaliapin's life off stage was colourful. The soprano Geraldine Farrar described him as 'A great blond cherub of a man, of superb physique, he had an uncanny gift for cosmetic metamorphosis, and adding to dramatic gifts a magnificent voice that rolled out like melodious thunder, it was easy for him to equal the triumphs of even Caruso those days! And what a fellow with the ladies!' Chaliapin, often unruly, imperious and egocentric, was the centre of any gathering, a bon viveur *and* raconteur *who set the pace in the vodka stakes.*

CHALIAPIN, FYODOR
1873 ~ 1938
RUSSIAN BASS

The first Russian singer to win international acclaim, Chaliapin remains to cognoscenti the ultimate singer-actor. On and off the stage, he was, as the Germans say, *ein Original*, a character. He set the standards and made his own rules.

Of humble origins, Chaliapin was apprenticed to a cobbler at the age of ten and four years later joined a travelling opera company in the chorus, alongside the writer Maxim Gorky. By 1896 he had studied singing, made a local reputation and become something of a celebrity in Moscow, but it was not until 1901 that he appeared outside Russia. At La Scala he was heard as Mefistofele in Boito's opera (a role which became one of his trade marks) and elsewhere in the standard bass repertoire (Mephistopheles in *Faust*, Leporello in *Don Giovanni* and Don Basilio in *The Barber*) but it was his towering portrayal of **Boris Godunov** that created a sensation in New York (1921–2). To this day, Boris and Chaliapin are synonymous to many.

CHRISTOFF, BORIS
B. 1918
BULGARIAN BASS

Perhaps *the* great bass singing actor of the post-war era. He first sang the title role in *Boris Godunov* at La Scala, Milan in 1949 and became closely identified with the role, almost as much as with his portrayal of King Philip in Verdi's *Don Carlos*.

DELLA CASA, LISA
B. 1919
SWISS SOPRANO

Like **Sena Jurinac** she had an enviable reputation as a singer of Mozart and Richard Strauss (her interpretations of Arabella and the Countess in *Capriccio* are reckoned to be definitive). Also a fine *lieder* singer. Retired 1974.

DOMINGO, PLACIDO
B. 1941
SPANISH TENOR

Number one or number two? You take your choice between him and **Pavarotti**. For many, he is the greatest actor *and* singer of the day, able with extraordinary and unusual versatility to stretch from Mozart to Wagner and on to the crossover market of popular songs.

He was born in Madrid but his family, travelling singers in a zarzuela troupe, moved to Mexico when he was eight. (He took time off in 1987 to raise money for the victims of the Mexican earthquake.) He joined the national opera in Mexico City ten years later and was the lead tenor with the Tel Aviv opera company at the age of twenty-one. The career rivalry between him and Pavarotti as portrayed in the press has been as unnecessary as it has been irrelevant. They are two different instruments which should be nothing but a pleasure to compare. Perhaps the Italian has the richer, more sonorous voice but there is no contest when it comes to range of work and acting ability.

By his own calculations, following his first engagement in 1957 he has sung more than seventy-five roles in over 1,300 performances. Elisabeth Schwarzkopf, the great German soprano, was once asked to name a contemporary opera singer who equalled the giants of her own era. She answered at once: 'Domingo'.

FERRIER, KATHLEEN
1912 ~ 1953
ENGLISH CONTRALTO

There can be few singers whose early deaths have been so widely mourned. Ferrier was at the height of her career when cancer struck. Those who heard her live testify that hers was perhaps the greatest contralto voice of the century, one that not even her many records fully captured. A delightful personality with a glowing stage presence, 'Our Kath' was a Lancashire lass whose first job was as a telephone operator. She created the title role in Britten's *Rape of Lucretia* and sang **Orfeo** at Glyndebourne (1947) and Coven Garden (1953). In a career of just ten years she became among the best-loved singers of her generation.

FLAGSTAD, KIRSTEN
1895 ~ 1962
NORWEGIAN SOPRANO

From 1935, when she made her American debut as Sieglinde in *Die Walküre*, she established herself as the leading Wagnerian soprano of the day. Her grand voice was, in other words, not a silky sensuous sound (like **Kiri Te Kanawa**) or a bright *coloratura* (like **Joan Sutherland**) but one that could soar above the orchestra in the loudest passages with effortless, resplendent power. At the Met in New York, Flagstad reigned supreme among nearly a dozen of the finest dramatic sopranos of the century. Before she retired in 1954 she sang Dido in Purcell's *Dido and Aeneas*. Her recording of 'Dido's Lament' is particularly moving.

FRENI, MIRELLA
B. 1935
ITALIAN SOPRANO

In a widely varied career, she has sung such roles as Mimi, Violetta, Marguerite and Susanna with great success and also, since about 1970 when her voice darkened, some of the heavier roles, including Amelia (*Simon Boccanegra*), Tatyana (*Eugene Onegin*) and Desdemona (*Otello*). A captivating stage personality.

GALLI-CURCI
AMELITA
1882 ~ 1963
ITALIAN SOPRANO

A previous generation grew up with scratchy old discs of Galli-Curci's inimitable trilling of such songs as 'Lo, Hear the Gentle Lark' and arias from long forgotten

works including 'The Shadow Song' from Meyerbeer's *Dinorah* and 'Charmant oiseau' from David's *La Perle du Brésil*. On all these records, the flute obbligato accompanying her forays into the higher realms served to underline the amazing range and agility of her voice. Even today, they are something of a wonder.

During the latter part of her career (1918 onwards) she fought a tendency to sing slightly flat and suffered from a goitre. She was forced to retire in 1936. One of the few major stars of the period who never appeared in opera in England.

GEDDA, NICOLAI
B. 1925
SWEDISH TENOR

Like his fellow Swede and contemporary **Elisabeth Söderström**, Gedda is an accomplished linguist, a gift which has helped him become one of the most versatile and broad-ranging of artists – everything from Bach to Barber (*Vanessa*). Especially at home in the French repertoire.

GIGLI, BENIAMINO
1890 ~ 1957
ITALIAN TENOR

The son of a poor shoemaker, he began his career in 1914 by winning first prize in an international contest held in Parma. 'We have found *the* tenor,' read the official report. Together with **Caruso**, De Reszke and a very few other lyrico-dramatic tenors, both his voice and delivery were unblemished. His acting, it's true, was fairly limited but after his first appearances at the Met, where he

appeared from 1920 to 1932, Gigli was hailed as Caruso's successor. Beginning in 1918 he made some 370 recordings. At the age of sixty, the beauty of his voice remained undiminished, his technique secure. His name is pronounced *Ben'ya-meen-oh Jee'lee*, not, as we once heard, 'Benjamin Giggly'.

GOBBI, TITO
1913 ~ 1984
ITALIAN BARITONE

A combination of fine acting ability, intelligence, musicianship and a voice of enormous character, made Gobbi one of the most important and revered operatic artists of his generation. His Scarpia (*Tosca*), thought to be definitive at the time, has been captured on film opposite **Callas** (in the second act). Apart from his distinguished Puccini and Verdi interpretations, he made a notable Figaro (*The Barber*) and Wozzeck.

HORNE, MARILYN
B. 1934
AMERICAN MEZZO–SOPRANO

A s a twenty-year-old, Horne's voice was used for the title role of the film *Carmen Jones*, but it was in 1963 that she had her first major success when she sang *Norma* with Joan Sutherland, followed by a concert performance of Rossini's *Semiramide*. It was in this repertoire (Rossini, Bellini, Handel) that she revealed herself as a truly great *coloratura* mezzo.

JURINAC, SENA
B. 1921
YUGOSLAV SOPRANO

C onnoisseurs of Mozart singing put Jurinac near the top of the list – her appearances at Glyndebourne (1949–56) are remembered with affection – but as her warm lyric voice altered she moved to heavier roles. In Richard Strauss's music, her Octavian in *Der Rosenkavalier* is among the finest (the Trio in the recording by Kleiber is one of the most moving things on record and has been known to reduce grown men to a pulp), to say nothing of the Composer in *Ariadne auf Naxos* and, though not opera, the *Four Last Songs*.

KRAUS, ALFREDO
B. 1927
SPANISH TENOR

B orn in the Canaries of Austrian descent, he made his début in Cairo (Duke of Mantua in *Rigoletto*) and has made his name in the Italian and French roles. Of the latter his des Grieux (*Manon*) and **Werther** are well worth hearing.

LEHMANN, LEHMANN AND LEHMANN

E ven opera buffs have been known to confuse Lilli with Liza and Liza with Lotte.

In terms of opera history, the most important of the three is **Lilli** *above* (1848–1929), a celebrated German soprano who created the parts of Woglinde, Helmwige and the Woodbird for Wagner. She was also given a life contract with the Berlin Opera House, and sang Isolde in the American première of *Tristan*. She made her American début as **Carmen** and followed it by singing Brünnhilde in *Die Walküre* five days later. Her operatic repertoire comprised 170 roles in 114 operas (German, Italian and French); her repertoire of songs exceeded 600. Reckoned to be one of the great voices of history.

Liza (1826–1918) was an English soprano who abandoned the stage after her marriage in order to concentrate on composition. The first English woman composer to achieve international success, her most enduring (and endearing) work is a setting of 'In a Persian Garden'.

Lotte *above* (1888–1976), a second German soprano, though no relation, also celebrated for her Wagnerian interpretations, though perhaps better remembered today as a famous Marschallin in *Der Rosenkavalier*. The occasion of her farewell recital in New York (1951) was movingly captured for posterity.

LUDWIG, CHRISTA
B. 1928
GERMAN MEZZO-SOPRANO

One of the truly great post-war singers (of any voice), with a remarkable range able to encompass Orlovsky in *Die Fledermaus*, which she sang in her 1946 Frankfurt début, Dorabella (*Così*), Cherubino (*The Marriage of Figaro*), and Octavian (*Der Rosenkavalier*) as well as dramatic soprano roles (Wagner, Leonore in *Fidelio* and Verdi's Lady Macbeth).

MARTINELLI GIOVANNI
1885 ~ 1969
ITALIAN TENOR

After his 1913 American début in *Tosca* and his first appearance at the Met a fortnight later as Rodolfo in *La Bohème*, Martinelli remained at the Met for thirty years. He sang Radames (*Aida*) 126 times there and made his final appearance in a production of *Turandot* in Seattle in 1967, when he was eighty-two. A great **Otello**.

MELBA, DAME NELLIE
1861 ~ 1931
AUSTRALIAN SOPRANO

Born Helen Porter Mitchell, Nellie Melba (a name she took after her native city of Melbourne) came to epitomize the *prima donna assoluta*, the imperious, self-assured star of the opera world. She was to the vocal arts what Paderewski was to the piano – the synonym for her profession. Although she was a limited actress, her voice (which can still be heard on ancient discs) was remarkably pure and even throughout its wide range (up to a top F). She was and a brilliant *coloratura* which made Gilda (*Rigoletto*), Violetta (*La Traviata*) and Rosina (*Barber of Seville*) her natural territory.

Gourmets as well as opera buffs remember her fondly: her universal popularity with the public was reflected in the creation by the Savoy's famous chef, Escoffier, of *Pêche Melba* (half a poached peach served with vanilla ice cream and a raspberry sauce), and also in the crisp, thin slices of toasted bread known as Melba toast, patented in 1929 by a certain Bert Weil, president of the Devonsheer Melba Corporation.

MELCHIOR, LAURITZ
1890 ~ 1973
DANISH-BORN AMERICAN TENOR

Between the wars, he was considered to be the nonpareil Wagnerian *Heldentenor* – 'heroic tenor'. Indeed, some consider him to be the finest of all time and his portrayal of Tristan (*Tristan und Isolde*) to be unsurpassed.

MERRILL, ROBERT
B. 1917
AMERICAN BARITONE

Began his career as a popular singer on the radio before making his operatic début in 1944. One of the mainstays of the Met after World War II, he is another artist who remained with the company for thirty years. His recording of the duet from *The Pearl Fishers* (with **Jussi Björling**) is a classic.

MILNES, SHERRILL
B. 1935
AMERICAN BARITONE

Since his début at the Met in 1965, he has been acclaimed for all his performances of the standard baritone repertoire from Scarpia (*Tosca*) and **Don Carlo** to Escamillo (*Carmen*) and, especially, **Don Giovanni**.

NILSSON, BIRGIT
B. 1918
SWEDISH SOPRANO

The Wagnerian soprano *par excellence* of the 1950s, 60s and 70s and the successor of Kirsten Flagstad, she had seemingly inexhaustible vocal powers and a commanding stage presence. Also a memorable **Turandot**, Elektra and Salome. Was still singing in the 1980s.

NORMAN, JESSYE
B. 1945
AMERICAN SOPRANO

Statuesque, enormously popular artist with a rich lyrico-dramatic voice, she is as impressive in Wagner, Richard Strauss and the French repertoire as she is in spirituals and the varied fare of her concert recitals. She has recorded many operas, but appeared in few.

PATTI, ADELINA
1843 ~ 1919
ITALIAN SOPRANO

Verdi proclaimed Patti the greatest singer he had ever heard; the elderly French composer Auber declared, 'I have never heard so perfect an artist as Patti'; and Queen Victoria was not alone among the great and good who wept on hearing her sing. Though her acting was rudimentary and her musical intelligence limited, she was for forty-five years the undisputed queen of the opera world, the most popular (and wealthiest) prima donna of the late nineteenth century.

At the height of her career she had a repertoire of forty-two operas. *Coloratura* roles were specialities (especially Rosina in *The Barber*) along with Marguerite (*Faust*), Leonora (*Il Trovatore*) and **Aida** (she gave the London première). Appearing in twenty-five consecutive seasons at Covent Garden, she had a clause in her contract excusing her from rehearsals ('they tire the voice'). In London she could command a single performance fee of £200; when she toured the United States in her own railroad car in 1881, it was $5,000. It is said that she had a pet parrot who was trained to scream 'Cash! Cash!', the method by which she insisted on payment. No cash, no Patti.

She married three times. With her third husband, the Swedish Baron Cederström, she lived in the magnificent Craig-y-Nos ('Rock of Night') Castle in Brecknock, South Wales. Here she had her own theatre, as well as a billiard room illuminated by the first electric lights to be installed in a country house in Britain.

PAVAROTTI
LUCIANO
B. 1935
ITALIAN TENOR

The son of a baker and a tobacco-factory worker, he began his career as a school teacher, also selling insurance. Now the Big Man is either number one or number two tenor in the world, depending on personal preference. Certainly there can be very few people in the world who have not heard of him – a distinction accorded to only a handful of people in each generation – so well publicized and marketed has he been. And with every justification, for a voice like his comes once in a generation, creamily smooth but with tremendous power and range (though he's been careful to avoid Wagner).

Making his debut in 1961 he quickly became an international star, much helped by his association with **Joan Sutherland**, both on stage and on record. Donizetti, Verdi and Puccini – this is his territory, the lyric, *bel canto* repertoire, the land of beautiful tone, high Cs, enormous aplomb and heartfelt sincerity.

Like many another tenor he is a gastronome, though more corpulent than most. His other – perhaps more suprising hobby – is horse breeding.

One thing is certain, however, that no one has done more to bring opera to the man in the street than this engaging giant among the all-time greats. The Three Tenors, 'Nessun Dorma' for the World Cup, Pavarotti in the Park ... what next?

PEARS, PETER
1910 ~ 1986
ENGLISH TENOR

No voice is so inextricably linked with one single composer as Peter Pears's is with Benjamin Britten, whose partner and muse he was for three decades. Albert Herring, Vere in *Billy Budd*, and Aschenbach in *Death in Venice* were all his creations sung with a voice of no great beauty but with a profound musicality and instantly recognizable timbre.

PONS AND PONSELLE
TWO SOPRANO CONTEMPORARIES

Lily Pons (1898–1976) was a stunning-looking French (later American) *coloratura* soprano who made her Met début as Lucia (*Lucia di Lammermoor*) in 1931, appearing there on and off until 1958. Despite a limited repertoire, she became quite extraordinarily popular, appearing in several mediocre films and even having a town in Maryland, USA named after her (Lilypons). She had a voice of enormous agility and a vivacious, captivating presence.

Rosa Ponselle (1897–1981) was an American soprano, the daughter of Italian immigrants who gave her the middle name of 'Melba'. 'Caruso in petticoats' she was

called, and indeed it was the great tenor who was instrumental in arranging her first appearance at the Met. She was one of the supreme interpreters of **Norma** and that, as has been said, is a role which distinguishes the truly great sopranos from the very good. Another famous Norma, **Maria Callas**, described Ponselle as 'the greatest singer of us all'. Quite a compliment.

POPP, LUCIA
B. 1939
CZECH SOPRANO

One of her early successes (1967) was as an entrancing Queen of the Night (**Magic Flute**). She has a wonderful stage presence as well as the kind of *coloratura* voice that can melt glaciers instead of shattering them. She is also a noted interpreter of Richard Strauss, especially Arabella and the Marschallin (***Der Rosenkavalier***).

PREY, HERMANN
B. 1929
GERMAN BARITONE

A noted Figaro (***The Barber***) and Count (***Figaro***) with impeccable diction, his versatility and technical skill mean he can do equal justice to anything from Wagner to *lieder*.

TWO FOR THE PRICE OF ONE
LEONTYNE AND MARGARET

Leontyne Price (b. 1927) is the American soprano whose career began with an outstanding Bess (***Porgy and Bess***) followed by one of the most glamorous and

vocally exciting **Aidas** in history. (In 1959 she sang the role at La Scala, the first black singer ever to appear there.) Her Leonora (***Il Trovatore***) was another triumph. Besides the rich warmth of her voice, she is a considerable actress.

Margaret Price (b. 1941) is a Welsh soprano who has made her reputation as an unrivalled singer of Mozart, having made her début at only twenty as Cherubino (***Marriage of Figaro***) with the Welsh National Opera. Verdi also suits her warm lyric voice – Desdemona in ***Otello*** and Elisabeth in ***Don Carlos***, for instance.

RAIMONDI RUGGIERO
B. 1941
ITALIAN BASS

Apart from his beautifully controlled, yet florid voice, Raimondi is a considerable actor with a commanding stage presence. His **Boris Godunov** has been highly praised, but he is probably best known for the title role of ***Don Giovanni***, which he first sang in 1969 and repeated most memorably in Joseph Losey's 1979 film of the opera.

RAMEY, SAMUEL
B. 1942
AMERICAN BASS

Made his professional debut in ***Carmen*** (as Zuniga) with the New York City Opera in 1973 and has since made his mark in the *coloratura* roles of Handel and Rossini, while he is equally at home in such lyrico-dramatic roles as **Don Giovanni**.

SCHWARZKOPF
ELISABETH
B. 1915
GERMAN SOPRANO

Her name, unkindly translated, is 'Betty Blackhead'. Among the great actress-musicians of the century, she first made her name as a refined singer of Mozart but went on to appear in the world première of Stravinsky's *The Rake's Progress*, also becoming one of the most memorable of Marschallins (*Der Rosenkavalier*) and securing an unsurpassed reputation as a *lieder* singer. On BBC radio's 'Desert Island Disks', all the records she chose were her own.

SCOTTO, RENATA
B. 1933
ITALIAN SOPRANO

A year after her début in Milan as Violetta in *La Traviata* (1953) she was singing at La Scala, and quickly establishing herself in the *bel canto–coloratura* repertoire, with her warm-toned lyric voice. Clarity of diction and elegant phrasing are among her hallmarks. A memorable **Madam Butterfly**.

SILLS, BEVERLY
B. 1929
AMERICAN SOPRANO

Originally Belle Miriam Silverman, she appeared in public for the first time on radio aged three under the name of 'Bubbles' (her nickname to this day). She has one of those winning personalities, which, combined with her intelligence and spectacular *coloratura* voice, made her many admirers in the 1950s and 1960s. She retired at the age of fifty to run (highly successfully) the New York City Opera.

SÖDERSTRÖM
ELISABETH
B. 1927
SWEDISH SOPRANO

Leaving aside her fresh lyric voice, she is an accomplished linguist and musician, abilities that have naturally led her into challenging roles (Emilia Marty in Janáček's *The Makropulos Affair* is a favourite) and through which she has acquired a wider than average repertoire, including Richard Strauss, Blomdahl, Mozart, Britten, Berg and much else. One of the finest singing actresses of her generation.

STADE
FREDERICA VON
B. 1945
AMERICAN MEZZO-SOPRANO

Among the most charming personalities and voices of the present day, she had a slow start to her career but is now making up for lost time, singing Rossini, Mozart and Richard Strauss as well as – and far more successfully than most who try it – the 'crossover market', with superb recordings of *Showboat* (Kern) and *Anything Goes* (Cole Porter). Certainly knows how to bring out the fun and wit of a piece.

SUPERVIA
CONCHITA
1895 ~ 1936
SPANISH MEZZO-SOPRANO

Although she died well over half a century ago, there are relatively few mezzos since who have matched her for sparkling exuberance and the sheer virtuosity of her *coloratura* technique. A tremendous personality comes over in the records she made (which are well worth hearing despite the hiss-and-crackle of the surfaces), particularly in her **Carmen** arias and as Rosina (*Barber of Seville*). She married the British industrialist Sir Ben Rubinstein in 1931 and died in London at the age of forty after childbirth.

SUTHERLAND
DAME JOAN
B. 1926
AUSTRALIAN SOPRANO

'La Stupenda' – a nickname the Italians gave her in 1961 after her Italian début in *Lucia* (1961). After Callas' retirement from the operatic stage, she was by far the best-known singer in the world, universally held in affection not just for having one of the finest voices in history but because of her down-to-earth personality and warm-hearted presence.

You tend to be a Callas freak or a Sutherland fan. The Callas camp will point to their idol's acting ability, her intelligence, the emotional truth of her singing, damning Sutherland for her lack of all these qualities. The Sutherland supporters will play any of her many recordings to demonstrate a technique, an evenness of tone and a vocal range that no one of her generation could equal. Perhaps more significant is the sheer natural beauty of the sound she produced. Her great roles were in the *bel canto–coloratura* repertoire (especially the nineteenth-century Italians) in which she was coached and encouraged by her husband, the conductor Richard Bonynge.

'Joanie' was made a Dame in 1978 and retired in 1990. Stupendous indeed.

TAUBER, RICHARD
1891–1948
AUSTRIAN-BORN ENGLISH TENOR

*T*he interpreter *par excellence* of Viennese operetta, especially those of Lehár (not surprisingly, since many roles were written for him), and any collection of vocal records must feature his uniquely charming voice. He made his début in 1912 as Tamino in *The Magic Flute* and it's often forgotten just how good a Mozart (and *lieder*) singer he was. Thankfully, there are some recordings still available to remind us.

TEBALDI, RENATA
B. 1922
ITALIAN SOPRANO

A supremely stylish lyrico-spinto voice. In the Italian *verismo* repertoire she could hold her own with any, even Callas, though she did not compete with her in the Bellini-Donizetti repertoire. Her **Tosca**, **Aida**, Desdemona (*Otello*) and (especially) Cio-Cio San (*Madame Butterfly*) were outstanding.

TE KANAWA
DAME KIRI
B. 1944
NEW ZEALAND SOPRANO

*T*oday, Dame Kiri is the best known (and possibly the most recorded) soprano in the world. Her looks, her charming girl-next-door public persona combined with one of the most beautiful-

sounding voices of the century has put her in the mega-star bracket, along with the Three Tenors, as the personification of the opera star of today. Millions saw and heard her radiant singing at the wedding of the Prince and Princess of Wales. She has sung all the major roles from Mozart and Verdi to Bizet and Bernstein. But, just as much as opera, she loves singing lighter music, and enjoyed great success in Bernstein's recording of *West Side Story*, as well as topping the charts with the Rugby World Cup theme song, '*World in Union*'.

TETRAZZINI, LUISA
1871 ~ 1940
ITALIAN SOPRANO

*O*ne of the most celebrated of *coloratura* sopranos – and one of the most buxom. (Perhaps Spaghetti Tetrazzini, which she

inspired, was the cause.) She was not much of an actress but that didn't seem to matter when she opened her mouth. Very few could – nor ever have – matched her effortless brilliance in virtuoso roles demanding high notes and dazzling passages. She is said to have earned over $5 million during her career (she retired in 1934), and at the height of her fame was paid a fee of $3,000 a performance. She died in poverty.

TURNER, DAME EVA
1892 ~ 1990
ENGLISH SOPRANO

A much-loved and remarkable dramatic soprano whose power and wide range (low G to top D) made her outstanding in Wagner and Verdi. It was quite something for an Oldham-born singer to be accepted by Toscanini and sing for him at La Scala (Freia and Sieglinde) which she did in 1924. Alfano (who completed Puccini's last opera) considered her to be the perfect **Turandot**. Listening to her recording of the role, one can hear why.

VICKERS, JON
B. 1926
CANADIAN TENOR

*I*f he's not *the Heldentenor* of the post-war era, he is certainly one of them. His commanding stage presence and vocal stamina have made him indispensable in Wagner and the heroic-tenor roles, notably, **Otello**, **Samson**, Pollione (*Norma*) and **Peter Grimes**, as well as a superb Canio (*Pagliacci*). He began his career as manager of a branch of Woolworth's.

INDEX

Numbers in **bold** refer to main sections

A

'Abends,will ich schlafen gehn'[Han & Gret] 53
Abigaille [Nabucco] 78
Abu Hassan 140
Acis and Galatea 127
Adalgisa [Norma] 79
'Addio del passato' [La Traviata] 109
'Addio, dolce svegliare' [Bohème] 29
Adele [Fledermaus] 46-7
'Adieu, notre petite table' [Manon] 67
Adina [L'Elisir d'Amore] 41
Adriana Lecouvreur 20
Africaine, L' (African Maid) 20, 129
Agathe [Freischütz] 49-50
'Ah fors'e lui ... Sempre libera' [Traviata] 109
'Ah fuyez, douce image' [Manon] 67
'Ah! je ris de me voir' [Faust] 43
'Ah Mimi, tu piu non torni' [Bohème] 29
'Ah, si, ben mio coll'essere' [Trovatore] 113
'Ai nostri monti' [Trovatore] 113
Aida 11, 21-3, 48, 81, 138, 150, 151, 152, 154
Akhnaten 23
Alberich [Ring] 94, 95, 96, 97
Albert [Werther] 115
Albert Herring 122, 152
Alceste 126
Alfano, Franco 114, 154
Alfio [Cav] 35
Alfred [Fledermaus] 46
Alfredo [Traviata] 109
Allen, Thomas 12, **144**
Almaviva, Count [Barber] 25-6
Almaviva, Count and Countess [Fig] 16, 69-70, 152
Amelia [Masked Ball] 23
Amico Fritz, L' 128
Amneris [Aida] 22-3
Amonasro [Aida] 22-3
'amor sull ali rosee, D' [Trovatore] 113
'amour est un oiseau rebelle, L' [Carmen] 33
Anckarstroem, Capt. [Masked Ball] 23-4
'Ancora un passo' [Butterfly] 62
Anderson, June 13, **144**
Angeles, Victoria de Los **144**
Angelina [Cenerentola] 36
Angelotti [Tosca] 106-7
'Anges purs!' [Faust] 43
Anna Bolena 123, 124, 144
Antonia [Tales of Hoffmann] 100, 101
Anvil Chorus [Trovatore] 113
Arabella [Capriccio] 16, 147, 152
'Ardon gl'incensi' [Lucia] 57
Ariadne auf Naxos 137
Arline [Bohemian Girl] 29-30
Arnheim, Count [Bohemian Girl] 29-30
'arreglito, El' 34
Arvidson, Mlle. [Masked Ball] 23-4
'As some day it may happen' [Mikado] 77
'As when the dove' [Acis and Galatea] 127
Aschenbach [Death in Venice] 152
Atalanta 127
Attila 138
'Au fond du temple saint' [Pearl Fishers] 86, 144
Auber, Daniel François Esprit **120**, 151

'aura amoroso, Un' [Così] 37
Aureliano in Palmira 13, 25
'Avant de quitter ces lieux' [Faust] 43
'Ave Maria' [Otello] 82
Azucena [Trovatore] 111-13

B

Bach, J S 18, 126, 130, 148
Bailey, Norman **144**
Baker, Dame Janet 15, **144**
Ballad of the Easy Life [Threepenny Opera] 103
Ballo in Maschera, Un 23-4, 138
Barber of Seville 12-13, 24-6, 36, 68, 123, 134, 135; singers 147, 149, 150, 151, 152, 153
Barbier, Jules 42, 100
Bartered Bride, The 26, 136
Bartolo, Dr [Barber & Fig] 24, 25-6, 69-70
Battaglia di Legnano, La 138
'Batti, batti, o bel Masetto' [Don Giovanni] 40
Beatrice di Tenda 121, 145
Beckmesser, Sixtus [Meistersinger] 71, 74
Beethoven, Ludwig van 18, **44-5**, 63, **120**, 136; and other composers 126, 127, 135, 139, 140
'Bei mannern' [Magic Flute] 66
'bel di vedremo, Un' [Butterfly] 62
'Bel insecte à l'aile dorée' [Orpheus] 81
'Bel raggio lusinghier' [Semiramide] 135
Belcore [L'Elisir d'Amore] 41
Bell Song [Lakmé] 13, 54
'Bella figlia dell'amore' [Rigoletto] 91
Belle Hélène, La 132
'Belle nuit, o nuit d'amour' [Tales of Hoff] 101
Bellini, Vincenzo 11, 12, **79**, **120-1**, 144, 149, 154
Beppe [Pag] 84-5
Berenice 127
Berganza, Teresa 15, **144**
Bergonzi, Carlo **144**
Berlioz, H 6, 11, 49, 85, 120, 129, 134, 140, 144
Bernstein, Leonard 145, 154
'Bess, you is my woman now' [Porgy & Bess] 89
'Bildnis ist bezaubernd schön, Dies' [Magic F] 66
Billy Budd 122, 152
Bizet, Georges 11, **31-4**, 85-6, **121-2**, 135, 144, 154
Björling, Jussi 16, **144**, 150
Blind, Dr [Fledermaus] 46
Bohème, La 16, 21, 23, **27-9**, 60, 67, 114, 133; compared with Tosca 103, 106; singers 16, 144, 145, 148, 150
Bohemian Girl, The 29-30
Boito, Arrigo 14, 50, 81, **122**, 147
Borgogna, Enrico di 123
Boris Godunov 12, 30, 131, 147, 152
Borodin, Alexander **123**
Bouillon, Princess [Adriana Lecouvreur] 20
'Braid the raven hair' [Mikado] 77
Brandenburgers in Bohemia, The 136
Bridal Chorus [Lohengrin] 55
Brigands, Les 132
'Brightly dawns our wedding day' [Mikado] 77
Britten, Benjamin 6, 11, **86**, **122**; singers 144, 148, 152, 153
Brown, Lucy and Tiger [Threepenny Opera] 103
'Bruderchen komm tanz'mit mir' [Han & Gret] 52
Brünnhilde [Ring] 16, 94-7, 145, 149
'Buona sera, mio signore' [Barber] 26

'Buon'giorno, signorine!' [Gondoliers] 51

C

Caballé, Montserrat 16, 123, **144**, 145
Calaf [Turandot] 114-15
Callas, Maria 7, 16, *103*, 123, 144, **145**, 149; compared with other singers 152, 153, 154
'Calumnia e un venticello, La' [Barber] 26
Calzabigi, Ranieri da 14, 80, 126
Cambiale di Matrimonio, La 134
Camille de Rosillon [Merry Widow] 75
Cammarano, Salvatore 56, 111
Can-Can [Orpheus in Underworld] 81
Canio [Pag] 83, 84-5, 146, 154
Capriccio 136, 147, 152
Capuleti e i Montecchi, I 121, 145
'Care selve' [Atalanta] 127
Carmen 15, 16, 21, **31-4**, 46, 74, 121-2, 137; singers 145, 149, 151, 152, 153
Carmen Jones 6, 32, 149
'carnival for life, A' [Graf von Luxemburg] 128
'Caro nome' [Rigoletto] 91
Carré, Michel 42, 85, 100
Carreras, José Maria 16, **144**, **145**
Caruso, Enrico 16, 29, 41, 84, **146**, 147, 148, 149
Cassio [Otello] 82
'Casta diva' [Norma] 12, 79
Catalogue Aria [Don Giovanni] 40
Cavalleria Rusticana 7, 14, 16, **34-5**, 68, 83-4, 128, 145
Cavaradossi [Tosca] 103, 106-7, 146
'Celeste Aida' [Aida] 23
Cenerentola, La 13, **36**, 135
Chaliapin, Feodor 12, 30, **147**
Champagne Aria [Don Giovanni] 40
Chanson Bohème [Carmen] 34
Charlotte [Werther] 115
Charpentier, Gustave 55-6
'Che faro senza Eurydice' [Orpheus & Eurydice] 80
'Che gelida manina' [Boheme] 29
'Che puro ciel' [Orpheus and Eurydice] 80
'Che soave zeffiretto' [Figaro] 70
'Che volo d'augelli ... Stridono lassù' [Pag] 85
'Ch'ella mi creda' [Fanciulla del West] 133
Cherubino [Figaro] 16, 69-70, 150, 152
Cheval de Bronze, Le 120
'Chi mi frena' [Lucia] 57
Chopin, Frédéric 18, 120-1
Chorus of the Hebrew Slaves [Nabucco] 78
Christoff, Boris 12, 30, **147**
Cid, Le 129
'Cielo e mar!' [Gioconda] 50
Cilea, Francesco 20
Cinderella 13, **36**, 135
Cio-Cio-San [Butterfly] 60, 62, 153, 154
Clemenza di Tito, La 131
Cobbler's Song [Meistersinger] 74
Columbine [Pag] 84-5
'Come friends, who plough the seas' [Pirates] 125
'Come soglio' [Così] 37
'Com'e gentil' [Don Pasquale] 40
'Comme autrefois dans la nuit sombre' [Pearl F] 86
Comte Ory, Le 135
'Contro un cor che accende amore' [Barber] 25
Coppelius [Tales of Hoffmann] 100-1

Corcoran, Capt and Josephine [*Pinafore*] 125
Così fan tutte **36-7**, 131, 144, 150
'*Credo in un Dio crudel*' [*Otello*] 82
Crespel, Councillor [*Tales of Hoffmann*] 101
Crown [*Porgy and Bess*] 88-9
Cunning Litttle Vixen, The 37, 128
D
Da Ponte, Lorenzo 14, 36, 37, 39, 68, **131**, 136
'*Dal tuo stellato soglio*' [*Mosè in Egitto*] 135
Daland, Capt [*Flying Dutchman*] 47
'*Dalla sua pace*' [*Don Giovanni*] 40
'*Dance a cachucha*' [*Gondoliers*] 51
Dance of the Blessed Spirits [*Orph & Eurydice*] 80
Dance of the Comedians [*Bartered Bride*] 26
Dance of the Hours [*Gioconda*] 50
Dandini [*Cenerentola*] 36
Danilowitsch, Count Danilo [*Merry Widow*] 75
Dapertutto [*Tales of Hoffmann*] 100, 101
Death in Venice 122, 152
Debussy, Claude 18, 127, 132, 135
'*Deh, non volerli vittime*' [*Norma*] 79
Delibes, Léo 53-4
Della Casa, Lisa **147**
'*Depuis le jour où je me suis donnée*' [*Louise*] 56
des Grieux [*Manon & Manon Lescaut*] 67-8, 149
Desdemona [*Otello*] 16, 82, 148, 152, 154
Despina [*Così*] 36
Di Luna, Count [*Trovatore*] 111-13, 144
'*Di quella pira*' [*Trovatore*] 113
'*Di tanti palpiti*' [*Tancredi*] 135
Diamants de la Couronne, Les 120
'*Dich teure Halle*' [*Tannhäuser*] 102
Dido and Aeneas 38, 133, 148
Dinorah 129, 148
'*Divinités du Styx*' [*Alceste*] 126
Djamileh 122
Dmitry [*Boris Godunov*] 30
'*Dolce Notte*' [*Butterfly*] 62
Doll Song [*Tales of Hoffmann*] 101
'*Dôme épais, le jasmin*' [*Lakmé*] 54
Domingo, Placido 7, 16, *81, 82*, 103, **147-8**
Domino Noir, Le 120
Don Alfonso [*Così*] 36-7
Don Alvaro [*Forza del Destino*] 49
Don Basilio [*Barber & Fig*] 12, 25-6, 69 147
Don Carlo [*Forza del Destino*] 49
Don Carlos 38, 138, 147, 151, 152
Don Giovanni 18, **39-40**, 100, 131, 141, 147,
   151, 152
Don José [*Carmen*] 32-4, 145
Don Ottavio [*Don Giovanni*] 40
Don Pasquale 40, 41, 123, 124
Don Pizarro [*Fidelio*] 44
Don Quichotte 129
Donizetti, Gaetano 11, 12, 78, **123-4**, 144, 151, 154
   operas 29, **40**, 41, 44, **56-7**, 111
Donna Anna [*Don Giovanni*] 40
Donna Elvira [*Don Giovanni*] 40
'*donna é mobile, La*' [*Rigoletto*] 12, 91, 137
'*Donna non vidi mai*' [*Manon Lescaut*] 68
Dorabella [*Così*] 36-7, 144, 150
'*Dove sei*' [*Rodelinda*] 127
'*Dove sono*' [*Figaro*] 70

D'Oyly Carte, Richard 51, 124, 125, 132
Dream Aria [*Manon*] 67
Dream Pantomime [*Hansel and Gretel*] 53
Drei Pintos, Die 140
du Locle, Camille 21, 38
Duke of Mantua [*Rigoletto*] 89, 90-1, 149
'*Duke or a Duchess, A*' [*Gondoliers*] 51
Dulcamara [*L'Elisir d'Amore*] 41
Dumb Girl of Portici, The 120
E
'*E lucevan le stelle*' [*Tosca*] 107
Easter Hymn [*Cav*] 35
'*Ecco ridente in cielo*' [*Barber*] 26
Edgar 27, 132, 133
Edgardo [*Lucia*] 57
'*Ein Mädchen oder Weibchen*' [*Magic Flute*] 66
Eine Nacht in Venedig 136
'*Einsam in trüben Tagen*' [*Lohengrin*] 55
Eisenstein, Gabriel von [*Fledermaus*] 46
Elektra 98, 136, 137, 151
Elisabeth de Valois [*Don Carlos*] 38, 152
Elisabeth [*Tannhäuser*] 101, 102
Elisir d'Amore, L' 41, 123, 124, 145
Elsa of Brabant [*Lohengrin*] 55
Emilia di Liverpool 123, 124
'*En fermant les yeux*' [*Manon*] 67
English Ring 29
Enrico [*Lucia*] 57
'*Entry of the Gods into Valhalla*' [*Ring*] 95
'*Eri tu che macchiavi quell'anima*' [*Ballo*] 24
Erik [*Flying Dutchman*] 47
Ernani 90, 137, 138
Ernesto [*Don Pasquale*] 40
Escamillo [*Carmen*] 32-4, 151
'*Esultate*' [*Otello*] 82
Etoile du Nord, L' 129
Eugene Onegin 42, 137, 148
Euryanthe 14, 140
Eva [*Meistersinger*] 71, 74
Evening Prayer [*Hansel and Gretel*] 53
Excursions of Mr Broucek, The 128
F
Fafner [*Ring*] 94, 95, 96
Falke, Dr [*Fledermaus*] 46
Falstaff 11, 14, 122, 137, 138
Fanciulla del West, La 133
'*Farewell, my love, farewell*' [*Frasquita*] 128
Fasolt [*Ring*] 94, 95
Faust 15, **42-3**, 49, 126-7, 147, 148, 151
Favorita, La 44, 123, 124
Fernando [*Favorite*] 44
Ferrando [*Così*] 36-7
Ferrando [*Trovatore*] 111-13
Ferrier, Kathleen 13, *80*, 127, **148**
Fidelio 16, 44-5, 49, 120, 139, 140, 150
Figaro [*Barber & Figaro*] 25-6, 68-70, 149, 152
Fille du Régiment, La 123, 124
'*Fin ch'han dal vino*' [*Don Giovanni*] 40
Finta Semplice, La 130
Fiordiligi [*Così*] 36-7
Flagstad, Kirsten **148**, 151
Fledermaus, Die 16, 18, **45-7**, 74, 136, 150
'*fleur que tu m'avais jetée, La*' [*Carmen*] 34
Fliegende Holländer, Der 47-8, 54, 139

Florestan [*Fidelio*] 44-5, 120
Flower Duet [*Butterfly*] 62
Flower Duet [*Lakmé*] 54
Flower Song [*Carmen*] 34
'*flowers that bloom in the spring, The*' [*Mikado*] 77
Fly Duet [*Orpheus in Underworld*] 81
Flying Dutchman, The 47-8, 54, 139
Force of Destiny, The 48-9, 138
Forester [*Cunning Vixen*] 37
Forza del Destino, La 48-9, 138
Fra Diavolo 120
Frasquita 128
Frau ohne Schatten, Die 137
'*Fredda ed immobile*' [*Barber*] 26
Freia [*Ring*] 94, 95, 154
Freischütz, Der 14, 16, **49-50**, 52, 122, 139, 140
Freni, Mirella **148**
Friederike 128
From the House of the Dead 128
'*furtiva lagrima, Una*' [*L'Elisir d'Amore*] 41
G
Galli-Curci, Amelita 13, 25, 57, **148**
Galli-Marié, Célestine 31, *33*
Gazza Ladra, La 135
Gedda, Nicolai **148**
Gershwin, George **87-9**, **124**
'*Gia nella notte*' [*Otello*] 82
Giacosa, Giuseppe 27, 60, 67, 103
Gianni Schicchi 50, 133
Gibichungs [*Ring*] 96-7
Gigli, Beniamino 41, 146, **148-9**
Gilbert & Sullivan 14, 51, **76-7**, 120, 122, **124-6**,
   132
Gilda [*Rigoletto*] 90-1, 150
Gille, Philippe 53, 67
Gioconda, La 50, 122, 132
Giordano, Umberto 16, 146
Giovanna d'Arco 138
'*Girls were made to love and kiss*' [*Paganini*] 128
Giuditta 128
Giulietta [*Tales of Hoffmann*] 100, 101
Giuseppe [*Gondoliers*] 51
Glass, Philip 23, **126**
Glawari, Hanna [*Merry Widow*] 74-5
'*Gloire immortelle*' [*Faust*] 43
Gluck, C 6, 11, 14, *80*, 81, 110, **126**, 140, 144
Gobbi, Tito 12, *103*, **149**
Golden Girl of the West, The 133
Goldenmane [*Cunning Vixen*] 37
Goldman, Shalom 23
Gondinet, Edmond 53
Gondoliers, The 51, 126
Götterdämmerung 47, 92, 94, **96-7**
Gottfried [*Lohengrin*] 55
Gounod, Charles 11, **42-3**, 94, **126-7**, 129, 144
Graf von Luxemburg, Der 128
Grand Duke, The 126
Grande Duchesse de Gerolstein, La 132
Grigory [*Boris Godunov*] 30
Grimaldo, Enzo [*Gioconda*] 50
Guglielmo [*Così*] 36-7
Gunther [*Ring*] 94, 97
Gutrüne [*Ring*] 94, 97
Gypsy Baron 136

H

'Habanera' [*Carmen*] 31, 33
'Hab' mir's gelobt' [*Rosenkavalier*] 99
Hagen [*Ring*] 94, 97
Halévy, Ludovic 31, 46, 67, 80, 121
Hammerstein, Oscar 32, 87
Handel, George Frideric 6, 12, 15, **127**, 133; singers 144, 149, 152
Hansel and Gretel 52-3, **127**, 140
'Happily coupled are we' [*Ruddigore*] 126
Harlequin [*Pag*] 84-5
Helen [*Paride ed Elena*] 126
Helmwige [*Ring*] 94, 149
'Here's a how-de-do' [*Mikado*] 77
Hermann, the Landgrave [*Tannhäuser*] 102
Heyward, (Edwin) DuBose 87
Hofmannsthal, Hugo von 14, 98, 136
'Holle Rache kocht in meinem herzen' [*Magic F*] 66
Horne, Marilyn 15, **149**
Huguenots, Les 129
Humming Chorus [*Butterfly*] 62
Humperdinck, Engelbert 14, **52-3**, **127**, 140
Hunding [*Ring*] 94, 95

I

'I am a courtier grave and serious' [*Gondoliers*] 51
'I am so proud ... To sit in solemn silence' [*Mik*] 77
'I am the captain of the Pinafore' [*Pinafore*] 125
'I am the monarch of the sea' [*Pinafore*] 125
'I am the very model ... Major-Gen'[*Pirates*] 125
I due foscari 138
'I got plenty o' nuttin'' [*Porgy and Bess*] 89
'I have a song to sing-o' [*Yeomen*] 126
'I stole the Prince' [*Gondoliers*] 51
'I'm called little Buttercup' [*HMS Pinafore*] 125
'I've got a little list' [*Mikado*] 77
Iago [*Otello*] 82
Iclanta 137
Idomeneo 130, 131
'If you want a receipt for that mystery'[*Pat'ce*] 125
'If you're anxious for to shine' [*Patience*] 125
'Il était un roi de Thule' [*Faust*] 43
'Il mio tesoro' [*Don Giovanni*] 40
Illica, Luigi 27, 60, 67, 103, 106
'In enterprise of martial kind' [*Gondoliers*] 51
'In fernem land' [*Lohengrin*] 55
'In quelle trine morbide' [*Manon Lescaut*] 68
'In questa reggia' [*Turandot*] 115
'Inaffia l'ugola' [*Otello*] 82
Inez [*Trovatore*] 111-13
'Inneggiamo, il Signor non è morte' [*Cav*] 35
Intermezzo [*Cav*] 14, 34, **35**
Intermezzo 137
Iolanthe 125
Ismaele [*Nabucco*] 78
'It ain't necessarily so' [*Porgy and Bess*] 89
Italiana in Algeri, L' 135

J

'Ja, das Studium der Weiber ist Schwer' [*Merry Widow*] 75
Jacquino [*Fidelio*] 44-5
Janáček, Leoš 14, **37**, **127-8**, 136, 153
'Je crois entendre encore' [*Pearl Fishers*] 86
Jenik [*Bartered Bride*] 26
Jenůfa 128

'Jerum! Jerum!' [*Meistersinger*] 74
Jerusalem 138
Jewel Song [*Faust*] 43
Jolie Fille de Perth, La 122
'Journey to the Rhine' [*Ring*] 47, 97
Juive, La 121
Julien [*Louise*] 56
Julius Caesar 127
Jupiter [*Orpheus in Underworld*] 81
Jurinac, Sena 147, **149**

K

'Kann mich auch an ein Madel erinnern' [*Rosenk*] 99
Kaspar [*Freischütz*] 49
Katya Kabanova 128
King of Clubs [*Love for Three Oranges*] 56
'Klange der heimat' [*Fledermaus*] 47
'Kleine Sandman bin ich, Der' [*Hans & Gret*] 52
Ko-Ko [*Mikado*] 76-7
Kraus, Alfredo **149**

L

'Là ci darem la mano' [*Don Giovanni*] 40
Lakmé 13, 16, **53-4**
Land des Lächelns, Das (Land of Smiles) 128
'Largo al Factotum' [*Barber*] 26
Laughing Song [*Fledermaus*] 47
'Legend of Kleinzack, The' [*Tales of Hoff*] 101
Lehár, Franz **74-5**, 128, 154
Lehmann, Lilli **149**
Lehmann, Liza **149**
Lehmann, Lotte **149-50**
Leïla [*Pearl Fishers*] 85-6
'Leise leise, fromme weise' [*Freischütz*] 50
Lensky [*Eugene Onegin*] 42
Leoncavallo, Ruggiero 16, 27, **83-5**, 128
Leonora [*Favorita*] 44
Leonora [*Forza del Destino*] 48-9
Leonora [*Trovatore*] 111-13, 151, 152
Leonore [*Fidelio*] 44-5, 150
Letter Duet [*Figaro*] 70
Letter Scene [*Eugene Onegin*] 42
'Libiamo, libiamo, ne'lieti calici' [*Traviata*] 109
Liebestod [*Tristan and Isolde*] 14, 47, 110
Liebesverbot, Das 139
Linda di Chamounix 124
Lindorf [*Tales of Hoffmann*] 100, 101
'Lippen schweigen' [*Merry Widow*] 75
Liszt, Franz 55, 94, 95, 99, 127, 135, 139
Liù [*Turandot*] 114-15
Loge [*Ring*] 94, 95, 96
Lohengrin 47, **54-5**, 120, 139
Lola [*Cav*] 35
Lombardi alla Prima Grociata, I 138
Louise 16, **55-6**
'Love breaks every bond' [*Graf von Lux*] 128
Love Duet [*Threepenny Opera*] 103
Love for Three Oranges 56
'Love in her eyes sits playing' [*Acis & Galatea*] 127
'Love,whence your magic power?'[*Land of Smiles*]128
Lucia di Lammermoor 13, 29, 44, **56-7**, 111, 123, 124; singers 145, 152, 153
Lucretia Borgia 124, 144
Ludwig, Christa 15, **150**

Luisa Miller 111, 138
Lustige Witwe, Die **74-5**, 116-17, 128

M

Macbeth 138, 150
Mack the Knife [*Threepenny Opera*] 103
Mad Scene [*Lucia*] 13, 29, 57
'Madamina' [*Don Giovanni*] 40
Madam Butterfly 16, 18, **58-62**, 133, 144, 153, 154
'Magic Fire Music' [*Ring*] 96, 97
Magic Flute 12, 13, 16, **63-6**, 131, 140, 152, 154
'Magnet hung in a hardware shop' [*Patience*] 125
Maid of Orleans, The 137
Makropoulos Affair, The 128, 153
Malatesta, Doctor [*Don Pasquale*] 40
Mallika [*Lakmé*] 54
'Man who would woo a fair...maid' [*Yeoman*] 126
Manon 67, 114, **129**, 144, 149
Manon Lescaut 27, **67-8**, 133
Manrico [*Trovatore*] 111-13
Marcellina [*Figaro*] 69-70
Marcello [*Bohème*] 27, 29
Marco [*Gondoliers*] 51
Mařenka [*Bartered Bride*] 26
Marguerite [*Faust*] 42-3, 148, 151
Maria Stuarda 124
Marriage of Figaro 16, 25, 39, **68-70**, 131; singers 148, 150, 152
Marschallin [*Rosenkavalier*] 98-9, 150, 152, 153
Martinelli, Giovanni **150**
Marty, Emilia [*Makropoulos Affair*] 153
Mascagni, Pietro 14, 16, **34-5**, 50, 68, 83, **128-9**
Maschere, Le (Masks) 128
Masked Ball, A **23-4**, 138
Massenet, Jules 11, **67**, 114, **115**, 129
Mastersingers see *Meistersinger*
Maurizio, Count of Saxony [*Adriana L*] 20
Max [*Freischütz*] 16, 49-50
Mazeppa 137
Medea 144, 145
'Meditation' [*Thaïs*] 129
Mefistofele 122, 147
Meilhac, Henri 31, 46, 67
'Mein Herr Marquis' [*Fledermaus*] 47
Meistersinger von Nürnberg, Die 47, **70-4**, 94, 101, 139, 144
Melba, Dame Nellie 25, 29, 57, **150**
Melchior, Lauritz 16, **150**
Mephistopheles [*Faust*] 12, 42-3, 147
'merriest fellows are we, The' [*Gondoliers*] 51
Merrill, Robert 12, 144, **150**
Merry Widow, The **74-5**, 116-17, 128
Meyerbeer, G 13, 15, 20, 47, 106, **129**, 137, 148
Micaela [*Carmen*] 32-3
Michonnet [*Adriana Lecouvreur*] 20
Mikado, The 51, **76-7**, 126
Milnes, Sherrill **151**
Mime [*Ring*] 94, 95, 96
Mimi [*Bohème*] 16, 27, 29, 60, 144, 148
'Mir ist so wunderbar' [*Fidelio*] 44
'Mira, O Norma' [*Norma*] 79
Miracle, Dr [*Tales of Hoffmann*] 100, 101
Mireille 127
Miserere [*Trovatore*] 113
'Mit mir keine Kammer dir zu klein' [*Rosenkav*] 99

'Mon coeur s'ouvre à ta voix' [Sam et Dal] 100
Monostatos [Magic Flute] 63, 66
Monteverdi, Claudio 6, 10, 11, 137, 144
'more humane Mikado ... , A' [Mikado] 77
Morgana, Fata [Love for Three Oranges] 56
Mosè in Egitto 134, 135
Mozart, Wolfgang A 14, 98, 121, 129, **130-1**, 136, 140; history of opera 6, 7, 11; operas 25, **36-7, 39-40, 63-6, 68-70**, 100; singers 12, 144, 147, 149, 152, 153, 154
Muette di Portici, La 120
Mussorgsky, Modest 30, 121, **131**
'My eyes are fully open ... '[Ruddigore] 126
'My name is John Wellington Wells' [Sorcerer] 125
N
Nabucco 78, 138
'Nacqui all'affanno...Non più mesta' [Cen'tola] 36
Nadir [Pearl Fishers] 85-6, 122
Nanki-Poo [Mikado] 76-7
Nedda [Pag] 84-5
Nemorino [L'Elisir d'Amore] 41, 145
Neris [Medea] 144
'Nessun Dorma' [Turandot] 7, 12, 85, 115, 151
'Never mind the why & wherefore' [Pinafore] 125
Nicklause [Tales of Hoffmann] 100, 101
Nightmare Song [Iolanthe] 125
Nilakantha [Lakmé] 53-4
Nilsson, Birgit 151
'Niun mi tema' [Otello] 82
'No, Pagliaccio non son!' [Pag] 85
'Non lo diro col labbro' [Ptolemy] 127
'Non mi dir' [Don Giovanni] 40
'Non più andrai' [Figaro] 70
'Non so più' [Figaro] 70
Norina [Don Pasquale] 40
Norma 79, 121, 149, 152, 154
Norman, Jessye 16, **151**
O
'O Colombina, il tenero fido Arlecchino' [Pag] 85
'O del mio dolce ardor' [Paride ed Elena] 126
'O du mein holder Abendstern' [Tannhäuser] 102
'O Isis und Osiris' [Magic Flute] 66
'O Lola' [Cav] 35
'O luce di quest'anima' [Linda di Chamounix] 124
'O maiden, my maiden' [Friederike] 128
'O mio babbino caro' [Gianni Schicchi] 50
'O namen - namenlose Freude!' [Fidelio] 45
'O paradiso!' [Africaine] 20
'O patria mia' [Aida] 23
'O sink'hernieder, Nacht der Liebe' [Tris & Is] 110
'O soave fanciulla' [Bohème] 29
'O terra, addio' [Aida] 23
'O welche lust' [Fidelio] 45
'O Zittre nicht' [Magic Flute] 66
'Obéissons, quand leur voix appelle' [Manon] 67
Oberon 140
Oberto 137
Ochs, Baron [Rosenkavalier] 98-9
Octavian [Rosenkavalier] 16, 98-9, 149, 150
Offenbach, J 11, 15, 31, 46, 68, 124-5, **131-2**, 136 operas 80-1, 100-1
'Oiseaux dans la charmille' [Tales of Hoff] 101
Olga [Eugene Onegin] 42
'Ombra mai fu' [Xerxes] 127

'On a tree by a river a little tom-tit' [Mikado] 77
'ora o Tirsi, è vaga e bella, L'' [Manon Lescaut] 68
Orford, Ellen [Peter Grimes] 86
Orlovsky [Fledermaus] 16, 46-7, 150
Orpheus and Eurydice 11, 80, 81, 110, 126, 148
Orpheus in the Underworld 80-1, 132
Ortrud [Lohengrin] 55
Ossian's Song [Werther] 115
Otello 11, 14, 81-2, 122, 134, 135, 138 singers 16, 148, 150, 151, 152, 154
'Où va la jeune Hindoue?' [Lakmé] 54
'Our dream of love' [Bartered Bride] 26
P
Paganini 128
Pagliacci 16, 34, 83-5, 128, 146, 154
Pamina [Magic Flute] 63, 66
'Pa-pa-pa' [Magic Flute] 66
Papagena and Papageno [Magic Flute] 63, 66
'Pari siamo' [Rigoletto] 91
Paride ed Elena 126
Paris [Paride ed Elena] 126
Parsifal 14, 139
Patience 125
'Patiently smiling' [Land of Smiles] 128
Patti, Adelina 25, 57, **151**
Pavarotti, L 15, 16, 41, 115, 146, 147-8, **151-2**
Peachum, J J and Mrs [Threepenny Opera] 103
Pearl Fishers, The 14, 85-6, 122, 144, 150
Pears, Peter 122, **152**
'Per pietà, ben mio, perdona' [Così] 37
Périchole, La 124-5, 132
Peter Grimes 86, 122, 154
Philip II of Spain [Don Carlos] 38, 147
'Piangi, fanciulla' [Rigoletto] 91
Piave, Francesco Maria 48, 89, 90, 108
Pilgrims' Chorus [Tannhäuser] 102
Pinafore, HMS 125
Pinkerton, B F and Kate [Butterfly] 60, 62, 144
Pirata, Il 144
Pirates of Penzance 125
Plaza-Toro, Duke and Duchess [Gondoliers] 51
Pogner, Veit [Meistersinger] 71
Pollione [Norma] 79, 154
Polly [Threepenny Opera] 103
Ponchielli, Amilcare 50, 122, 132
Pons, Lily **152**
Ponselle, Rosa 48, **152**
Pooh-Bah [Mikado] 76-7
'Poor wand'ring one' [Pirates of Penzance] 125
Popp, Lucia **152**
'Porgi amor' [Figaro] 70
Porgy and Bess 87-9, 124, **152**
'Pourquoi me réveiller' [Werther] 115
Preciosa 140
'Près des ramparts de Seville' [Carmen] 34
Prey, Hermann **152**
Price, Leontyne **152**
Price, Margaret **152**
Prince Igor 122
Princess Ida 76, 126
'Printemps qui commence' [Samson et Dalila] 100
Prisoners' Chorus [Fidelio] 45
'Prithee pretty maiden' [Patience] 125
'Private buffoon...light-hearted loon' [Yeomen] 126

Prokofiev, Serge 56
Prophète, Le 129
Ptolemy 127
Puccini 6, 11, 16, 50, **132-3**; operas 27-9, **60-2, 67-8, 103-7, 114-15**; singers 15, 144, 146, 149, 151, 154
Purcell, Henry 11, 38, **133**, 144, 148
Puritani, I 121
Q
'Qual fiamma avea nel guardo' [Pag] 85
'Quando me'n vo' [Bohème] 29
Queen of the Night [Magic Flute] 12, 13, 16, 63, 66, 152
Queen of Spades 137
'Quel guardo il cavaliere' [Don Pasquale] 40
'Questa o quella' [Rigoletto] 90, 91
R
Rackstraw, Ralph [HMS Pinafore] 125
Radames [Aida] 22-3, 150, 151
Raimondi, Ruggiero 12, **152**
Ramey, Samuel 12, **152**
Rape of Lucretia 148
'Recondita armonia' [Tosca] 107
'Regnava nel silenzio' [Lucia] 57
'regular royal Queen, A' [Gondoliers] 51
Reine de Saba, La 127
Rheingold, Das 92, 94, **95**, 97
Rhinemaidens [Ring] 94, 95, 96, 97
Rice Aria [Tancredi] 135
Ride of the Valkyries [Ring] 94, 95-6
'Ridi Pagliaccio' [Pag] 85
Rienzi 54, 122, 139
Rigoletto 81, 89-91, 108, 111, 137, 138; singers 144, 146, 149, 150
Rimsky-Korsakov, Nikolai 30, 122, 131
Ring des Nibelungen, Der (Ring cycle) 11, 18, 47, 49, 54, 110, 138-9, 140; operas 92-7; singers 16, 144, 145, 148, 149, 154
Rinuccio [Gianni Schicchi] 50
'Rising early in the morning' [Gondoliers] 51
'Ritorna vincitor' [Aida] 23
Robert le Diable 129
Roberto Devereux 124
Rodelinda 127
Rodolfo [Bohème] 16, 27, 29, 144, 145, 150
Romani, Felice 41, 79
'Romanza' [Favorita] 44
Roméo et Juliette 126, 127
Rondine, La 132, 133
Rondo Aria [Cenerentola] 36
Rosalinde [Fledermaus] 46-7
Rosenkavalier 16, 98-9, 136-7, 149, 150, 152, 153
Rosina [Barber & Figaro] 24-6, 69-70, 150, 151, 153
Rossini, Gioacchino 7, 11, 12, 13, 68, 70, **134-5**; operas 24-6, 36; singers 144, 149, 152, 153; & other composers 78, 92, 120, 123, 125, 129, 131
'Ruddier than the cherry' [Acis and Galatea] 127
Ruddigore 126
Ruffini, Giovanni 40
S
Sabina, Karel 26
Sachs, Hans [Meistersinger] 71, 74, 144
Saint-Saëns, Camille 94, 99-100, 135

'Salce, salce, salce' [Otello] 82
Salome 98, 136, 137, 151
'Salut! demeure chaste et pure' [Faust] 43
Samson et Dalila 99-100, 135, 154
Santuzza [Cav] 7, 35, 145
Sarastro [Magic Flute] 63, 66
'Say not love is a dream' [Graf von Lux] 128
Scala di Seta, La 135
Scarpia [Tosca] 103, 106-7, 144, 149, 151
Schoenbergg, Arnold 14, 110, 139
Schwarzkopf, Elisabeth 148, 153
Schweigsame Frau, Die 136, 137
Scotto, Renata 153
Scribe, Eugène 20, 23, 41, 44, 120, 129
'Se tradirmi tu potrai' [Lucia] 57
'Sea interludes' [Peter Grimes] 86
'Seguidilla' [Carmen] 34
'Selig wie die Sonne' [Meistersinger] 74
Selika [Africaine] 20
Semiramide 134, 135, 149
Senta [Flying Dutchman] 47-8
Seraglio, Il 131
Sharpears [Cunning Vixen] 37
'Si, mi chiamana Mimi' [Bohème] 29
'Si può ... Un nido di memoire' [Pag] 85
'Siciliano' [Cav] 35
Siegfried 52, 92, 93, 94, 96, 110
Siegfried [Ring] 47, 94, 96, 97
Sieglinde [Ring] 94, 95, 96, 148, 154
Siegmund [Ring] 94, 95, 96
Signor Bruschino, Il 135
'Signor, una parola' [Cenerentola] 36
Sills, Beverly 145, 153
Silvio [Pag] 84-5
Simon Boccanegra 138, 148
Simoni, Renato 114
Smetana, Bedřich 26, 135-6
'Soave sia il vento' [Cosi] 37
Söderström, Elisabeth 148, 153
'Sola, perduta, abbandonata' [Manon Lescaut] 68
Soldier Song [Threepenny Opera] 103
Soldiers' Chorus [Faust] 43
'Solenne in quest'ora' [Forza del Destino] 49
Sonnambula, La 121
Sophie [Rosenkavalier] 98-9
Sorcerer, The 125
Spalanzani [Tales of Hoffmann] 100-1
Sparafucile [Rigoletto] 90-1
Spinning Chorus [Flying Dutchman] 48
'Spirito gentil' [Favorita] 44
Stade, Frederica von 153
Stella [Tales of Hoffmann] 100, 101
Straniera, La 145
Strauss, Johann II 45-6, 98, 125, 128, 136
Strauss, Richard 11, 14, 98-9, 136-7; singers
    144, 147, 149, 151, 152, 153
Stravinsky, Igor 11, 127, 136, 153
'Stride la vampa!' [Trovatore] 113
'Suicidio!' [Gioconda] 50
Sullivan, Sir Arthur see Gilbert and Sullivan
'Summertime' [Porgy and Bess] 89
'sun, whose rays are all ablaze, The' [Mikado] 77
Supervia, Conchita 15, 153
Susanna [Figaro] 69-70, 148

Sutherland, Joan 7, 13, 16, 57, 79, 100, 123,
    153-4; and other singers 144, 145, 148, 149, 151
T
'Tacea la notte placida' [Trovatore] 113
Taddeo [Pag] 84-5
'Take a pair of sparkling eyes' [Gondoliers] 51
Tales of Hoffmann 17, 100-1, 132
Tamino [Magic Flute] 63, 66, 154
Tancredi 134, 135
Tannhäuser 47, 54, 71, 101-2, 139, 140
Tatyana [Eugene Onegin] 42, 148
Tauber, Richard 128, 154
Tchaikovsky, Piotr Ilyich 42, 94, 121, 137
Te Kanawa, Dame Kiri 16, 36, 148, 154
Tebaldi, Renata 154
Tetrazzini, Luisa 154
Thaddeus [Bohemian Girl] 29-30
Thaïs 129
'There's a boat dat's leaving soon' [Porgy & B] 89
Thespis 124, 125
'Three little maids from school' [Mikado] 76-7
Three Norns, The [Ring] 94, 96
Threepenny Opera 102-3, 140
'Time was when love and I ... '[Sorcerer] 125
Tonio [Pag] 84-5
Toreador's Song [Carmen] 31, 34
Tosca 15, 103-7, 114, 133
    singers 16, 144, 146, 149, 150, 151, 154
Toscanini, Arturo 27, 83, 114, 126, 154
'Traft ihr das Schiff' [Flying Dutchman] 48
Traviata, La 48, 81, 89, 108-9, 111, 137, 138;
    singers 145, 148, 150, 153
Trial by Jury 124, 125, 132
'tringles des sistres tintaient, Les' [Carmen] 34
Tristan and Isolde 14, 47, 71, 94, 110, 122, 139;
    singers 145, 149, 150
Trittico, Il 50, 133
Trovatore, Il 14, 48, 89, 108, 111-13, 137, 138
    singers 144, 151, 152
Turandot 17, 85, 114-15, 132, 133; singers 150,
    151, 154
Turiddu [Cav] 35
Turn of the Screw, The 122
Turner, Dame Eva 114, 115, 154
'Tutti i fior' [Butterfly] 62
'Twenty lovesick maidens we' [Patience] 125
U
'Un di felice' [Traviata] 109
Un giorno di regno 78
'Un tal gioco' [Pag] 85
'Una vergine, un angel di Dio' [Favorita] 44
'Una voce poco fa' [Barber] 12, 13, 26
Utopia Limited 126
V
'Va crudele' [Norma] 79
'Va, pensiero, sull'ali dorate' [Nabucco] 78
Valkyries [Ring] 92, 94, 95-7, 148, 149
Vanessa 148
Vasco da Gama [Africaine] 20
Vasek [Bartered Bride] 26
'Vecchia zimarra' [Bohème] 29
Vêpres Sciciliennes, Les 138
Verdi, G 7, 11, 14, 15, 35, 42, 92, 106, 137-8;
    operas 21-4, 38, 48-9, 78, 81-2, 89-91; 108-9,

111-13; and other composers 120, 122, 123,
    129, 132; singers 12, 144, 147, 149, 150, 151,
    152, 154
vergine degli angeli, La' [Forza del Destino] 49
'Verranno a te sull'aure' [Lucia] 57
'Vesti la giubba' [Pag] 84, 85, 146
Vickers, Jon 154
Vie Parisienne, La 132
'Vilja, oh Vilja' [Merry Widow] 75
Villi, Le 27, 132, 133
Violetta [Traviata] 108-9, 145, 148, 150, 153
'Vissi d'arte' [Tosca] 15, 107
'Viva, il vino spumeggiante' [Cav] 35
'Vogelfänger bin ich ja, Der' [Magic Flute] 66
'Voi che sapete' [Figaro] 70
'Voi lo sapete' [Cav] 35
'Votre toast je peux le rendre' [Carmen] 34
W
Wagner, Cosima 139
Wagner, Richard 11, 14, 15, 16, 18, 138-9;
    operas 47-8, 54-5, 70-4, 92-7, 101-2, 110;
    other composers 50, 52, 79, 85, 120, 129, 132,
    135, 136; Bizet 31, 121; Rossini 92, 134; Verdi
    81, 138; Weber 49, 140; singers 144, 146-52,
    154
Walküre, Die 92, 94, 95-6, 97, 148, 149
Walther von Stolzing [Meistersinger] 71, 74
Waltrante [Ring] 94, 97
Waltz Song [Bohème] 29
Waltz Song [Merry Widow] 75
'wandering minstrel I, A' [Mikado] 77
'Waterloo House young man, A' [Patience] 125
Weber, Carl 11, 14, 49-50, 129, 139, 140
Wedding Procession [Lohengrin] 55
Wedding Song [Threepenny Opera] 103
Weill, Kurt 102-3, 140
Wellington Wells, John [Sorcerer] 125
Werther 115, 129, 149
West Side Story 145, 154
'When a felon's not engaged ...'[Pirates] 125
'When a merry maiden marries ' [Gondoliers] 51
'When a wooer goes a-wooing' [Yeomen] 125
'When all night long a chap remains' [Iol] 125
'When Britain really ruled the waves' [Iol] 125
'When I first put this uniform on' [Patience] 125
'When I was a lad I served a term' [Pinafore] 125
'When I was called to the Bar' [Trial by Jury] 125
'When I went to the Bar' [Iolanthe] 125
'When lying awake with a dismal headache'[Iol] 125
William Tell 70, 135
Willow Song [Otello] 82
'Willow, tit willow' [Mikado] 77
'With a cat-like tread' [Pirates] 125
Woglinde [Ring] 94, 149
Wolfram von Eschenbach [Tannhäuser] 102
Wotan [Ring] 93, 94, 95, 96, 97, 144
X, Y & Z
Xerxes 127
Yeomen of the Guard, The 51, 126
'You are my heart's delight'[Land of Smiles] 128
Yum-Yum [Mikado] 76-7
Zauberflöte, Die see Magic Flute
'Zingarella, La' [Trovatore] 113
Zurga [Pearl Fishers] 85-6, 122

ABOUT THE AUTHOR

JEREMY NICHOLAS is an actor, composer and writer. His one-man show *Three Men in a Boat* ran for four months in London's West End, received an Olivier award nomination and was filmed for Channel Four. He starred in the TV series of *The Good Companions*, *The Pickwick Papers* and *Wish Me Luck* as well as the last six months of *Crossroads*. Frequently to be heard on the radio in one of the many features and series he has written, most recently he has presented *The Tingle Factor* for Radio 4 and *In Tune* for Radio 3. Jeremy has also composed 150 songs for Robert Robinson's *Stop The Week* and the scores for several major TV dramas. He has had two books published, *Raspberries and Other Trifles* and *Godowsky, the Pianists' Pianist*.

SPECIAL OPERA TICKET OFFER

Opera North, the Royal Opera House, English National Opera, Scottish Opera and Welsh National Opera are offering generous discounts off selected performances in 1993 to readers of *Beginner's Guide to Opera*. To obtain further details, please contact the opera company of your choice on the following telephone numbers, then send the enclosed voucher to the *Box Office* at the addresses below:

OPERA NORTH
Grand Theatre
New Briggate · Leeds LS1 6NU
tel: 0532 445326

ENGLISH NATIONAL OPERA
London Coliseum
St. Martins Lane · London WC2N 44ES
tel: 071 836 0111 ext 420

THE ROYAL OPERA HOUSE
Covent Garden · London WC2E 9DD
tel: 071 240 1200 ext 298

SCOTTISH OPERA
39 Elmbank Crescent · Glasgow G2 4PT
tel: 041 248 4567 contact Cara Pell

EACH VOUCHER MAY BE USED ONLY ONCE
OFFER SUBJECT TO AVAILABILITY

WELSH NATIONAL OPERA
John Street · Cardiff CF1 4SP
tel: 0222 464 666
contact: Marketing (office hours)

PLUS, you can win a year's worth of tickets at either Opera North or Scottish Opera. Everyone who takes up an opera ticket offer with either of these two companies will be entered in a prize draw for a subscription for either Opera North's Leeds 1993/94 season or Scottish Opera's 1993/94 Glasgow season. This prize is open to current non-subscribers. Ring the companies to find out more.